THE FULL TURN OF THE WHEEL

by

Peter May CMILT, MIRTE

ROADS AND ROAD TRANSPORT HISTORY ASSOCIATION

British Library Cataloguing in Publication Data
A Record for this book is available at the British Library
ISBN 978-0-9552876-1-9

Printed by R. Booth Limited, Antron Hill, Mabe, Penryn, Cornwall, TR10 9HH.

Cover. Guy Warrior Light Eight 225 SPA ready to leave for Hamburg from Guildway (see Chapter 7) with a timber-framed structure for a house. It was Guildway's first ever export. Driver John Hard looks on as Dennis Lockhart, Guildway director and the author shake hands.

Published by the Roads and Road Transport Association Limited, 124 Shenstone Avenue, Norton, Stourbridge, West Midlands, DY8 3EJ.
Founded in 1992 to support historical research
E-mail: RoadsandRTHA@aol.com
Website: www.rrtha.org.uk

Contents

The author, Peter May, in 1957.

Preface

The wheel, for us, started turning somewhere around 1920, and stopped in 1997, some 77 years later.

I have always had the thought to write this narrative for some time. It was in July 2003, that an article appeared in the journal of the Road Haulage Association, *"The Road Way"*, which said that there were some reasonable records and histories of a few of the larger road haulage companies of yesteryear, but virtually none for the small private enterprises which 'mushroomed' from those early years. That article in *"The Road Way"* set my mind searching and prompted me to get going on the project. Obviously it is really a family history, of a family business mixed up together. All families have their stories to tell, which are peculiar to them and the particular pursuits that they have followed, all interesting in their own right and infinitely diverse. It so happened that ours was involved with motorcars, trucks and buses.

Having decided to start on this monologue, the misgivings began to surface, mainly those of memory - or lack of it. I have forgotten so very much of the happenings, good or bad, of my lifetime, that one thinks - have I got enough to offer, are my memories accurate and true to write about them? Is it really interesting to others? Maybe it is to me, but not to others. And then, so what? Much of this was so many years ago that even if some of it is unintentionally inaccurate, there really is no one to argue with me or correct it.

Furthermore, I then realised that I am only doing this for our own family, a potted history of our own affairs, which will give an insight, albeit sketchy, of how things were a few years back and very much, I have no doubt, to the surprise of our grandchildren. At this point, I realised that I wanted to do this and must therefore make a mental commitment to see it through. I found it interesting that the thought process was stimulated, in that several things from the past resurfaced and the whole concept of the writing became more established and clear, in that it would be a bigger job than I had thought, and that I had to start at the beginning.

I had long since realised that we all live in an ever-changing world. Always have - always will. Charles Darwin was right in that, in life everything is slowly evolving and is therefore accompanied by inevitable change.

Looking back over my own eighty-two years, the 'ever-changing world' falls into some sort of perspective, as one constantly compares the present with the past, but even then, only a smattering of what has gone on flits through the mind. How those things of such concern and worry at the time, have now passed by and are no longer of any consequence or importance. Others followed and again, have gone. Therefore need we have worried in the first place? This is what is called 'being wise after the event'.

I hope that I have produced a book of interest and entertainment to readers, who can then make comparisons, whatever their backgrounds, with their own experiences in this ever-changing world.

My thanks to Mrs Sarah Cashmore for her extremely patient and highly efficient word processing, and to Mrs Maureen Harris for proof-reading and producing a long list of necessary corrections. To our daughters Jan and Judith for doing the same, to the Roads and Road Transport History Association for taking on the publishing of the book and The Kithead Trust for details of the pre-war bus fleet. Finally, to my wife June for her patience and fortitude, in having to listen to bits of this over and over again.

Peter May,
Helston
January 2007.

1. The first twenty years

My father, Dick May, was born in 1889 and lived for 98 years. He was christened Dick and not Richard. Tragically his father, Joshua, was killed in an accident whilst cleaning out a steam boiler at Pullman's Tannery in Godalming. He was aged 36 years. He left a widow and nine children. I understand that the eldest daughter, Bessie, one year older than my father, had a lot to do with the bringing up of the family. She would have been about twelve at the time. My grandmother Ellen, whom I never met, went out of her mind, as there was of course no state or other assistance. She was for many years an inmate of Warren Road Hospital, Guildford, although she lived well into her nineties. Quite a collection of the May family lived very close to each other in somewhat primitive dwellings, virtually under the Ockford Road known as 'Frogs Hole'. There lived Dick May's grandmother, who supplemented her grandchildren's food with bread and dripping and the like. There was also a soup kitchen in Godalming once or twice a week, costing a penny a bowl.

My mother was born in 1891. She was Winifred Gladys Curel. Her father, Regimental Sergeant Major George Curel, was, prior to the 1914 war, a cook and controller of the Cadet Force, on the staff at King Edward's School, Witley. He re-enlisted into the Army in 1914, was injured in France, came home for one week's leave and sadly died. He was very highly regarded by the Governors and pupils at the school. The name Curel is derived from the French, Huguenot. George Curel was a strong supporter of the Temperance Society. I must confess that such a conviction no longer exists within his successive generations! He left two daughters, Ethel and Winifred and a son, George.

My mother was brought up in Gosport and used the ferry (fare - one half penny) to Portsmouth from Gosport for piano lessons. At this time, George Curel senior was serving in the Army, prior to 1914. The family then moved and lived at King Edward's School, Witley until my Grandfather's death. My grandmother, Jesse, then built a house in nearby Wormley, known as the 'Laurels'. This must have been approximately 1919-1920. It was in 1920 that Winifred's and Dick's lives really converged. They married on 7th April 1920.

Back to Dick May, stories of hardship abound. He did a large paper round before school. His round was some five miles return, location - Charterhouse Hill. This is very long and very steep and how an undernourished boy, with literally his toes out of his shoes, could carry enough papers for the number of houses involved is quite incredible, they are very heavy. He also did an evening round. One of his brothers, another Joshua, also had a similar paper round. He related that they were allowed a concession, to arrive at school by 9.45 am. If they were late, it was the cane. He also related that everyone had to pay two pence per week to the school. He often arrived with one penny, the other having gone to the soup kitchen. Once more, the cane.

Many of the shops in Godalming were open-fronted. This enabled Dick, on his way to school, to 'collect' in passing, the odd cake or bun that came to hand. School was, we believe, a patchy affair. However, Dick May and several of his contemporaries emerged extremely upright and respected citizens, several of them creating and developing businesses, most of which went on into third generations. Something that they all had on leaving school at thirteen were the three 'R's - Reading, Riting and Rithmetic - again, a changing world.

Dick started work at Godalming Old Station, which was a goods depot. The Passenger Station was a little further down the line, which was, and is, the main line from London to Portsmouth, then part of the Southern Railway. Part of his duties was the writing out of consignment notes for delivery of the goods from the rail to customer. Unless the railway employee concerned had good spelling and copperplate writing, then he would not get the job!

These notes were then 'spiked' on a vertical spike mounted on a circular wooden base. There were hundreds of them, probably never to be looked at again.

This is the story of a family business, which became involved in the developing industry of road transport. It was at this point that I woke up to the fact that I am writing about things that happened in my time, some seventy years ago. I realised that not many people would know what I am writing about. It is necessary to now try to explain the then system and for most, it could become a boring history lesson, but you don't have to read it.

From about 1910 to say 1940, much development took place with regard to the motor vehicle. I have always held the simple view that the following happened - the rail took over from the horse and the road took over from the rail. Too simple? Maybe, but I think it is fundamental. Transport means movement of people and goods. Therefore movement by all means should be included, thus bringing in movement by sea and air, including waterways and indeed by human feet. The dimension broadens into international movement. It follows therefore, that the subject must be, or should be, looked at overall and comprehensively by governments. That has not happened and regretfully, I cannot see it happening for the foreseeable future. However, back to the railways.

Let us take a small section of the then Southern Railway, London to Portsmouth line, being Guildford, Farncombe, Godalming, Milford, Witley and Haslemere, the section Dick May worked on. Most of these stations had sidings off the main line to and from which the trucks, both open and covered, were shunted most days as required. Say a goods or freight train arrived at Godalming Goods Station from London. The Station's own small locomotive 'lived' there and would sort out the various trucks consigned to the stations above, in progressive order.

There was always a Guard's Van at the rear of the train that carried the red rear light (which was a polished oil lamp). This van had to be unhooked on arrival at the first destination and pushed out of the way and then reconnected at the rear on leaving for the next station. Of course, before they could leave the loaded trucks at their consigned station, they had to pull out the empty ones to make room to leave the loaded ones in the sidings and so on. This was known as shunting. When shunting was completed at a particular station, they would have to run on the main line between passenger train movements, to their next destination.

All of this was controlled by semaphore signals. That was a red and white or black and white 'arm' on a gantry beside the track - horizontal for stop or dropped to go. They were controlled and operated by the signalman in the signal box who also operated the railway crossing gates. The signals were changed by the pulling of heavy levers in the signal box and by a series of pulleys and wires. The movement of the signal arm covered or uncovered the red or green lens and this was lit by a paraffin lamp placed high up, behind the signal arm. These lamps all had to be changed daily and Dick had to do this by climbing the ladder on the signal gantry, while the shunting train stopped and waited for this to be done. These lamps were a sight to be seen, put out at various stations all cleaned, trimmed and refilled and polished like new.

The trucks were coupled or uncoupled by a simple but very heavy three-link chain, each end link on a hook on each truck. The 'shunter' used a 'shunting pole' and as the trucks met each other being pushed by the locomotive, he had to lift this heavy link with the pole and quickly hook it onto the approaching truck. Tragically, at Milford Station on a wet day, the shunter slipped and his head was crushed between the truck buffers. He was the husband of a cousin of mine. Although everybody tried, including me through our solicitors, to get compensation for his widow and three young children, none was forthcoming. It was called in those days, 'an act of God'.

The point about all this is that these railway trucks had to be emptied or filled at these various small stations and this is where road haulage comes into the picture. This function had been carried out by horse and cart and this method survived in London and other cities well into the mid-century. I could tell many stories about this but it is another subject. Incidentally, Elstead, our village, was famous for growing carrots and they were taken to Milford Station in horse-drawn wagons, destined for Covent Garden Market and then horse drawn from railroad to the market.

These operators were called Railway Cartage Agents and many haulage contractors started with their horses and carts and progressed to motor lorries in this way. During the early days of transition from horse to road, the heavier work was carried out by the steam traction engines for road use and these were eventually pushed out by petrol and diesel engined lorries and by taxation, as the road tax was calculated on the unladen weight and of course, traction engines were very heavy. Many of what became the larger road haulage companies evolved in this way.

It is interesting to reflect that the word 'haulage' was usually used because, from the horse and cart origins, goods were 'pulled' or 'hauled' on carts, not carried. This was because we had an improving road system as the years passed by. This was not so in many other countries, for example in the desert or mountainous terrain, the pack animals, donkeys, mules, camels etc carried the goods and often still do! As the spectrum changed, not only by road but by sea and air and passenger movement became much greater, the word 'transport' gradually took on a much wider meaning, so road haulage contractors became road transport contractors.

When I was a small boy, nine or ten years old, it was my delight, if and when we were in the vicinity of, Milford Station, to persuade my mother to stop and park and accompany me on to the footbridge which crossed both up and down the lines. When the train, having stopped, started to move, we would watch the signalman pull the levers and wind the great wheel that closed the gates to road traffic. I would probably get a wave and a toot on the whistle from the train driver. If we were up there when a fast train came through, we could see it coming from afar, very fast, roar underneath us with much dust and wind and disappear into the distance. A great thrill, but really I was scared stiff although would never admit to that!

Little did I know then, that by the 'turning of our wheel', I would in the future spend many hours, most of it with a large shovel, emptying trucks of coal, twelve tons per truck, at that very station, in those very sidings.

My father joined the Army in 1910, at nearby Aldershot, as the wages on the railway were not very good. I imagine that the prospect of an adequate supply of food on a regular basis, from wherever the Army sent you, and an adequate supply of boots was a major attraction. He joined the Seventh Hussars; a cavalry regiment and served his time in Persia (Iran) and India 'chasing Brigands' as he called it, somewhere near the North West Frontier (Afghanistan?). He became a Rough Riding Instructor and had a pretty tough time and many stories to tell.

He enjoyed a horse ride whenever possible in later life. He won a Military Medal (MM) and was twice mentioned in despatches. Because of the intervening 1914 -1918 war, he did not get home until 1920, having been away some ten years, but arrived home with a special marriage licence in his pocket as they had become engaged before he went abroad. Whilst away he had been sending money home to Winifred from his army pay, which was banked towards their future. From this time information is a bit sketchy.

Dick May in dress uniform of *The Queen's Own Seventh* Hussars, and Winifred Curel probably taken soon after he joined the Army in 1910.

As I stated earlier, my parents married in April 1920. It is a staggering thought that they did not see each other or speak to each other for some ten years and then were married immediately on his return to this country. For a somewhat sheltered and perhaps not very worldly young woman, to be precipitated into the married state and to be living in two rooms in someone else's house, must have been quite daunting. These two rooms were rented in Avenue Row, Milford Road, Elstead, Surrey.

The author, photographed in his pram, circa 1925. In the background, the general goods vehicle used by my father for his local carriers round. It was signwritten "D. May, General Carrier - Elstead, Shackleford, Eashing, Hurtmore, Godalming, Guildford."

They had arranged to purchase a small 'carriers business', the business bit of the deal apparently more hypothetical than factual. It seemed to consist of one van, able to carry five hundred weight or, one quarter of a ton, or two hundred and fifty kilos. The deal was that the vendor would stay and teach Dick May to drive the thing. In the event, when the money came through and was paid over, the gentleman was no longer available for driving instruction. It is fortunate that the traffic densities and speeds were much lower than the present day and there were no driving tests! However, they survived that and organised to park the van just down the road, at the rear of 'Ham Cottages'. So, now we are in business. For the benefit of the Reader, the 'purchased business' had nothing to do with the railway cartage to which I referred earlier. Obviously, if a customer instructed to take a consignment to or from a local station, then that would be done. Quite a lot of these small consignments were labelled 'to be collected' and they would be waiting in the Station Parcels Office.

The town of Godalming is five miles from Elstead, in the opposite direction five miles from Farnham, ten miles from Guildford, some nine miles from Aldershot and thirty-five miles from London and thirty-five miles from Portsmouth. This gives some idea of the location of Elstead in Surrey.

I do remember in Godalming High Street, such shops as Liptons, Home & Colonial, Maypole, International stores and a local firm, Burgess Stores, all selling groceries. All of the other trades were there as well. Ironmongery, furniture, drapery, clothing, butchers, chemists etc. It was the delivery of the products of these shops, which provided a substantial amount of business for the carrier, as well as the parcels that arrived at the station for collection and parcels from the villages taken to the station for despatch. When a shop had a consignment for Elstead or other outlying villages, they would place a white card with a large black 'M' on it, in their shop window and Dick May would call in and collect whatever.

This is exactly how it was done for Pickfords or Carter Paterson or Chaplins in London and larger towns elsewhere. Communication to and from the villages and towns was either by foot, by taxi (pony and trap), by bicycle, by letter or by telephone, which was in its infancy and somewhat scarce. No doubt many people in Elstead went to where Mr and Mrs May lived and gave a verbal instruction.

However it was done, it seemed to work because it would appear that Mays prospered, because it was not very long before they changed the quarter-ton van for a one-ton vehicle.

The Ford model TT 1-tonner, replacement for the original ¼ ton van. It could carry parcels and up to nine passengers on wooden longitudinal benches. Note the roll-up canvas curtains.

Now we have a new situation. Remember that rurally there were no buses, but this vehicle could carry up to nine passengers - one beside the driver and four each side, gaining access from the rear. Therefore, whilst collecting and delivering parcels, the odd passenger or two could get to and from town. Among the goods carried, they often had prescriptions from the chemists, which of course had to be same day delivery. Therefore, when no one else was available, my mother would have to deliver these packages by bicycle. I remember her often saying that to do this on winter evenings, with a flickering paraffin lamp for a 'headlight' on the bicycle, that she was petrified. This I can well understand because where she sometimes had to go was to a place called 'Cutt Mill' which was, and still is to this day, very rural, sparsely inhabited and very spooky, but the job had to be done.

Progress must have been pretty good, because from their digs at Avenue Row, they had acquired a house called 'Ludlow House', in the Thursley Road in Elstead. These premises had a good side access to a yard behind and a quite useful, quite high shed, into which parked the one-ton van. There was attached to the house a small shop from which were sold sweets, biscuits and a few groceries. I do not know whether this came with the house or was started by my parents, I rather think that it was already there. On 29th December 1922 their first child, my sister Christine, was born at Ludlow House. So from 1920 to 1922 they had become well established. Next door was Rose Cottage where lived a Mr Caesar (his name? Yes you guessed it, was Julius, Julius Caesar) with his daughter Mary and he was by all accounts a very nice old man. During this time, Sir Edgar Horne, from 'Aldro' (now a public school) at Shackelford approached my father to start a bus service from Elstead to Godalming, through Shackelford and Hurtmore, which was substantially one of his carrier routes.

Our first house, *Ludlow House*, in Elstead. The small shop is located at the far end of the building with the side access to yard beyond it.

The project was financed by four people. By the end of the first year, my father and mother had bought out, in full, the other three. On 14th March 1924, I was born at Ludlow House. Later, I recall my mother saying that she was standing by the window, having initial pains, when Dick May pulled up in his bus outside, was joking with his passengers, but much to her dismay drove off without looking her way. In those days there was always a village nurse, a midwife, known as the 'mole catcher', not far away. Her duty seemed to have been to assist people into this world and at the other end, to assist them out! After my arrival, a pale, blue-eyed, blond, curly-headed boy, I was parked in a high-wheeled pram of the day, under the apple tree in the yard. My mother said that people would take a peep, drop their eyelids and shake their heads thinking that this little lad was not long for this world! I am pleased to relate that nearly eighty years on, I am very well and have been throughout. I have been extremely lucky.

Another little episode at Ludlow House has been reported. Old Julius Caesar was slowly putting out rows of cabbage plants. By that time, I was mobile and crawling. I had crawled through a gap in the hedge into next-door's garden and followed Julius by pulling out all of the plants, one by one. Julius only chuckled. My parents purchased from the church a virgin site of some two acres, 400 yards down the Thursley Road from Ludlow House, known as The Glebe Meadow.

Young Peter May. Petrol was contained in two-gallon cans. This was the only method of storing petrol to fuel the buses.

They built a workshop, later adding a small showroom on the front, a four-bedroom house and installed two petrol pumps on the forecourt and eventually, established a car repair business and filling station. This was undoubtedly a move dictated by my mother, who really was the brains behind the outfit and very forward looking. How useful that area of land was to be. A further turn of the wheel had been completed and here starts another chapter. Ludlow House, later on became a butcher's shop, owned by Arthur Russell.

Bill Matthews, who lived at School Cottages, kept a pig in his back garden, fed largely on 'scraps' that could be easily collected from nearby residents. Therefore, every so often the pig would be 'ready'. Like its owner, it was very fat and would only waddle. Bill, with his somewhat tired, button-through cardigan, his treble-chinned red face, topped by a seasoned flat cap, completed with a pair of very well used wellies, would teeth grip his permanent burnt-out cigarette and attempt to persuade piggy to walk the 400 yards to his doom. This, it was very reluctant to do and each heavy step was accompanied by continuous ear-splitting squealing, right up to the previously mentioned 'useful shed' at the rear of Ludlow House where Arthur was waiting and where in due course, peace and tranquillity would return.

I have said that the land and the new buildings were the beginning of a new chapter. They were, in that from an early photograph of the new premises, a distinct change had taken place within the business. I have very little information of this period on which to work and I can only estimate the approximate date (in years) of some of the happenings.

I have deduced that the new yard must have been operative by 1926 or 1927. During those six years I conclude that many of the Godalming shops and businesses previously mentioned, had purchased their own delivery vans and several of the grocers had amalgamated, whereby one or two vans could cover the work. The setting up of the May's Bus Service increased the flow of people to and from the villages and towns and most would therefore carry their own purchases. If this happened two or three times per day according to the frequency of the bus service, it would quickly dilute the need for a carrier. The opposite happened with the buses, with increasing passengers, added to which, the buses had a parcel compartment usually near the door for a few packages costing so much a package, collected by the recipient waiting for it at the relevant bus stop.

The growing fleet, photographed outside Ludlow House in 1926. Prior to the 1930 Act and the appointment of the Traffic Commissioners, buses were authorised and licensed by the local Police Chief, in our case, the Superintendent of Police, at Godalming, Surrey. The leading vehicle is a Guy, registration PD 2136 and behind it is Fiat PD 7199 with a Ford model 'T' bringing up the rear.

From photograph on page 19, it is evident that there was no small van, no one-ton van but five buses. It had become an omnibus operation, plus one motor taxi, which my mother had learned to drive. There were at least three employees and a few casuals. From 'digs' in Avenue Row and one very small van, they had progressed to a new garage, new house, large yard, five buses and a large car and a family of two children. This really was a spectacular achievement in six years, one of enterprise and dedication to the job and continuous hard work.

An additional bus route, to and from Godalming and Farnham, via Elstead had been started. The Godalming cinema, with its corrugated iron roof, known as the 'Bug Pit' was the subject of a special run on Saturday evenings to bring home the cinemagoers. It was said that when it rained, the noise on the roof obliterated the sound track - or were the films still silent? Also, the first Saturday evening performance at the Aldershot Hippodrome would be met, possibly about 7.30 pm. By using May's bus from Elstead to Farnham there were plenty of buses onwards to Aldershot. People would go to

Aldershot for Saturday shopping, have tea then go to the Hippodrome (live stage), so May's ran a bus to enable them to get home to Elstead. Saturday shopping in Godalming and Farnham was active; therefore Saturday buses were always packed.

There were many hop fields in the area and during the hop-picking season the local ladies were taken to work before the first bus service was started and they were collected at around 5 pm. They were paid Saturday midday and usually adjourned to the nearest pub, but getting them out was another thing!

This view shows only the rear of the Maxwell 'char-a-banc' with the fold-down pram hood just visible at the extreme rear. Hope for fine weather!

The summer opened up the previously unknown coastal outings. They would have been mainly to Portsmouth, Brighton, Littlehampton, Bognor and perhaps Worthing, but nothing mattered to the customers so long as they went for a day out. The modern day difference between a bus and a coach, was then the bus and the 'char-a-banc'. This was usually an open-topped vehicle, with a large 'pram-hood' folded down at the rear. Although there must have been some form of side protection from the elements, none was evident from photographs. There was a long board running along each side, which was a step. There was no centre gangway, but rows of full width seats with a little door at each end of each row of seats.

Breakdowns and failures were all part of the scene and provided many a talking point. For instance, on these early machines there were no electrics. Probably the front lights were driven by acetylene or paraffin and the single rear light would have been fed by paraffin. On windy nights, the passengers at the rear would transmit, row of seats by row of seats to the driver that the vehicle was on fire. Whilst travelling the 'growl' from the rear axle rendered speech impossible. My mother said that on a still evening, the char-a-banc would be heard leaving the A3 at Milford, some three miles away. It was an American 'Maxwell'.

Maxwell bus PC 9906, photographed in Queen Street, Godalming, ready to depart on an excursion to Brighton. The fleet livery was red. The bus was new in the spring of 1923 but only remained in service with us until November 1924.

However, back to the fire. An inspection by at least half the passengers, would confirm that the rear light was on fire! Action would then be taken by a few, whilst the remainder would advise until the matter was resolved. To start up again, the driver would have to crank up the engine, from the front, but always pull the handle up not down. They were prone to 'kick', which if one were pushing down, a broken arm could easily result! By pulling it up, one could at least let go and try again. Eventually order would be restored and the journey completed, minus a rear light. It must have been quite a pantomime in the event of a rainstorm, to stop and erect the great hood, but it appeared that nothing ever upset anyone. There was always talk around the village of the great fun and enjoyment and happening that went on with regard to May's bus outings. They certainly contributed much to the social world of the local community.

A regular happening, I think annually, but either bi-annually or tri-annually and this was The Aldershot Tattoo. It was a highly spectacular and highly colourful military entertainment. It took place in the open-air evenings at the Rushmoor Arena, on military land, behind the Garrison Church at Aldershot. It was essentially held in the dark to obtain the full effect of the searchlights and the colourful lighting, therefore it finished quite late. It was a well-known event, lavishly presented on a large scale with many Regimental Bands in full dress uniform, including the pipes and drums, the whole thing terminating with the full power of the massed bands. The Tattoo went on for at least six nights, maybe ten. If it rained, most vehicles had to be towed out. It was often three or four in the morning when the vehicles finally finished, but the early morning work still had to be done.

The fourteen-seat Fiat 'coach', PD 7199, our most comfortable vehicle.

My mother took on a ticket agency for the Tattoo and was meticulous with its organisation. With enquiries from the surrounding areas, she would make block bookings way before the event. Each block of 25 to 30 from one location would mean the hiring of a bus. Apart from the commission on the ticket sales, it generated traffic for May's red buses and very useful revenue.

This expansion of the bus industry was obviously not confined to Elstead, it was going on all over the place. Several large companies were building up all over the country and near to us was the Aldershot and District Traction Company Limited. It covered a large part of Surrey and a large part of Hampshire. Adjoining its territory, southwards and towards the coast was the Southdown Motor Services Limited that radiated from Brighton and covered the whole of Sussex. If one looks at a map of the Aldershot and District services, it was very comprehensive and it fitted very neatly with Southdown's boundaries. What a revelation to discover that both companies, whilst totally independent of each other, were both part-owned by the Southern Railway!

With the rapid growth of the industry, it was inevitable that interference, or control would be required by the politicians. It is a pity that the thinking in those early days was not more fundamental and carried out by knowledgeable people from a cross section of industry and Government, but non-political. But it wasn't and still is not. What eventually emerged from Government was legislation to licence the routes being operated by bus companies, whereby some hypothetical protection could be afforded to the railways. A case of closing the stable door after the horse had bolted. What was coming was the Road Traffic Act 1930, which affected public service vehicles, or passenger vehicles and the Road and Rail Traffic Act 1933 which concerned itself with licensing of goods vehicles.

Godalming High Street with our Guy bus PD 2136 on the service to Elstead before sale of the bus business to Aldershot & District.

Referring to the above-mentioned Aldershot and District route map, one could see 'holes' in it and May's red buses were one of those small 'holes'. As the large companies could afford to pay lawyers to look at the proposed legislation and predict the outcome and its effect, they quickly saw that whatever routes they were operating, when the legislation came into force, 1930 in this case, they would get an automatic grant for those routes for starters! The timing of this was 1927. So they set about quietly monitoring 'black holes', ours included. The outcome was that they offered to buy May's red buses out - the vehicles and the staff, not the premises. The alternative? We will run a bus in front of you and if necessary, another behind for as long as it takes. It must be said from what I could learn, that they offered a very fair market price for the operation, produced no undue pressure onto my parents, but made it abundantly clear, what they would and could do. What would you have done? In the event the deal was done at the end of 1927 and for many years afterwards, two buses (one on each of the original routes) were garaged on the premises for a very fair rent. The relationship with 'All the lot and risk it' as it became known, survived and it was a very good one.

Again, in this ever-changing world and by a further turning of the wheel, May's faced another situation, but there was no reason to give up and they did not.

The bus fleet at Glebe Meadow in 1927. From left to right, car TP 4191 Ford model T Ford Tudor with my mother at the wheel, the two Guy buses PF 8777 and PD 2136, Ford model T bus TP 837, and the two Charabancs. The nearer Guy bus is on pneumatic tyres.

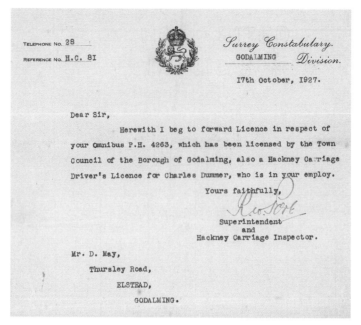

Before the 1930 Road Traffic Act and the appointment of Traffic Commissioners, buses and drivers were licensed by the local Town Council, through the medium of the Superintendent of Police. The covering letter for the licence for omnibus PH 4263 and driver Charles Dummer, dated 17th October 1927. The registration number quoted is thought to be an error for PH 4623.

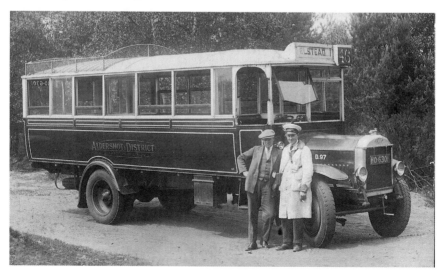

The new order in Elstead after sale to *Aldershot & District* – 1924 Dennis 4-ton HO 6301 with Dennis 36-seat bodywork. Pictured are driver Bill Adams (left) and conductor Reg Adams (no relation).

2. A taste of local history

This period, the nineteen twenties and through to 1939 was one of very great change. It was really throughout Europe, where many changes were running parallel to our own to a greater or lesser degree. Such things as cars, trucks, plumbing, electricity, piped water, radio (known as wireless), telephones, steam power, then diesel, the development of aircraft, TV etc. This subject is better left to the historians, but my point is that Elstead and District would have been typical of many and subject to the same changes.

I do not know whether my parents sat down and considered their new situation - no bus business, possibly a nice chunk of capital in the bank from the sale of the bus business - a new but nearly empty premises, or did this money go to pay off debts, or had they already some new ideas? However, on they went and a few interesting developments did take place. There was already another established filling station and taxi service in the village on the Milford - Farnham road adjoining the village green, owned by Mr and Mrs Chandler. They must have felt some concern on the arrival of May's garage and petrol pumps. Indeed, Mrs Chandler operated a taxi, being a pony and trap, which she drove. There was quite a demand for this, to and from the main line station. When Mrs May learned to drive and May's had a motor taxi, there was I understand, quite a bit of feeling! I am pleased to say that subsequently the relationship was first class and the Chandlers are still there, now well into the fourth generation. By the way, the May's 'taxi' was actually a large motor-car and not, as possibly comes to mind, a 'London cab' type of vehicle. It was known as 'private hire', not as 'taxi'.

From now on, the workshop was utilised as a shop and a small showroom from which many items were displayed and sold. This was near the road and the petrol pumps. The remainder of the building, which was quite large and included an 'inspection pit', had become a vehicle workshop for the servicing and repair of motorcars and for bicycle repairs. How many people today could straighten up a buckled bicycle wheel, or replace two or three broken spokes? From the shop were sold all sorts of bicycle spares, many tyres and tubes, 28" x 1½" or 26" x 1¼". I mentioned spokes for wheels, different lengths for different sizes of wheel. They were all there. All sizes of ball bearings, brake blocks, pedal rubbers, chains, cotter pins, puncture outfits, valve rubber, bicycle pumps, bells, mudguards, carbide etc.

Early vehicle lighting on buses, lorries, cars, motor cycles and pedal cycles would nearly all have been acetylene. The exception was Henry Ford, who used electric lighting on his Model T years before anyone else. We supplied acetylene lighting equipment for bicycles. This used calcium carbide as fuel and was supplied in round tins, about two inches in diameter and some twelve inches high, with a tightly sealed lid. It was in crystal form, approximately ¼ inch lumps. For those interested, it is chemically known as CaC_2. It had to be kept very dry. Some of the crystals would be put into a container known as a generator that fastened to the bicycle frame. Another container, holding water would be fitted nearby. By admitting small quantities of water via a screw-down valve, acetylene gas - C_2H_2, would be generated. A rubber tube would carry the gas to the lamp in which would be a special burner or jet. Open the front of the lamp and apply a match! With a reflector in the back of the lamp, a reasonable amount of light would be forthcoming. We sold lots and lots of tins of carbide, 6d each (2½p). An alternative form of lighting was paraffin, which also required a match to start it going. Eventually lamps became powered by dry batteries, battery number 800, a double-cell battery for front lights, and U2 for the smaller rear light.

We also sold a significant number of new cycles. These were mainly 'Hercules', a typical price £4-19-11, one old penny short of £5. My mother issued a card to the customer showing the date and amount paid, usually 2s 6d or half a crown, weekly. There were eight half-crowns to the pound so payment would take about forty weeks. No doubt there was some deposit and some interest. One year they sold one hundred bikes. Another quite unrelated line, on a display stand were various Ingersoll watches, five shillings each.

Up to 1933, there was no electricity in Elstead. The workshop was lit very poorly, with town gas - note, not natural gas. Radio sets, known as 'wireless' sets were driven by a 120-volt (v) high tension dry battery, a 9v Grid Bias battery and a 2v lead acid or 'wet' accumulator. The 120v battery would last for several months and was relatively expensive. The Grid Bias was small and narrow and would be adjustable by various plugholes or sockets, giving 2½ volts, 5 volts, 7½ volts and up to 9 volts, stepping up by moving the plug, as the battery ran down. It lasted a long time and was not very expensive. The final battery was a 2v accumulator filled with sulphuric acid. This, when fully charged, would last for about one week and then required recharging. Therefore, most people had two of these, one in use and one on charge.

With the arrival of electricity, May's bought a charging plant. It was a Hobart Rotary Converter and could charge one 12v car battery, two 6v car batteries and about twenty 2v accumulators in four rows of five. We painted numbers on the accumulators allocated to each customer and usually spent Saturday afternoon exchanging the weekly accumulators. For four pence old money a time. These things were a bit of a nightmare in that the terminals would corrode and break off. We had to keep them topped up with distilled water to keep the plates covered. The liquid from the battery was neat sulphuric acid and it took great delight in burning little holes into one's clothing that appeared a few days later as holes surrounded by miniature rainbows of colour, and this was the first that we knew of yet another pair of trousers ruined.

Of course, we used to supply these batteries and accumulators as required. Occasionally we would notice that one or two of these chargeable batteries would become old and no longer hold their charge and we would inform the customer to this effect. Before long he would arrive with a new accumulator, not purchased from us, with his number painted on. It would soon become apparent that someone had lost one of his or her new accumulators. We would probably discover, on examination, that the number had been altered on the one that the customer had brought into us as a replacement for his original. We found that the best way to sort this one out, was by direct confrontation, seldom was lasting damage done.

Before the arrival of electricity, some of the 'big houses' had their own small generating sets. Some of these had an assembly of large accumulators similar to the wireless variety, but much larger and therefore able to store much more energy. There was a stationary engine, usually a Petter or a Lister. This drove a dynamo by means of a belt and would thereby charge these storage batteries. It would give a certain amount of direct current lighting, usually 12 volts, by the simple act of switching on. If the set had no storage accumulator, then one could only obtain light by starting the engine. If the engine stopped, the light stopped. Only light was obtained this way, not power as we know it today.

These engines were started from cold with petrol and when warmed, would switch over to paraffin. I had the job on Saturdays of delivering, by means of a handcart, cans and cans of paraffin in two-gallon cans and collecting the empties.

My Saturdays were usually taken up with wireless batteries, accumulators, paraffin deliveries, or perhaps cleaning someone's bicycle. One interesting application of generating electricity was down at Elstead Mill. This was once a woollen mill, but at this time a private house. There Mrs Bentley, the owner, had harnessed the water wheel to a dynamo, as they were then called. This was charging a large 'bank' of accumulator batteries, which gave a very liberal supply of electricity. Periodically, we would have to go and tend to this apparatus as required. The maintenance was very little and of course the power supply, that is waterpower, was free. In the workshop, with the coming of electricity, as well as the battery-charging plant previously mentioned, the petrol pumps were soon changed from hand-operated to electric. Four-poster car hoists appeared and the air compressor. Try to operate today without electricity!

I commented earlier about the situation after the sale of the buses. In fact, apart from the activities that I have described there was quite a lot happening. They were operating two one and a half ton Ford tipper lorries. Tipping was achieved by two handles, one handle and one man each side. Winding these handles rotated a shaft behind the cab, which turned a vertical 'worm', which lifted the body - if one could. As I said earlier, The Glebe Meadow was some two acres. The vehicles were kept busy delivering ballast and sand, which was dug by hand from the rear of these two acres to a depth of several feet and was delivered 'as dug' in one and one half cubic yard loads. In addition, they dredged river sand from the River Wey, situated at the lower boundary of The Glebe Meadow and reached by a track for the cows at Stacey's Farm next door. The track led to the water meadow below. Across the water meadow could be seen the Elstead Mill, a lovely building, still standing and well preserved now as a restaurant.

The new house at Glebe Meadow next to Grandma Jesse Curel's house. It was built on land purchased from Winifred and Dick May for £70 in March 1927. Pictured is Dick May with Christine and Peter and "Old Bill".

As a child I could lie in bed and hear the water rushing over the water wheel, which was very soothing. Sometimes the water would be diverted to a parallel channel that bypassed the wheel, when the wheel stopped, all would be silent. On these occasions, I would not sleep so well as I sorely missed the comforting sound of the water. The dredging of the river sand was primitive in the extreme. The local blacksmith, Guy Bovington at the Elstead Forge, had made for May's a sort of inverted coal scuttle. It was really a copy of a five-gallon oil drum with an open front and had many holes to allow the water to drain out. It was attached to a long wooden pole at the rear of the drum. We had a flat-bottomed punt, with a small standing deck at each end. The 'dredgers' would drop the coal scuttle into the river, with the pole uppermost and standing on the deck would drag the scuttle along the riverbed thus filling with sand. Then pull it out of the river and allow it to drain, then lift it up, swing round though 180° and lift it higher to tip the sand into the punt. When full, the punt would be 'poled' along to the river bank to the foot of the property. It was then shovelled on to the bank. Then away for some more.

Dick May filling up Peter's car with "Old Bill" as the passenger.

The supply would vary according to the time of year, rainfall and therefore flow of water, this being the controlling factor. Flood time would bring along plenty of sand, particularly on the river bends. In times of short supply, they would have to pole further up the river to find supplies. After all this, the lorry would come along and again shovel the sand onto the vehicle for delivery, delivered for something like three shillings per cubic yard on average. The local sand pits under the Hogs Back, called Runfold, were plentiful and a cubic yard was measured by a bottomless box with four lifting handles measuring 1 yard, by 1 yard, by 1 yard. When full and levelled at the top, it could be lifted by two men and leave a heap of sand to be loaded, which was one cubic yard. River sand was cleaner and 'sharper' than dug sand from the Runfold Belt and would be used for quality plastering work. A competitor, Frank Harber, with his Morris-Commercial lorry would be doing the same thing a few miles away at Eashing Bridge.

A young Peter May, with Roger the dog in a 1928 Austin Seven. Years later, June had a similar machine in which she drove many miles with the children. I sold it for £5 and have never been forgiven!

I mentioned that among other activities, they were operating Ford tippers and this is probably the embryo of the haulage or transport business that came later. The lorries were well exercised by the apparently very strong demand for the supply and delivery of the 'home dug' aggregates, which went straight out to the builders' jobs and the same for the home dredged river sand. After the lower end of The Glebe Meadow had been excavated, it was turned into a very nice landscaped sunken garden.

Here was introduced the local Bargate Stone from Godalming. It was available as flat, crazy paving, large intricate rockery stones with nooks and crannies to harbour all sorts of alpine plants, and dressed walling stone. These products were also supplied and delivered by the May's. We had in this sunken garden a lovely supply of 'sharp' watercress from the constant supply of fresh clear spring water from the surrounding hills, the only way to grow watercress. Another commodity was the Farnham path gravel, sticky and heavy, but it made excellent paths and drives.

The gardening and landscaping was carried out by our own staff, during any slack period of work, they were never stood off if work was scarce. All of this was going on among and in addition to the accumulators, the private hire car, the car and bicycle repairs etc. As the aggregate supply at Glebe Meadow was soon 'dug out', it left the front half of the property on which were the workshop, the house and the petrol pumps at road level as original.

Another property was acquired one and one half miles away, which was fairly remote and near the same River Wey. Here they started digging again for aggregates. This time they had a very primitive screening plant, which graded the size and mix of the ballast. It was driven by a petrol engine and series of belts, was a bit rickety and could be towed about the site. All was dug by hand. The pit was reached from the road by a long un-surfaced lane called 'Ham Lane'. I would go with the driver because I would drive the lorry down the lane to the quarry and back again when loaded. By pulling on the steering wheel to keep me forward, I could just reach the pedals and see just enough through the screen! At about ten years old, very good training! Obviously our activity and scope was very limited. The supply of aggregates was becoming big business and large areas of land were being developed for the purpose.

Excavators, conveyor belts and large storage hoppers with different sizes and grades became available, which rendered May's 'hand digging' somewhat obsolete and the property which was known as 'Ham Lane' was sold a few years later. Nevertheless, it was very surprising looking back how many customers, mainly builders, used these services. Not only sand and ballast, but many more uses for the lorries were building up. Movement of bricks, coal, horse manure, topsoil, site clearance, birch faggots (for wood ovens for bread making), eggs (boxed from a poultry farm), to London and other destinations.

Ladham's Nurseries at Elstead House with lots of land behind attended many flower shows in Surrey, Sussex and London. The Royal Horticultural Society's hall at Ecclestone Square was a regular. Here Ladham's would set up a 'rockery' with the Godalming Bargate rockery stones and their own alpine plants grown at Elstead. All the gear and equipment would be loaded at Elstead and taken to the destination. The stand would then be set up by Ladham's Reg Pritchard who ran the nursery. Those rockery stones were very heavy but everything had to be manhandled. These displays were very skilfully done and the variety of plants, shrubs and landscapes exhibited by different nurseries was diverse. Some of the bigger shows were as good as the Chelsea Flower Show and indeed, we did for several years carry to and from the Chelsea Flower Show.

The clearing of these shows was always a late finish. Usually Saturday, sometimes Sunday evenings and probably 6.30 pm before we could start to break down the stand and load the lorry. Always a problem to grab a trolley to carry the goods out to the parking bay, there were never enough of them. At the end of the London shows, the locals would be waiting outside. All of those magnificent and exotic cut flowers, although several days old but well preserved, would be up for grabs, all given away to anyone who asked. It was usually well after midnight when we finished and we would unload Monday morning.

The local rural district council began hiring one and a half ton tipping vehicles on day or part day hire, daily hire rate 28 shillings or three shillings per hour. An increasing amount of the work required a non-tipping but longer platformed vehicle for bulkier loads.

The first lorry, PL 5117, a 2-ton Ford, bought in 1931. Note the hand-operated petrol pumps, the left-hand pump dispensed Redline Glico (Anglo-American Oil), centre probably Dominion Motor Spirit and the right-hand pump National Benzole.

In addition, a detachable cover or 'tilt' could be fabricated with an ash frame and fitted tarpaulin sheet, which could be lifted on and off. These were made by Joe Hogger in Godalming. You now have an open truck with drop-sides or a covered vehicle of the required length. From the Aldershot and District Guildford depot was purchased an ex-bus minus its body. On this Dennis chassis was built a lorry cab and body. The bus depot was very near to the Dennis Bros factory at Guildford and nearby there were the bodybuilding premises of Mr Gash. Into these premises was wheeled the Dennis, work commenced and completed and the finished article was well inspected and greatly admired. But - when the great day arrived to collect the vehicle, it would not come out as it was built too high for the doorway, requiring a certain amount of demolition of the workshop and producing a few red faces. I think that it was not a very satisfactory vehicle and after a couple of years was sold and replaced by a new 2-ton Bedford drop-side truck for which was made a new 'tilt'.

From 1928 to 1933, the pattern of the lorry world was obviously changing, as was the motorcar, servicing and repair side of the business. The car population was increasing, therefore so was the repair and servicing. The production of home-dug ballast and home-dredged river sand was decreasing to small orders. Whilst the variety of goods carried and the variety of customers using small tipping vehicles was quite wide, the 'tipping' world was becoming more and more reliant on the local council's day work. Also working on hire to other local operators on an 'as required' basis, provided some revenue. However, when the council ran out of money each year, from around December until the following March, two vehicles spent most of their time parked up behind the garage building, whilst the third vehicle, the non-tipping Dennis and then the Bedford, had other work and with the aforementioned 'tilt' it became a covered vehicle, whereby covered work such as household removals provided another activity. The council contract was by tender and usually the competition came from two Guildford operators, one of which J. Bentley owned a Runfold sand pit and the other, Benjamin Heath. It was a very tense time during February awaiting the outcome of our tender, which obviously we did not always win.

If these vehicles were used during the winter and the weather was frosty, then the water had to be drained from the radiator every night. That involved turning a very greasy and stiff tap underneath and another inaccessible and stiff tap at the back of the engine. Going out at 7 am the next morning probably meant the use of a blowlamp to thaw the water tap, wrapped in a sack at the front of the building. This assumes that the watering can could be found, when two trips with the can would be required. A self-starter, if fitted, relied on a six-volt battery and was more of an ornament than anything else.

So, cranking up from the starting handle was the norm. Thinking of modern vehicle comforts, it is quite impossible to compare these with the vehicles that we had. For instance, the seats were usually utterly worn out, being once covered with a sort of rexine, now ripped to pieces and releasing several coil springs some of which had broken, presenting several very sharp protrusions. The remedy was a folded heavy twill corn sack, but the sharp points still found their way through! Underneath the seat was the petrol tank. The floorboard, literally boards, were rattling about loose on the floor as the fixings were long since defunct and many draughts and water 'lived' inside the cab!

The windscreen was a split affair. A top half screen from one side to the other that opened, the bottom half fixed. There should have been a rubber seal between the two halves but the words are 'should have been'. The rain that blew in ensured that the driver had wet knees. The wiper was a single blade some nine inches long that described a small arc at eye level. It was usually a suction type of wiper that, as one applied the accelerator to climb a hill, the vacuum stopped and so did the wiper! The door windows were ordinary plate glass and slamming the door broke the glass, which remained in about three pieces, rattling inside the door. Therefore it was pointless to replace it. Again the cure was a thick sack pinched over the top of the door. There was only one mirror so the occasional lifting of the sack was quite useful. Brakes and lighting (one rear light only) were in keeping with the rest of it. Of course the traffic conditions and the lack of rules and regulations were equally different, therefore relative. To complete the picture, there was a hand-operated tipping gear behind the cab, but when the vehicle was loaded it was quite impossible to tip the load by oneself. The vehicle that I have partially described was really an American Chevrolet (General Motors), with a Bedford badge, before they started manufacturing Bedfords at Luton as Vauxhall Motors. It was almost certainly of 1930 vintage. At this time, these were the types of tool with which we had to work, in common with other operators. There was no money to keep the thing as maintained as it should have been, just make do and mend until it became a total wreck.

The winter was the most difficult time to find work for the staff, but the various activities as described kept it going, including gardening and painting. It is interesting to hear that when Mrs Court Treatt, from the Elstead Mill, wished to go shopping at Harrods, the car, which at the time was a large Armstrong-Siddeley, would drop her at Harrods and then wait outside until she chose to emerge from the store. Imagine doing that today! One of the lorry drivers, who were also amateur mechanics, would do the driving. On one occasion, Mrs Court Treatt asked the driver, "if his fingernails were in mourning?" At Harrods, the driver would not leave the car in case she came out, so they always went armed with a bottle under the front seat, for obvious reasons. They had learned the hard way.

It was not all work. There were a few holidays. Writing about the Armstrong Siddeley reminds me of family camping holidays. This was a most unlikely activity for our family, but I remember my mother cooking on a Primus stove, protected from the wind with a three-sided biscuit tin, on Killiecrankie Pass in Scotland, whilst I was fascinated by the double-headed (two-engined) steam trains struggling up the pass on the adjacent railway line. I think that my sister and I slept in the back of the car, one on the back seat and one on the floor. At different times, we made John o'Groats, Land's End and South Wales.

South Wales was during the depression and it was quite frightening to us kids to see large numbers of unemployed and hungry men standing about in the towns devoid of all hope and self respect. We must have looked very ostentatious and prosperous, driving past in our big motorcar. No wonder that the looks we received were somewhat belligerent! Looking back on this episode and being so young and impressionable, it was an object lesson. It was a total surprise to me to discover that there would be so many people, all out of work, in the same town, all with the same problem. We were out of the protection and the environment of our little Surrey village and were precipitated into "how the other half lived", or rather did not live! It was a lesson that we needed to learn and it certainly had its effect.

During these early years, I was a pupil at Elstead Church School, from five years to eleven years of age and was part of the village community. I lived three minutes from the school, three minutes from the Church and as described, we lived at our place of work. On one side was a working Farm, Stacey's Farm and on the other, the Cemetery. This I called the Elstead underground or, the dead centre of Elstead. At this time the cemetery was still 'operative' and as kids, we witnessed many burials, by peeping through the railings. We understood that at midnight on a clear moonlit night, we could call up a ghost by dancing round an old grave, number 7, seven times. My sister and I sometimes with a few others, only ever managed at latest ten o' clock and after seven turns, would bolt home breathless, without ever seeing the apparition. Charlie Fitken was the gravedigger. He always wore 'whirlers', tied just below the knee to stop "the mice from running up his trouser legs". Into this whirler he pushed a dibber, a flat sharpened piece of wood for scraping off any soil clinging to his spade. He kept this clean and shiny, the easier to work. I noticed that this was no problem as he was digging clean ballast, from the same vein that we had dug from Glebe Meadow next door. At the funeral, Charlie would always be in attendance, behind the yew trees, armed with his spade, just in case a little final trimming of the sides was required to allow the coffin to descend. When one of the 'gentry' died, the grave would likely be lined. Charlie would peg the inside with wire netting to enable him to completely cover the inside of the grave with sprigs of laurel leaves. Quite how this assisted the soul of the departed into heaven I never discovered. After all of the mourners had gone, then most of the local women, all regulars when there was a funeral and who waited respectfully outside the cemetery, had slowly walked past the grave and every label on every wreath and bunch of flowers had been carefully read and noted, then Charlie could complete his task of 'filling in'. In common with other villages and communities, Elstead had a few characters, but as we were living among them, it probably took several years to realise and appreciate the fact.

It was usual most summers for the army to leave Aldershot and come to Hankley Common for manoeuvres. It was a really massive affair taking two or three days for regiment after regiment of Cavalry, Infantry, Royal Army Service Corp and all the others to pass over the river bridge into Elstead through the village, past the church and so out onto the Common. All of this was horse-drawn and accompanied by the full Regimental Bands leading each contingent - many of them. It was a transformation on the Common with rows of tents of all shapes, rows and rows of tethered horses, each with its own net of hay. How they watered them I do not know.

There were lines of gun limbers with highly polished artillery guns hooked on behind, General Service Wagons with stoves, equipment, ammunition etc. There was a freshly laid system of telephone wires all the way back to Aldershot and thousands of troops. A complete army on the move! Enterprising traders from Aldershot quickly arrived and set up 'shop', selling fruit, sweets, soft drinks and odds and ends to the troops. It certainly appeared that the organisation that the army had developed was highly efficient, perhaps a little clumsy or heavy handed, but they seem to have covered all requirements.

Whilst this army game was going on, there was a new well being dug by a local builder - Mr A.J. Tracy. This was near the edge of the Hankley Common, where a house was being built and was passed by the arriving Army. As the well became deeper, so stages were set up inside the circular hole being dug. The deepest man threw his excavations up to the lowest stage above. In turn, another man threw it up to the next stage and at the top, keeping it clear, was one 'Siddy Bowler'. He was an ex-service man himself and was passionately fond of military bands. He was a keen member of the British Legion and in the bar, after a couple of pints, he was well known for prancing around going "pomp de pompity pom, pom" with his clenched fists to his mouth as an imitation instrument and in his element. He was always happy and cheerful and liked by everyone. Back to the well. Siddy had to pull up and remove the ladders whilst his mates were digging as the ladders were in the way. With the arrival and passing of the Regimental Bands, 'Siddy' dropped his shovel and joined the following marching troops! The story does not recall for how long he was gone, but he would have been blissfully happy! I can only hope that his mates were released before nightfall.

Jack Elliott was a lengthman. That was the term used for a Parish Council employee, who, supplied with a wheelbarrow, shovel and broom, would sweep and clean up the verges of the roads running through the village. He would have a certain 'length' to keep clean. Jack Elliott was a lengthman as was his father before him. Jack was not the brightest of individuals and unfortunately for him, he stuttered quite badly. One day a motorist stopped and asked Jack the way to Thursley. Jack said "you go up this ro...ro... road for about thr...thr...three miles and turn le...le...left - oh bugger off, you could be there while I am telling you!" Another story tells of Jack, after a row with his wife saying - "I told her, I don't wa...wa...want yer tea, so I drank a cup and ca...ca...came out!"

Another colourful character was Mr A.J. Tracy, the local builder. He was a most kindly man and did all that he could for the village community. He was notoriously absent-minded and his driving was equally absent-minded. He drove a small open truck. He would leave his yard, emerging onto the Farnham Road from behind a high wall, straight across over the village green, bump, bump, across the Thursley Road onto another green and park outside his house without stopping or looking either left or right and he always got away with it. One of his workmen known as 'Tippy' Stillwell had one leg shorter than the other. This meant that the foot on the short leg had to be on 'tip toe' when he walked, hence the name 'Tippy'.

On the way to Milford was a very sharp, humped bridge - Oxenford Bridge and we as kids always asked mother to drive quickly over the bridge which would throw us up into the air from the back seat of the car. Well one morning, Mr Tracy was taking Tippy and one other to a job at Milford. Tippy being seated in the back with his legs dangling over the road. I do not need to relate what happened to Tippy. He was left behind at Oxenford Bridge! Further to this, the man still with Mr Tracy said "well Mr Tracy, you did say that we were going to Tilford, not Milford!" "Dang bust it, sonny" he said, "we had better go back", Tilford was in the opposite direction. Tippy was collected unharmed and away they went to Tilford. On arrival

Mr Tracy, then drew a plan of the job with a stick, in a pile of sand and all was well except that the lorry driver, Bill Pierce, arrived and loaded up the sand. Despite all of this, there is still a thriving business to this day being operated by the third generation.

The Post Office was operated by Vic Martin and his wife in the Milford Road. It had a highly polished mahogany counter, bare except for an equally highly polished set of scales with a neat pile of brass weights in ounces, for weighing letters and parcels, overlorded by Vic with his winged celluloid collar and was supported by his wife who hovered in the background. At the rear of the Post Office and little lower down, was a marvel of modern science, a telephone switchboard. This consisted of a vertical panel of sockets, one for each number of the telephone being called. The caller was connected by the operator, who pulled up a long wire cord from a horizontal panel in front of her and plugged it into the appropriate socket. She then turned a small handle in front of her that rang the bell of the telephone being called. She then had to wait for the call to finish before disconnecting the connection.

That was all fine, except that it was a twenty-four hour job, so that if someone made a call during the night, the poor operator would have to get up and then wait for the call to finish. It is not surprising that the operator became the most 'knowledgeable' person in the village. She had to act like the 'three wise monkeys - Hear no Evil, See no Evil, Speak no Evil', but she knew plenty!

The telegram 'boy' was Mrs Martin's sister, Bessie Blackman. She was always dressed in black from top to toe, including a large wide brimmed hat, also black. She had a very high bicycle, which, due to the efforts of climbing on to it, caused her to push it on most local trips. She delivered the telegrams in little buff coloured envelopes and always went through the farce of not knowing the contents when delivering it although she had read it at the Post Office when it arrived. The stock phrase was - "I hope it is not bad news!"

It is interesting to note that some of the original telephone numbers which started at number one and so on are still going. William Etherington was number one, A.J. Tracy & Son Ltd were seven, Glazier and Ellis were thirty three, D May by now known as May's Motors were thirty four and George Chandler Ltd thirty five. Of course there are several other numbers in front of the original numbers nowadays, but there are still some links. Soon after the telephones were installed, William Etherington was reputed to having used it as follows - first came - "number please" from the operator, "Get me Dick May of Elstead, don't want no number, tell 'im its Willy a callin" and it worked.

However, the Post Master, Vic Martin had a very serious problem, his telephone operator, 'Miss' somebody, had become pregnant. This situation, when presented to Mr and Mrs Martin a couple of the highest integrity and soaked in the doctrine of the Congregational Church - indeed they lived almost next door to it - would have been devastating! Immediate action was taken whereby the 'Miss' someone was spirited away, no information given, to make it appear that it had never happened and that was that.

My mother's sister, Aunt Ethel, (left) with a friend.

During this period, my parents had sold a plot of land to my grandmother Jesse Curel, who built a new house next door to ours and sold 'The Laurels', her previous house at Witley. My mother's spinster sister Ethel, lived with my grandmother. Their brother, George, also lived in Elstead some two miles distant and he had four daughters. He had served with the Twenty First Lancers and had joined up, as did Dick May, at Aldershot. So my grandmother had three children, all of them in Elstead. For some years George worked for his brother-in-law driving a lorry, but they eventually fell out. Neither of them found it difficult to do that.

The Garage business, by now known as May's Motors, had employed a working manager cum-salesman-cum-general hand, who greatly assisted my mother who did all of the bookwork and most of the thinking. The one thing that was far reaching during this period was the 1933 Road and

Rail Traffic Act - more of that later. I was from 9 years of age to 15 years during this phase. I spent as much time as possible travelling around on the lorries. I moved from Elstead Primary School, to Farnham Grammar School – in 1935.

Grandma Jesse Curel taken at "Shirley", the new house in Elstead, in 1928.

Mention was made earlier of William Etherington. He came from very humble beginnings and his proudest boast was that he was or rather had been - "the poorest boy in the parish" and as such, had received some form of parish relief, obviously the early days of social security. He now had a "Wood Business" and a very good one. There were several large estates around Elstead and all had their own extensive Coppices or Copses. They were usually operated on a seven-year cycle and to the owner, were a source of revenue, as was the field of grass or corn.

Willy would contract to cut and husband the copse and to buy the product wood, which was quite diverse. Properly handled, it was ready again in seven years time. The land was usually wet and unusable as arable or grassland and would otherwise go wild. Today many of these areas have matured into beautiful and natural woodlands, glorified by primroses and bluebells. The main product was chestnut, birch, hazel or 'Powder Wood' which was alder, usually from the water meadows. Apparently, this alder was used for making gunpowder, hence the name.

Willy Etherington was able to supply the necessary. Everything was used from the copse. Willy's men had worked for him for years and years, as he was by now no longer a young man. Their skills with the 'hand bill' (a hand axe) and axe were superb. Chestnut posts and poles, posts and rails for chestnut fencing and chestnut palings for fencing, bark strippings for borders and mulching, timbers for cart shed roofing - hand-made etc. Young birch trees were cut just before they came into leaf in early March when the whole birch wood had a pinky, mauve hue to it, but as yet no leaf. They were made into faggots (bundles) and stacked about the woods. We would come along with a lorry and hopefully dodge the birch tree roots remaining, as they would easily wreck a tyre.

We would load these faggots (butts outwards) and deliver to bakeries in Churt, Runfold and two in Elstead for heating the 'wood ovens' for bread making. They were stacked into ricks for use as required, until the next year's supply came along. The best way, in fact in those days the only way, to draw the product out to the road, was by horse and cart. Willy had two of these and nightly they could be seen plodding their grateful way home, always loaded with product from the woodlands, to store in the yard. All otherwise non useable woodland cuttings from the trees were collected and brought home known as 'cord wood' and converted into logs for the Saturday log delivery round. The hazel wood was special in that the 'woodland craftsmen' would, in the woods, make those lovely hurdles and stack them where they were made awaiting collection and ultimately to the customer. They were always oversold.

Willy, because of his upbringing was extremely frugal - he had to be. He could not drive. He travelled his working area, which was extensive, around the various estates by bicycle. His woolly jumper was a collection of holes connected by woollen strands. He always wore mittens (fingerless gloves) and heavy hobnail boots. When in rain, he strung a heavy twill sack over his shoulders, tied round his neck by a piece of string. This is the best bit and perfectly true, the front tyre of his bicycle, which was completely worn through exposing the inner tube, was sewn together by binder twine (agricultural string), in order to achieve a few more miles!

One would imagine, from what I have described above, that he was a right scrooge. Not true. He was not. Willy and his wife Lou had no children. Rumour has it that in their large kitchen, were two large cupboards. On the left, one would be frequented by Lou, as it contained the gin bottle. On the right, the second would be visited by Willy as it contained the whisky bottle. However, occasionally Willy would visit the local hostelry on his way home. It was not unknown for his bicycle, now being pushed not ridden, to lead him to an open ditch, usually dry, alongside the Thursley Road. It was quite normal for some local to assist him to re-navigate and point him in the direction homewards. Although no children, I understand that they brought up more than one child, thereby giving them a home, which otherwise they would not have had.

I recall three names of his workforce 'Twinger Bonner', who spent many evening hours at the saw bench cutting logs, 'Tuppeny Birchett', why 'Tuppeny' is not known and 'Nobby Clarke'. Nobby was a lovely simple soul. One day, whilst leaning on his bicycle, he confided to me that he was concerned about his wife's health. "Why, what's the matter Nob?" I said. "Well Pete" he said, "She's got a collision of wind and water." One more thing, a pair of semi-detached houses, top side of the Recreation Ground came up for auction. Willy bought them. Sadly, Inland Revenue wanted to know where the money came from, as according to his tax returns, he could not afford them. However, he survived it!

We eventually supplied him with an ex-army Bedford truck and thereafter maintained it for him. Here ends the chapter on Willy Etherington. Frugal though he was, he was a most straightforward and honest man and added much to my experience of life as it unfolded.

Talking of Willy Etherington's horses calls to mind another important activity of shoeing horses. Guy Bovington was the village Blacksmith. There were quite a number of heavy working horses around the village and they all required shoes. As well as the horses for carts, traps and riding and one pony for Clem Reid's milk round, Guy made them all. He also did all sorts of general ironwork as required. In those days there was no oxy-acetylene or electric welding.

Everything was heated in a 'Coke Breeze' fuelled furnace. A large lever worked a large bellows pumped by hand, which blew the coke into a red hot mass, showering out sparks through which the iron was passed and held by a pair of tongs until it was red hot. Therefore the blacksmith worked with one hand, the other doing the pumping until the material came out of the fire.

The metal, whilst still red, was held with the tongs and hammered into shape on the anvil, being periodically dipped into a trough of cold water to adjust it to the correct temperature. The traditional shape of an anvil is much more sophisticated than it would first appear as it allows all sorts of shapes to be beaten out of red-hot steel, more than one would imagine. Like humans, horses' feet are all different sizes and shoes were therefore individually made, starting with a piece of flat bar. Even the nail holes, some square, some round, were punched out of the softened metal. Every so often it would require reheating to further the process. The forge building was divided into two compartments. The inner contained the forge, the bellows, the water troughs, the tongs, the anvil, hammers etc and lengths of various sized flat bar and lots of unfinished gates, hinges, pick axes for sharpening, things to repair and so on.

The other compartment was where the horse to be shod stood. There would be the usual top and bottom half door leading to the outside. For regular customers, particularly the heavy horses, their sizes would be known and the shoes would have been previously made, therefore only requiring fitting. The blacksmith would wear a thick leather apron, turn his back to the horse's head and hold its foreleg between his thighs, holding its hoof in his hand with the bottom face of the hoof facing upwards. The old shoe would have been removed and the new one heated and then laid onto the hoof where it would burn its impression onto the hoof. From these burn marks would be seen the profile of the 'fit' of the shoe. The hoof would then be cut if necessary, with a curved knife and finished off with a coarse rasp file. When a good fit was obtained the shoe would be nailed to the hoof. The smell of the burning hoof was to me, horrible!

The blacksmith had to contend sometimes with a frightened horse with mighty kicking power. However, providing he knew what he was doing and avoided going 'too deep', or nailing in the wrong place, the horse would feel nothing as the hoof is something like our finger nails, having no actual feeling. I have gone on at some length on this subject as it was a most important factor in everyday life and now the blacksmith and his important role have quite gone as there are many modern facilities that replace the blacksmith. Modern horseshoeing would be done by a farrier, but that is nothing like the same thing as the village blacksmith.

You might also ask what this has to do with May's Motors, or haulage contracting. The answer is nothing. I trust though that it is of interest to the reader.

As I am writing in this vein, there is quite a lot more about this period which hopefully will add background to the situation at that time of my life, therefore I might was well carry on, because it is in the context of the unfolding story.

May's Motors had by now, acquired an Austin Car Agency. Our distributor was Messrs H.A. Jackson of Godalming, from whom we ordered our new cars. The Agency was then much simpler than today, but we did sell quite a few new vehicles over a period of years. The car workshop was by now quite busy and most of the custom was very local and very personal. Nevertheless, a new car was quite an event, good for us and the customer. There were no car transporters, so cars were driven down by road. The vehicles had to be treated very carefully until run-in, a recommended thirty m.p.h. for 1000 miles. Drivers were paid 'job and finish', so the quicker they could complete the delivery and then arrange a lift back to Longbridge, Birmingham, the better for them. Quite a bit of engine damage could be inflicted due to overheating, causing partial engine seizure and possible permanent harm.

The solution was to get Mr May to collect the car from the factory. This entailed setting sail in the Armstrong-Siddeley, complete with me and sometimes my sister, but certainly my grandmother from next door, my father and my mother who would drive the Armstrong home. My grandmother was a 'large lady' in her seventies and very dominant who still retained a somewhat Victorian attitude. The trip to and from Birmingham was an excursion not to be missed by Grandma. She and Dick May conducted a fairly abrasive relationship over the years, so the journey home had a much better atmosphere as Dick was driving the new Austin.

The amazing thing about Grandma was her ability to climb into the rear seat of the car, complete with a large black hat with a long hat pin driven from one side to the other of her large mass of grey hair, to keep the hat in place and there she would stay, until we arrived home! The other thing was her infallible and detailed memory of every town and village and other landmarks of the journey through which we passed. Also, it was a break for daughter Ethel who looked after her rather demanding and dictatorial mother. It so happened, that I was one of the few that got on quite well with the 'old girl'.

The business of retailing petrol was another experience and that certainly has gone through a 'changing world'. We sold 'Redline' (Anglo American Oil Co.) and National Benzole for several years and later on we became 'Esso'. The letters 's' and 'o' making Esso mean Standard Oil (of America). There was a period when tanker drivers would come hawking petrol and do a deal for a load of petrol. This was their job. The brand? - R.O.P. - the company being Russian Oil Products.

We were not on a main road so that much of our petrol sales were on monthly account. The traders with several vehicles - cars, vans, etc like builders or other substantial businesses were obviously the best customers, but of course the credit risk was higher and it was always the same ones who owed the most and were the slowest payers, or went bust.

The other extreme was the type, and there were several of them, who bought very little petrol and who sat blowing their horn if we were inside and then after serving them with one or two gallons, we would have to dip the oil, top up the radiator, top up the battery with distilled water and then check their tyre pressures - all for free of course! The other filling station in the village, George Chandler, sold Shell petrol. We had some customers who used us for everything except petrol.

When pressing some of the private car customers for money for petrol or repairs to their car, it was not unusual to be confronted by a very irate customer who considered it to be most inconsiderate of us to want money when they had school fees to pay! It proved that all that glitters is not gold!

They used to say ..."that their car would not run well on Esso, much better on Shell," and it took us some time to understand this, as if they changed their car, the same thing happened. It turned out that they were Shell shareholders!

And so the whole operation went on. The haulage side, two 1½- ton tippers and one two-ton non-tipper continued much as before, with the tippers working mainly for the local council March to December and the other one on general work. As well as the Ladham's Nursery work and other work as described, it was running all over the south delivering new tables for Vann Bridge Table Works. Whenever I could go, I did, with Reg Adams the driver. He was a bus conductor on one of the Aldershot and District buses garaged in our yard and was made redundant one Christmas Eve and my parents took him on at thirty shillings per week, plus his midday meal. He worked for us until he retired at about seventy years old. When he finished driving we employed him on the switchboard until failing eyesight stopped that. He died aged ninety-one, for many years totally blind.

In 1935 I left Elstead School and was sent to Farnham Grammar School, leaving there in 1940. I was a choirboy at Elstead, perhaps looking more angelic than was truly the case. In addition, I would 'blow' the organ if required and ring the bells, one in each hand and one on the left foot. The Sunday morning 'parade' is worth a mention. Services were 11 am, 3 pm children, 6.30 pm Evensong. The morning service was attended by the 'Gentry' and those who thought they were. It was all-important to be seen, particularly by the Rector. Each would go to their 'own' pew and woe betide anyone who got there first, they would be quietly moved. Of course most of these people were genuine and very natural and contributed much to the community, but as usual, there were a few who tried but without much success.

One old dear ran the children's Sunday School, across in the school, having some twelve small children for about forty minutes before the morning service and would arrive at the church limping on her stick, at two minutes to eleven for maximum effect, with the kids in their Sunday best, who would quietly occupy their allotted pews. Just before the sermon started, the children were allowed to leave while the old dear would have to remain seated throughout the remainder of the service because of a 'weak heart'. She was so pious! She remained so, well into her nineties.

The Evensong was totally different. None of the Sunday morning parade would attend the evening service. The evening congregation always consisted of non-assuming people, wives, husbands, mums - none of the pretence of the morning. It is quite surprising that this impression came through so strongly to me so early in life, but it would be wrong to over generalise. My mother would play the organ occasionally if asked in emergency, if the usual organist could not. He was the local school Headmaster.

Many, if not most of the people were customers of ours. It is quite revealing how much one can learn about one's fellow creatures, by working for them and with them over a number of years. During the course of these happenings, the 1933 Road and Rail Traffic Act had been brought into force.

The Armstrong-Siddeley car, PG 99, with the family enjoying a picnic, somewhere on holiday. The absence of my mother in the photograph indicates that she was the photographer. Note the hood folded down at the rear.

3. The decade before the War

It is therefore necessary to describe the very minimum of this Act as it certainly affected the future of road haulage in this country. Its intention was to restrict the growth of road haulage in favour of the railways. It was typical of Government action by people who did not understand the railways or the road haulage industry, but who made life very difficult for those employed in either industry.

Sufficient to say that it did not, long term, prevent the growth of road haulage and if one looks at the state of the railways, it is more than evident how dreadful that outcome has become. They still do not learn from past mistakes. However, it is not the purpose of this book to become involved in the theories or solutions to this problem. The basics were that all vehicles classified as 'Goods Vehicles', had to be licensed under 'A', 'B' or 'C' licences. An 'A' licence allowed carriage of goods for anyone, anywhere but not one's own goods. 'B' licences allowed conditional carriage of goods for specified goods, for specified customers according to granted conditions, but own goods anywhere. 'C' licence, own goods anywhere, none for other people.

At the time, 1933, my parents would not have had much knowledge of the Act or its consequences, or indeed, bothered over much about it. They would have applied for a licence to meet the legal requirement applicable then. They still supplied sand, ballast, Bargate Stone, Farnham path gravel etc. from the surrounding pits as an aftermath of their own digging and dredging operations. Therefore, as they were carrying their own goods, purchased from the pits, until they had been delivered and sold - the term used was supplied and delivered. Therefore this would require a 'B' licence. For example, the 'B' licence for their two small tippers were "Building and Civil Engineering goods within 30 miles, other goods within 20 miles of Elstead Post Office. That meant haulage of those goods for other people. They could carry their own goods anywhere. For instance suppose they supplied and delivered a load of walling stone from Dorset for a customer in Elstead, or any other commodity that they owned, it was permissible.

The grant for the other vehicle, the non-tipper, read according to the work that it was doing at the time, something like this..."Furniture and effects within 150 miles. Goods for Ladham's Nurseries within 60 miles, Eggs for Dean's Poultry Farm within 40 miles, other goods within 20 miles of Elstead Post Office".

The stupid thing about it that was that the vehicle never carried our own goods and could therefore have been specified an 'A' licence. My parents did not understand that they could have mixed 'A' and 'B' licences. Also, as circumstances changed - losing a customer, gaining a new one, different goods, different destinations - required an application to vary the conditions on the licence. This was open to objection from the railways and from other road operators and required supporting evidence to achieve the change. This was costly, very long-winded and often farcical. There were very many other rules and regulations involved with this matter and I have tried to give only the 'bare bones', just to hopefully maintain the context of the story.

Rather similar to the large bus companies as described previously and the 1930 Road Traffic Act, larger haulage companies would have afforded and obtained expert advice and prepared themselves more fully for the effects of the new Act. For the smaller man, struggling to keep going, he would have accepted the need to apply for the new licence with the minimum of form filling and certainly not understanding the implications. Meantime village life and the activities of May's Motors went on.

As stated, there was the cemetery on one side of Glebe Meadow and a working farm called Stacey's Farm on the other. There were two or three more heavy horses which required new shoes every so often by Guy Bovington. As kids we used to go up into the hayloft above the stables and feed hay into the machine for cutting up into chaff and push it down to the horses below. On the other side of the yard were the cow stalls. The cows would come up from the water meadows below and automatically go into their own stall for milking twice a day.

Grass would be cut with a two-horse knife-mower, left to dry, turned with a horse drawn 'tedder' once or twice and then loaded onto a horse-drawn, four-wheeled cart by hand, brought up to the yard and made into a hay rick and then thatched with straw, to be used for winter feed. Similarly corn would be cut with a horse-drawn binder. This cut the corn and tied it into bundles or sheaves and dropped them regularly along the field.

They would then be hand-stacked vertically, in stacks of approximately five or six sheaves and allowed to dry. Again collected and stacked in a rick and thatched to keep out the water until the steam threshing tackle arrived to thrash out the corn during the winter. The traction engine, the threshing drum, a van, sometimes an elevator and a water cart would arrive hissing and clanking from its previous job, anxious to start again. To see that lot dragged, pushed and manoeuvred into position by the engine, having got it into the farmyard in the first place, to get the Engine lined up with the thresher, to fit the great driving-belt to operate the machine, was really awe-inspiring to watch. When ready there would be the threshing. Today, one man on a combine harvester and one on a tractor/trailer.

The days of Stacey's Farm were drawing to a close. There was granddad Ellis with his white flowing beard, his son Walter Ellis and his wife living at the farm, their son Gerald and wife, with two sons, lived nearby in 'Apple Tree Cottage'. Their main income was milk. Gerald operated the milk round with a Jowett van. His mother had a dairy down steps from her large farmhouse kitchen. Here she would 'separate' the cream from the very full rich milk with a hand-operated centrifuge. We would have delivered daily a small pot of cream, contained in a 'Shipham's Paste' jar, for one penny. The farm ceased operating and was sold. The main building eventually became a very nice British Legion Club, donated by Mr J.N. Billmeir. My father, a founder member of the Legion, was the person who really planted and nurtured the 'seed' for that to happen. The farmland was sold, some for housing and other fields to neighbouring farmers.

Gerald Ellis built a new dairy nearly opposite the Village Hall on some of the ex-farm's land. He purchased his milk from other farms surrounding the village, collected it each evening, pasteurised and bottled it ready for next morning delivery. This only left 'Blacklands Farm' and Clem Reid with his Pony and cart and their own milk rounds. Clem had milk in a large churn and dipped a ladle into the churn that was a stamped half pint or one-pint ladle. This went directly into the customers' jugs.

Gerald used May's for keeping his van going. The van had to contend with some three hundred stops and starts per day, six days (or was it seven?) per week. Everything used to wear out, door hinges, door catches, driver's seat, starter motor, all road springs and suspension shackles, engine, clutch, gearbox - the lot!

It was a Ford 10 cwt. E83W Van. Nothing was normally done to it until it broke. It was uncanny how the engine would pack up at Christmas each year. We would then set about an engine exchange at some time over the holiday and the gearbox would normally collapse at Easter time. At least it was warmer at Easter, lying underneath it with eyes full of falling mud, as we struggled to get it together. Poor Gerald would tell how he went all the way to a remote cottage up a very rough track on Hankley Common, the delivery would be a maximum of one pint and often he would get there only to be told "none today - thank you Mr Ellis!"

He really was so placid, I never heard him complain. His accounting system was a large drawer in his house. Our auditor, who was the same person as Gerald's told us that each year he was confronted with hundreds of little milk delivery duplicates, from his daily deliveries, which he simply emptied daily into the drawer. Eventually he purchased all of his milk from Unigate, who delivered it ready bottled and crated and took away the dirty bottles daily. During the hot weather, this was carried out at night. Gerald's son, also Gerald, carried on with the business until his own retirement.

I mentioned earlier that it was in 1933 that the Dennis lorry was replaced with the first new Bedford, a 2-ton long wheelbase drop-side truck and again as I said earlier, complete with a liftable, therefore removable 'tilt', making it into a covered vehicle when required. This facility, as with the previous Dennis Lorry, was used for household removals, These were mainly for farm workers moving from one farm to another and usually on a Saturday and from one 'tied' house to another. We invariably completed the loading with a mixture of kids, chickens, wire netting, soap, pet rabbits, coal, garden tools and the 'wife' perched precariously on a kitchen chair purposely left out, and wedged on the above articles!

The first new Bedford, a WHG model of 2-tons capacity, APF 418, new in December 1933, moving someone's caravan in its early days. One big improvement on this vehicle was the fitting of a one-piece windscreen, hinged at the top. Only one rear-view mirror and one rear light was the legal requirement in those days.

If there was a distance involved from collection point to delivery, we would make a periodic stop to check if all was well and complete. There would usually be two of us on the lorry and the male member of the family being moved would wedge himself into the cab with us to "show us the way". Sometimes they were pleased to leave the ex-farm, sometimes not pleased. It obviously depended on the farmer concerned. At the rear of the vehicle there was only a canvas sheet, fastened at the top, no doors. This was tied back to allow light and vision to the occupants peering out. I do not know why no one seemed to be overcome by exhaust fumes, as there were plenty. I suppose they were different to farm yard smells! If there was a distance involved such as Norwich or similar, it would mean a very early start. The packing and loading would take perhaps four hours, then the return journey and, on arrival the unloading, probably to find that the wardrobe would not go up the stairs. We have even removed an upstairs window to achieve this before today. Sometimes it was so late that the prime object was to get the beds installed and leave them to it, complete with tired and hungry kids, dog, chickens, rabbits, etc. Often they were entering a completely strange and unknown world and employer.

Removals were real pioneering stuff for us, as was much more of the business. In applying for a Carrier's Licence from scratch, they had to apply for conditions as existing at that time. This explains the wording among other conditions on the grant of that 'B' licence, "Furniture and Effects, within 150 miles of Elstead Post Office". The 150 miles was a bit of fiction anyway but it was granted.

The 1930s was a time when our 'wheel was slowly turning' and the 'changing world' was of course, still changing. I was six years to 15 years old, being of 1924 vintage. It did not appear to be a 'changing world' to any extent, probably because my greatest activity was dealing with school and with the process of growing up. Our life was really The Business. It was the means of survival. It was my parents' creation and took priority. That is not to say that there was no recreation, no fun, no family life - there was, and of course, village life.

Alongside Stacey's Farm was Hope Street. A terrace of very small houses, two up and two down were very primitive. Further down the lane, lived and worked Henry Young. He sat in his shed making birch brooms, the birch no doubt supplied by Willy Etherington. Henry would require a year's supply as the birch material was only any good just before it came into leaf, the same as the 'Faggots' for the bread ovens.

Henry came to Dick May one day and asked for a favour. Could Dick collect a corpse from Hope Street, "the coffin would fit into May's wagon a treat". My father went round at about six 'o' clock to collect it to take it to Headley, about eight miles up the road. It sounded a bit rowdy and Dick could not make himself heard because there was so much noise. Eventually Henry Young came downstairs and said "Shan't want you cos Lord Jesus not ready for him". Dick was invited in and went up the stairs to find the 'corpse' sitting up in bed drinking hot elderberry wine whilst someone in the corner played the violin.

It was almost certain that the winter rain would cause the River Wey to flood. This was below our premises where we dredged river sand and one of the water meadows where the cows grazed in summer. We could see The Mill House. If flooding happened it would look like a lake in front of the Mill instead of a river. We would receive a telephone call from the owner Mrs Bentley, "could we please come straight away and carry her (very nice) furniture upstairs, from her ground floor lounge". It could have perhaps twelve to fifteen inches of water throughout the ground floor.

A float for Elstead Carnival, sometime in the early 1930s. Dick May is "Mrs Tubb", the tall man looks like Henry Ellis of *Glazier & Ellis*, and on the left of Henry is Siddy Bowler, who abandoned the Welldiggers to follow the band.

The few years before the war were nationally fairly depressed, particularly the farming industry and the increasing talk of trouble in central Europe did not help very much. Whilst our Garage side was slowly developing, the 'Developing Haulage Business' was not. We still had the same old two tippers and the one, newer, 1933 Bedford. Haulage contractors were all competing for any job going, all using similar equipment and by and large would never say no to a job if they felt that there was the slightest possibility that they would manage it. The restrictions imposed by the new Act would be interpreted by the operator as widely as the imagination would allow. For instance, in our own case "Furniture and Effects, 150 miles" really meant Household Removals, 150 miles so we were carrying new tables for "Vann Bridge Table Works" all over the South. We considered that tables were furniture, so on we went. One bold operator, Fred Henden of Pirbright, running about six lorries, all Fords and all 5-ton drop-side trucks, had written on his vehicles "Anything, Anywhere, Anytime". Today's Trade Descriptions Act might question the accuracy of that statement, in view of the diversity of things that needed moving. However, Fred was doing nothing wrong and ran a good business. Imagine the enforcement problems that emerged from all of these different licence conditions and other new regulations, including the new keeping of records, or Driver's Log Books that had to be kept.

Any change of operation could mean a variation to the licence. We would have to prove the need perhaps before a Licensing Authority's Traffic Court to achieve the variation and the application could well have received objections from the railways and perhaps, from other lorry operators. One can see the difficulty of "proving the need", more than likely before the event of the job happening. Therefore, if a company was tendering for a job and needed transport, and if they got the job, for us it would mean perhaps an extra vehicle. Well, what would probably happen would be that if the job came off, the operator would start work on it anyway. We obviously had no sympathy for the 1933 Act and would have no compunction about breaking the law, if we thought that we could get away with it. I have deliberately over simplified and understated much of this subject out of pity for the reader, but it became a very big subject and a legal minefield.

The early haulage contractor, the entrepreneur, was in the main, a hard working, non-sophisticated fair-minded person. These were the people who pioneered the haulage business, the small firms. The larger companies of the same period were quite different, but probably developed from the merging and amalgamations of smaller companies anyway. The people that I am writing about would almost certainly have had no financial training at all and no business training. They would be prepared to work for 'a fair price for a fair job'. They would be resourceful and they had to be. There would be no set start and finish times. They were quite prepared to work hard for a living.

I would have to suggest that most, if not all of us, as we are included, when confronted with the new regulations set about getting around them if possible. Over a period of time, vehicle size could be increased, fleet size would creep up, licence conditions would be varied and improved, the odd 'A' licence would be acquired, contract licences obtained and so on. This process was long and hard so there was a certain amount of illegal working involved, in other words we became legal by operating illegally. When we saw someone else doing it later we would moan about it, but that's life! I was still at school for the first six years of the Road and Rail Traffic Act, so did not really know much about it, but had quite a bit to do with it later on.

Perhaps it was stress or frustration born of the foregoing, but it was a pity that my father had such a volatile temper, without much logic attached to it. He would fly up in the air over some thing when it would often have been better to have kept quiet. On one occasion many years ago, he answered the phone to one of our then best customers, Mr Gordon of Weyburn Engineering Co. Mr Gordon was apparently of similar disposition and was yelling down the phone alleging that our vehicle, as ordered, was late. The result was a head-on verbal collision and we lost all of their work for the next forty years. We did eventually resume working.

The "old man" would argue, usually without logic and having stirred it up, would leave someone else to clear up the mess and he would clear off and completely forget it! This was often very difficult for my mother and sometimes members of staff. There was a similar temper problem with old George Chandler, down the road at the other garage. George Taylor who lived nearby as a small boy, had made himself a bicycle. This was achieved by visiting the local dump at Woodside Farm where a collection of old bikes, prams, wheelbarrows and so on, could usually be found. George had created this machine from scrap, but it was totally brakeless. Old George Chandler was carrying two buckets of water for the horses across the yard when young George Taylor came flying into the yard and completely flattened old George and his buckets. He was so angry that he went and fetched an axe and chopped the bicycle into two separate pieces.

The same George Taylor was naturally mechanically minded particularly with engines. He later became our fleet engineer. Many years ago, Ron Tracy from the builder's family, was building an extension to his house. There was a concrete mixer there on site, George and his friend "Fizz" Reffold, were wandering about the village in the dark, at about ten 'o' clock when they came across the mixer. Fizz found the starting handle in the drum of the mixer. He fitted it on to the engine and proceeded to wind. George knew exactly how to set and 'tickle' the carburettor, so whilst Fizz was winding, she burst into life and carried on running - pom, pom, pom, pom. This was the signal for the two of them to rapidly disappear into the night. Poor Ron Tracy had to get up and come down to stop the thing.

One of my greatest fascinations was the arrival and operation and departure of the annual Village Fair. It would arrive during a Thursday in June, open Friday evening, Saturday afternoon and evening and leave Sunday. Whilst a lorry can only pull one trailer, a Showman can pull three or four trailers. This is a concession gained by the Showman's Guild. They, like us had to apply for a 'C' licence to carry their own goods. Each vehicle and trailer had to have its own disc on display. My fascination was with those magnificent great Showman's traction engines.

I would rush home from school, run 300 yards down to the Village Green and watch every movement and action that was carried out by the staff and their engines. I would watch for hours. They would tow their beautiful great four wheeled caravans into position, all polished copper and chrome, their ornate cut-glass mirrors, their highly painted wheels etc complete with smoking chimney from their coal fired-cooking range.

Entrance was in the centre on the side. There were three wide steps. The caravan was carefully placed whereby most of the stalls and rides could be seen by Madam, the owner's wife, who spent most of her time sitting on the top step. She would wear a large black apron with a wide and deep pocket sewn on the front. During the opening hours, staff would frequently come to the caravan and pass over the money to The Missus.

I would watch the engines manoeuvre, drag or winch the trailers into position to unload their cargoes and then pull away empty out of the way. The 'Roundabout' or 'Galloping Horses' was loaded on the trailers piece-by-piece in the right sequence to allow progressive rebuilding of the Roundabout at the next site. This machine was built around the centre engine, mounted on its own four wheels. A beautiful, small, self -contained steam engine that drove the Roundabout round and round and it drove the wonderful organ with its moving 'Musicians' as well. The Roundabout was completely built around this machine, with the coal smoke emerging from the central chimney at the top.

All of the electrics, mainly for hundreds of coloured lights, were generated by the big engines which had a front-mounted dynamo driven by a flat belt from the engine flywheel. The engine would quietly, gently and smoothly tick over, generating light for as long as you wished, providing that you fed it with plenty of coal and water. It was always shining bright and highly polished. The work was very heavy and very labour intensive and the men would be filthy at the end of the setting up. However, despite the fact that they had to carry all of the water to their caravans, they emerged in the evening to operate the rides spick and span.

Starting very late on Saturday evening, after shut down, they would start dismantling the whole lot. I was not interested in having money when the Fair was operating, to ride on various things. I could quite happily watch the machinery performing throughout and Sunday would find me there again, watching. However, my aunt Ethel would take my sister and I and her brother's four girls from the other end of the village to the Fair on the Saturday, which we all enjoyed. It was finished off Saturday evening by a visit from 'Fishy Stevens' from Farnham, who arrived in his van with hot fish and chips, with plenty of salt and vinegar.

Bob Pearce (Garage Manager), Peter May, Dick May, Peter Pearce with the Armstrong-Siddeley car at Hammersmith Bridge en route to Olympia for Dick May to leave for Sudetenland in 1939. The trip was cancelled the next day.

In 1938, Neville Chamberlain, with his Appeasement Policy and his politicians decided to send a peacekeeping force to Sudetenland, to prevent Hitler from invading Czechoslovakia, or something like that. It was a non-armed civilian force set up by the British Legion. Dick May was elected as one of the people to go. They were to assemble one Sunday at Olympia. My mother, with us, delivered Dick in the Armstrong-Siddeley to Olympia. We have photographs taken from Hammersmith Bridge with my father with his peaked cap and a British Legion badge, armed with a walking stick. The next day, the whole thing was cancelled. I reckon just as well, or for us the whole course of history would have been changed.

On 3rd September 1939, it was a Sunday. I was at home and I heard on the radio that war had been declared. My mother happened to be playing the organ at Elstead Church for the 11 am service. I went into the rear of the church via the vestry, whispered to my mother the news and it was announced from the pulpit.

Before this chapter is closed I would add one little fact. I mentioned earlier that sometimes I rang the church bells. It was customary to ring the old year out and the new year in, at midnight on New Year's Eve. Old Billy Pierce, who taught me, grew too old to do this. Perhaps I was too young. However, for one or two years, I went on my own at 11.45 pm on New Year's Eve into that dark and creepy old church to ring. The process was to ring normally one, two, three, one, two, three, until about two minutes to midnight. Then strike twelve on the toll bell. Then at past midnight, wind all three ropes together, clang them all together, then go home. I think that I am the last person, so far, to do this, but that may not be true as several years have passed since I left Elstead. At the outbreak of war all church bell ringing stopped only to be used in the event of invasion. Fortunately that did not happen!

Among the vehicles visible in this view are (left to right) a new Ford Popular, Ford Y type, Morris Eight, the Armstrong-Siddeley "taxi", new Morris Ten and another new Ford Popular on our trade plate 890 PA, issued to May's Motors by Surrey County Council. The Armstrong Siddeley PG 99 had been replaced with a later model PJ 2249.

4. Wartime - 1939

My ever-changing world certainly underwent a dramatic change on 3rd September 1939 by the outbreak of war. I was fifteen years old at the time and took my examinations in 1940. The subjects that I had to take were English, History, Geography, French written, French oral, Mathematics, Physics and Chemistry. The best achievement would be Matriculation, the second a General School's Certificate, or a failure. In the event of a failure, it was take the whole lot again. We could not go back and just retake a failed subject. I missed Matriculation by one subject because I failed History. I achieved a good General School Certificate by passing all other subjects. I had left school and started work before the exam results had arrived, so I could not have gone back to school to retake exams anyway.

Up to this time the business had progressed as a combined garage filling station, car dealership and repair shop and by now, four small lorries working mainly locally. It had become a Limited Company in 1935. To build up a haulage business was, from 1933 onwards, an uphill task. Every change of circumstance and connection with Carrier's Licensing had to be applied for, subjected to objection from both the Railways and other road operators and the applicant had to establish "proof of need". Even to replacing an old vehicle with another, no more than an increase of half a ton in unladen weight on the replacement vehicle would be granted automatically.

The variation could be granted by the Licensing Authority without a Public Inquiry, at his discretion, if no objection had been received within the prescribed objection period. However there would almost certainly be an objection from the railways, which often resulted in a complete farce. We would obtain evidence of need by persuading a customer who wished us to carry his goods over a certain distance or destination to attend the Traffic Court and explain why the Railways could not efficiently carry out this task if granted. We would then have a condition attached to our 'B' licence authorising carriage of whatever for that customer to specified places or a specified radius from base.

The snag with that was that we could not head home with other people's goods. Therefore, the further away the delivery point was, the less likely that the customer would be able to afford to pay a two-way rate. If the customer had traffic each way we could quite easily obtain a 'Contract A licence' to work for that customer exclusively, without restriction. This required full-time work for the vehicle, as it could not work for anyone else.

We therefore finished up with a variety of goods, destinations and named customers on a variety of vehicles, specified on the licence. Therefore, it was inevitable that the wrong vehicle was in the wrong place at the wrong time. A nightmare for the operator and for the enforcement officers. Of course, an 'A' licence had none of these problems, except that to obtain an increase in the size of the vehicle or to increase the number of vehicles would be an even bigger battle. By now there were solicitors and consultants who specialised in these matters and who conducted the Application for the operator or the objectors in the Traffic Courts, the "Judge" being the Licensing Authority. In subsequent years on several occasions, I quivered in these courts and felt quite humiliated by these "arrogant experts", who set out to make one feel very much like the "peasant up from the country".

It is easy to understand from the aforementioned that with the business overall to keep going, my parents would have found that the 1933 legislation was, to say the least, extremely daunting. The original grant for the licence, which would have been more or less as asked for, was adequate for the two little tippers "Building and Civil Engineering goods within 30 miles, other goods within 20 miles of Elstead Post Office". Had they asked for an 'A' licence for one vehicle in 1933, they would probably have got it. But they did not know or understand that at the time and could not be expected to know.

The war of course presented a totally new situation. In 1940, the great scare was invasion from Europe. The Government decided to build a defence system of "Pill Boxes" across the country, at strategic points, defending roads and bridges. In addition, many road bridges were fitted with 'tank traps' which were often short lengths of railway lines ready to be slotted into concreted squares and let into the bridge's road surface, so that these vertical steels prevented all wheeled vehicles, except bicycles, from crossing and would be covered by cross-fire from the "Pill Boxes". This operation required many tons of aggregate and cement to be carried to the sites to make concrete. All of the concrete was mixed on site. We were instructed to carry this material from the pit or quarry to these various sites.

Many of the 1939/40 vintage lorries were commandeered by the army, leaving the likes of us, with the 'old bangers' to move things about with great urgency. The poor old things were puffing and blowing like a winded horse, suffering from overwork and severe over-loading. When loaded they struggled uphill and were extremely difficult to stop downhill, as the brakes were very poor, even when the vehicle was new several years earlier.

Leaving school in 1940, I found myself immediately on the road, delivering this precious aggregate, full time. The minimum age for a driving licence was seventeen years and I was then about eight months short of that age. When the local "Copper" saw me coming, he would slowly turn round and look away as I drove past! Another priority was the delivering of filled sand bags from the Runfold Pits to build "blast walls" in front of the large windows of certain hospitals. At Botley's Park Hospital, Chertsey as it was then known, was a section for male and female patients who suffered from mental problems.

When we first started delivering these sand bags the inmates would be waiting inside the gates. They would swarm all over the lorry and ride to the unloading point. On arrival they would scatter the bags in all directions. Flying sand bags everywhere. One poor soul picked up a bag under each arm, weighing some twenty-five kilos each and jumped complete with sand bags, from the lorry onto the ground where he collapsed from the impact. After a few days they gave up this activity and would run round the block and hide when we arrived, but would ride on the empty lorry tack to the main gate.

Their Recreation Room apparently had a "One Armed Bandit" installed. This was an early design, which exhibited the jackpot, which was seven pounds fifty in sixpences, little silver coins - forty to the pound. This was behind a glass panel. It took sixpence, pull the handle and three drums rotated. If three 'cherries' came up when the drums stopped, the jackpot came cascading out. The machine immediately replaced the jackpot from a container above and refilled the compartment with the glass panel. This encouraged the player to continue feeding the thing with sixpences in the hope of another jackpot.

These machines became all the rage and were installed in pubs and clubs. With the wonderful lack of logic of the lawmakers, pubs were not allowed to use real money. Money was changed over the bar for tokens the size of sixpences and addicted players would stand for hours feeding into the machine. When it coughed up various amounts of tokens as winnings, or indeed the jackpot, the tokens were exchanged over the bar again for money, theoretically to buy goods over the bar. Clubs were allowed to use real money.

Experience found that many people became 'hooked' on the thing and almost always put back in at least as much that it had paid out and usually more. The clubs did particularly well out of these machines. However, the machine in the Recreation Room at the hospital went bust and was removed because the winnings received by the inmates went into their pockets and not back into the 'One Armed Bandit'. The moral of this story is, who was it that had the mental problem?

It is not my purpose to go into lengthy and detailed descriptions of the happenings in wartime Britain. There have been many volumes written by many people far more capable than I on this subject. Sufficient to say, that everyone and everything was geared to the war effort. As I said earlier it was all a totally new situation and experience. There was no disagreement on the purpose. Our entire future, both individually and as a nation, was on the line and a very narrow line at that. Whatever needed doing, at least an attempt to do it, was made by everyone. On looking back, it was surprising how often an impossibility was achieved.

Our own little business had its functions and activities slotted in, progressively, as the priorities emerged. Our garage business had petrol pumps for fuel for local consumption, a repair workshop for local cars, vans and other essential vehicles from the milkman, the baker, the candlestick maker and so on. We also now had four old lorries continually required to fetch and carry this, that and the other. Of course, there were many similar enterprises to our own throughout the neighbouring districts and indeed throughout the country.

I think that perhaps one feature of the situation was that we were a rural community adjoining other rural communities, in our case centred more or less on the south side of Guildford. Obviously others were centred on the north, east and west of Guildford. As a result, most had some knowledge of, or acquaintance with the other and had perhaps in the past, some dealings with them. We were well known to some extent to the local authority, which was mainly Guildford and from here came many of the directives, priorities and requests for assistance that were emerging all the time. All of us were suffering from shortages of everything, particularly staff. As the forces were built up our labour force became the "very young" or the "very old", but all had determination. I can only describe the "Rural Scene", as I have no knowledge or experience of the problems or solutions suffered or solved by the built-up areas or the cities. But I am sure that they were no easier or fundamentally different.

Returning to the lorries as the main subject of this book. I mentioned earlier that we now had four commercial vehicles. All were now Bedfords and each with a carrying capacity of two tons. From the limited records and sketchy information available, it became obvious that the demand for May's Motors services was increasing.

Hence the extra tipper. Repeat business for sand and aggregates came from many local builders and civil engineering companies and for lorry hire on an hourly or day rate basis, work from the local authority, including Surrey County Council etc. It was also surprising to find that there were and had been many requests for quotations over the years from some London coal factors, who were tendering for boiler coal supplies for local hospitals, often involving sometimes as much as one thousand tons per annum. This all came through Milford, Godalming or Witley Stations. All of this tonnage had to be hand shovelled from the railway truck onto the lorry and often hand-shovelled off through a door at the hospital boiler house. The average railway truck would hold probably twelve tons. We would put up some extra sideboards on the lorry for coal and therefore manage three tons instead of two, for each journey. We would have a few days in which to clear the railway truck. If we had not cleared it, we would have to pay 'demurrage' to the railway until the truck was cleared.

The Ministry of Transport became the Ministry of War Transport and we came under their control. The 'A' and 'B' licences were suspended and we were issued with Defence Permits. We then started on a job working for Callender's Cables, who subsequently became British Insulated Callender's Cables. They had to build one hundred and twenty four pylons for an electricity grid supply from Godalming to Byfleet. At the time, we did not realise the significance of this project. It obviously carried a high priority, but there was no information or publicity produced. For me, it was a very interesting civil engineering job. I had our one non-tipping lorry and had to move all of the equipment and materials by hand from pylon to pylon as the line progressed. It was extremely hard work and went on in all weathers, seven days a week.

There were no digging or lifting machines, except for a large concrete mixer and two heavy-duty pumps and everything was lifted or shovelled on and off the lorry and moved to the next pylon position. I would collect the workforce, mainly Irish (hard men), with the lorry each morning from Farncombe near Godalming, work on site all day and return them in the evening. They had to hand-dig each of the holes for the four legs of the pylons. These holes were large and deep and were filled with concrete, with the leg concreted in the centre protruding from the ground, to which were bolted the pylon structures assembled on site.

The route, directly from Godalming to Byfleet was almost totally through fields, many of which were low-lying and through the winter had high water tables. Consequently digging holes soon reached water. Then they had to be "framed", 6" x 6" elm or oak timbers about six to eight feet long each, set up in a square as they dug down and "backed" by elm boards, driven down behind the frame, this forming a "box". As they dug down deeper, another frame was constructed, a few feet further down and the elm boards driven down further. Of course, sometimes the water just poured in to the hole. The pumps were started and then ran if necessary, non-stop, day and night to try to allow the excavation to reach the required depth.

Imagine the effort required from those men, to dig with shovels and to maintain that depth. Then the "boxes" had to be set up to hold the concrete, known as "shuttering", until the concrete set and so held the protruding "foot" of the pylon for later construction. Then the timber had to be retrieved, the hole filled in and the surplus excavated soil cleared up and so on to the next pylon.

Where the water table was high, it was not unusual to find next morning, that the depth of the hole was less than the night before. Other extremes were, that on a particularly difficult hole, the soil was saturated and the pumps were pumping "liquid soil". The result was that the "walls" of the hole, holding the timbers together, collapsed from behind, leaving a large circular mud hole.

My skills as driver were quickly enhanced, as running about in wet fields and wet gateways and avoiding getting "stuck" with a vehicle designed for road use only, was certainly an acquired art. When stuck, much digging at the rear wheels, throwing dry sand or ballast under the wheels and "all hands on deck" to push the vehicle into mobility. Revving the engine, thus spinning the wheels, was not the answer. And so it went on for some fifteen months. I still had no idea of the purpose behind all of this, except that it was an overhead high voltage electricity supply, from Godalming to Byfleet.

Again on reflection, there was never an apparent shortage of essentials. Petrol for the lorry (or coupons), petrol for the mixer and the pumps, no problem. Timber for frames, timber boards, cement, sand, ballast, all delivered in. All of the components for the pylons, including nuts, bolts and washers, all galvanised, on to the insulators and the cable on the large drums. The labour force was produced and accommodated and tough they were. Old George, a Godalming man, was among other things, in charge of brewing the tea twice daily.

We had an official ration of tea, sugar and milk. It was "brewed" in a blackened bucket over bits of scrap wood. If we were near a stream, the mugs would get a rinse or two. It is a wonder that we did not get "foot and mouth" disease. Eventually the line when finished merged into a much bigger and heavier grid near Byfleet. Apparently, Godalming, an early pioneer of electric street lighting, had a surplus of generating capacity. This was transmitted to Weybridge and finished up at Vickers Factory at Brooklands. Here, unbeknown to us, Vickers was producing ever-increasing numbers of military aircraft, thus requiring an increased supply of electric power.

Across the road (the A3) was built Wisley Aerodrome. The unfinished planes from Weybridge were flown to Wisley for completion. In addition, Hawker Aircraft at nearby Kingston, were making fighter planes, "Hurricanes", as quickly as they could. This was all happening under the Ministry of Aircraft production. Of course, at the time, it was all "hush, hush" and very few people realised quite what was going on, or the real scale of things.

The first Bedford, APF 418, in 1942 and about to be retired. Note the white wing tips, white bumper and the mask on the nearside headlamp. The offside one has its bulb removed to conform with wartime "blackout" regulations.

During this period, the oldest of our three tippers developed a 'terminal illness'. It emitted hefty knocking noises deep down inside the engine. New vehicles were allocated by the Ministry of War Transport (MWT). The vehicle inspector from the peacetime Ministry of Transport, in our case the South Eastern Traffic Area, had to inspect the 'ailing' machine. It took him very few minutes to decide that the poor old thing had reached the end of the road. We were granted a permit for a new Bedford. The factory was at Luton. At the outbreak of war, the Bedford truck was subjected to many detailed differences in design that turned it into a military vehicle. From the very large numbers being produced at Luton, a civilian version was produced, allocated on permit.

There were two main differences. The wheels and tyres and road springs were changed on the civilian lorry compared to the army vehicle. The second main difference was that the army truck was rated a three-ton carrying capacity and the civilian version, five-ton, otherwise virtually the same lorry. In 1942, the cost including the tipping gear and body was £415-12-6d.

In view of the urgency and priorities of this job, it was essential to keep the lorry running somehow and remarkably, we did. The mileage worked was small and we were never more then twenty-five miles from our yard. The beauty of the wartime Bedford was that almost all of its bits and spares were inter-changeable, so that in an emergency we could "rob" another vehicle for some spare or another and make good later. However, the treatment that my old lorry received on the sites that I have described did not improve its condition. All maintenance and repairs had to be carried out from about 6.30 in the evening, until seven a.m. and by me. On one occasion, a cylinder head gasket was required, so I went off to Guildford to a bus operator during the night, found a company who had night cleaners and borrowed a head gasket. Came home, fitted it and went to work (just) on time in the morning. Somehow or other, the lorry never failed completely during that job. Sometimes I would perform a temporary operation on it at night in order to get the gang to work in the morning and return to our yard to catch up.

Late one afternoon, in the winter we were about to have the canopy lifted on, to return the gang to Farncombe and I noticed a small hole in the cover of the differential gear on the rear axle and it was leaking oil. This was serious, as the hole had been made from something inside the axle. I trusted that it retained enough oil to get me home, which it did. I then removed the damaged cover and found that a rivet, which with others, held the crown wheel to its carrier, had sheared and bits were floating about inside, one of which had battered its way out. I could only remove the broken rivet, but could in no way replace it. It was one of several. I found an old cover plate (very lucky!) and so got to work in the morning. The abuse that the transmission was suffering in the fields was taking its toll and complete failure was not far away.

Another piece of luck. We had already submitted a request for a new vehicle permit and the Examiner had authorised this. It was now a matter of waiting for the new lorry to arrive, before the old one totally gave up and it did arrive in time, cost £405-3-0d.

5. More 'Wartime'

After the power line job was finished, we were involved in distributing heavy boxes of lard and margarine from a cold store in Guildford to local shops. This on a covered lorry with only canvas curtains at the rear, with no security or temperature controls whatsoever. Here we were, running around with up to five tons of rationed foodstuffs on board at any one time, and never experienced any problems.

Because of the increasing incidence of enemy bombing and the damage therefrom, there were many more household removals needing to be carried out. Many of our garage and motor car customers had family members affected by this, therefore the majority of this work originated locally. Our customers - mainly parents, certainly relatives of these customers, were rearranging their lives and accommodating their sons, daughters, grandchildren, uncles, aunts etc. Several of these moves were urgent, some immediate. For instance, we had more than one occasion of an unexploded bomb being in the basement, or in neighbouring properties.

We were as pleased to get loaded and heading for home, as our customers. Most of this work was concentrated on London and to a lesser degree, Portsmouth, although many other parts of the country came into this type of operation. 'Mother' would not have been very thrilled to have seen daughter's prized piano, trussed up like a parcel using lorry ropes and descending from the balcony of the second floor of some dwelling off Kensington High Street, but it was the quickest way down. There was also considerable movement to and from military married quarters. Often, when servicemen were posted overseas their wives and families would move back to 'mum' in the country, pending better times.

With the developing Air Raid Precautions (A.R.P.), later renamed Civil Defence, all sorts of activities were emerging. Our garage became the base for three vehicles provided by the authorities. They were converted into 'Ambulances'. One was a American Chevrolet van, the second an old, large Austin Twenty car with a two-stretcher canvas-covered body fixed on the rear half, the front end of the car being retained. The third was an ex-army six-wheeled Morris-Commercial truck, which had been built to army specification as an ambulance. Its vintage was probably mid-nineteen thirties but it had received very little use and had been extracted from some obscure Ministry of Defence storage depot.

These vehicles were to be driven by volunteers - all female, who were trained for this by my father. These ladies came from the surrounding villages and could not exactly be described as young, but all were keen to contribute their best to the war effort! Most of them were very good drivers, but one or two never would be. In the event of an incident, the casualties would have been well advised to seek "alternative arrangements". However, they meant well and tried hard.

ARP took over one council house at West Hill, Elstead and arranged a direct telephone to headquarters in Guildford. Volunteers were required for night-time to monitor any possible enemy activity. It will be remembered that the threat of invasion was uppermost in the thinking, therefore things could happen at night. The council house was equipped with bunk beds and blankets and of course, a tea ration. Several of us took part on a rota system to sleep there, giving seven nights coverage. We would usually go straight to work from there, according to circumstances.

At that time, any aeroplane activity caused an alert. We would go to a nearby hill where, if any raids were going on, either in London or on the South Coast, we could see the glow in the sky and the searchlights sweeping the sky. We were more or less on the flight path from the south coast to London and it was "this bit in between" where much activity often took place, with our fighter aircraft trying to intercept the German bombers. On one occasion a fleeing enemy plane unloaded his sixteen bombs on nearby Hankley Common, fortunately without damage. Our purpose was to monitor any such activity, to locate the incident and give early reports to Control at Guildford. We had been supplied with an ex-army 350cc Royal Enfield motorcycle, to enable us to find any such incident that might occur on our patch. There were many areas of open common land in our district where German planes could attempt to drop parachutists.

As the number of different activities grew, so did the need for training. The organisations were quickly 'welded' into the civil defence. Red Cross, St John's Ambulance, Air Raid Wardens, Rescue Services, Auxiliary Fire Service, Special Constabulary, WVS, Home Guard, Observer Corps, Auxiliary Nursing and many others, with most of these people working by day. Older people emerged from their retirement, but one way or another, it was a formidable force! I mention training. Several "exercises" were set up to simulate bomb damage that required the rescue services and first aid. As a result of a few local exercises with local people, Red Cross and ARP particularly, one or two of us got involved in acting as casualties. This developed into an effective and more realistic scenario for the rescuer and first aid people to practice their skills. My mate Peter Perry and I had been involved in one or two village concerts in the village hall. These consisted of any individual acts or talents that could be found and would be put together by someone who would act as producer. Perry and I would concoct our own script, which we would present on stage as BBC news bulletins. This meant that we needed no make up and no scenery, only a microphone. In addition we could read the script, not learn it. However these concerts were well supported and much enjoyed. Entertainment was pretty scarce at the time. The concerts were essentially local. We always found that the same pattern emerged. Our 'news bulletins' were always on local matters and about local people. We found that we could be as rude as we liked about people. The most important thing was to not leave them out as that would upset them!

I suppose that it was as a result of these activities, that I got roped in to act as a casualty. We had to learn the symptoms of a particular injury for a particular incident. As we became more efficient so did the make-up. For instance a small lamb chop bone, taped to an arm or leg would become a compound fracture. The bone would protrude from a large swelling, made from putty and discoloured to look bruised. Blood with an oily basis and covered in dirt and dust would be added. We would be made up to look to be in complete shock. If anyone touched the 'fracture', it would produce a suitable reaction and sometimes an unexpected reaction from the rescuer or first aid person. Many of these presentations were very realistic. On one occasion, Susan Lloyd (Red Cross), called our own Elstead doctor to me, by which time they had got me into the Casualty Station (Village Hall), as she was convinced that I really had been in an accident!

I have never forgotten when I consented to be buried under a collapsed building, as a result of bombing. The farm next door, as previously mentioned, had been closed down and sold, together with its surrounding land to the local builder A.J. Tracy Ltd. It had become a builder's yard and the local salvage dump for all collectibles such as old iron, aluminium, timber, in fact anything re-usable for the war effort. There was plenty of brick and rubble and it was here I was "buried", having been previously made up with the appropriate injuries. We had arranged for a long four-inch drainpipe to be laid from my face area to the outside of the mock up, to enable me to breathe. It had also been arranged that Ron Tracy would stand guard at the far end of the pipe, which might otherwise have become blocked or been covered with rubble during the rescue. Thankfully, Ron faithfully carried out his duties. Care had to be taken by the rescuers in moving about and in moving materials, not to inflict more damage on the casualty. This of course, was all part of the training. We took this activity very seriously and it was necessary to be as realistic as possible. I would be more than reluctant to ever do this again, although at the time I was many years younger, even so, very glad to be "discovered and released!"

The Casualties Union as it came to be known, was in ever-greater demand. In my case, the extremely long and erratic hours that we worked severely restricted the time that I could spend 'casualty' working. Despite this, I had many requests together with colleagues, to attend "incidents" from way outside of our area. Fortunately for us, we were never called upon to apply our learning in rescue or first aid as a result of enemy action. However, it must be said that none of this that I have written in any way compares with where the trouble really was, that is in our main cities of London, Coventry, Portsmouth and so on. The fact that I am talking about training and possible incidents recedes and fades, compared to the real thing. To think back on the suffering, the injuries, the tragedies inflicted upon the people of these cities, it was not initially a matter of training and make-believe, there was no time for training. It was learn the hard way. They did and they eventually overcame, but we must never forget the terrible physical and mental scars left upon the people and the landscape.

Surrey County Council had purchased a property that had been the subject of a direct hit by a bomb. It had been a fairly large house with a large garden and had been very badly smashed up. It was situated in Leatherhead and it was turned into a training centre for the whole of the county. The Elstead team had been scheduled to attend on a certain Sunday morning for training exercise at Leatherhead. The facilities were good and the management was good, whereby the site could be set up to whatever the particular exercise required, so a programme was normally set out in advance. As there were eight or ten people involved from Elstead on this occasion, I was to drive the ex-army Morris-Commercial ambulance with these people on board to and from Leatherhead and then to act as a casualty.

We had discovered that the vehicle had a primitive form of heating for the comfort of the patients during winter. This was achieved by routeing the exhaust pipe through the stretcher department. In the summer, the exhaust was diverted underneath the vehicle as normal. This was controlled by the driver by means of a lever which diverted the exhaust into whichever pipe was selected. On this occasion, for a bit of fun, I and my colleague who was up front with me, thought that we would give our passengers a "warm-up" so we opened up the heater. What we did not know was that the pipe had rusted through somewhere and was discharging exhaust fumes onto the customers, carbon monoxide of course. This could have been serious but fortunately, it was no worse than a few headaches.

On arrival at Leatherhead, I was to act casualty for some other team and scheduled to be trapped under some fallen roof timbers, therefore I was on my own waiting to be called for makeup. I came across an open door of a shed, which was obviously the central point of the public address system, because in the centre stood a microphone. I mentioned earlier that I had been involved in a few theatricals and I had become pretty good at impersonating the great man himself, Winston Churchill. Despite the extreme tensions and nervous strains that the whole population was experiencing at this time, Churchill never faltered in his resolve that we would never give in, quote - "We shall never surrender!" There was no television so the most used media was the radio. Therefore, when Churchill made a broadcast, everyone stopped to listen. There I am, on my own with the microphone. For a lark I launched forth into a 'Churchill broadcast', which I was making up as I went along. From the open door, I could see several different activities going on round about the place. I then realised that everyone had stopped to listen to the "broadcast" and I was fast running out of words. There was only one thing that I could do - STOP, get smartly out of the shed and then saunter off and this I did! I suppose it was put down to radio failure but just as well, as what I was saying was incoherent anyway.

With the constant threat of a German invasion ever present, the authorities determined to make things as difficult as possible for them should they arrive. One of their moves was to make as many of the petrol filling stations as possible "dry". So our place was therefore to remain with empty tanks. Supplies were concentrated into the larger main road sites that could be better defended.

After that, along came the army who requisitioned two of our tanks and pumps and filled them with petrol for use in army vehicles working in the area. Similarly, Civil Defence took another tank for their use, including supplies for the three ancient ambulances stationed on our premises. The fourth pump was left in peace. This meant that we had to give coupons and cash to our drivers to buy fuel on the road. There were no credit cards then. One side effect of this was that sooner or later, the odd driver would build up a reserve of coupons, say five or ten gallon units. He would "economise" by freewheeling down hill, taking short cuts to save mileage, creating fictitious diversions and thereby requiring extra miles that were also fiction. The point is that a five or ten gallon petrol coupon was worth money. Not only that, he had been given the money to buy that five or ten gallons of petrol as well. With us, there was only one instance of this with a non-regular driver, but with a larger company it would have been quite significant.

Also tied up with the invasion scare was the decision to remove place names of towns and villages and to remove signposts along the roads to disorientate the enemy. This made life more difficult for the likes of us collecting and delivering things about the country. Some people would be reluctant to answer if we asked the way to somewhere or to ask where we were and this, despite the fact that we did not look much like an invading German army! Another difficulty after dark was trying to find your way home having only one masked headlight during the blackouts. It was the same for everyone.

As a result of the war, part of St. Thomas's Hospital moved from London. This was built in the chestnut woods at Hyde Stile, Milford. The site was quite difficult for large vehicles. For instance, London Brick Company's eight-wheeled vehicles could not enter because they were very heavy and only suitable for hard road use. They would be hand-unloaded at the roadside. We would have to load these bricks onto our small, lighter tippers, making three or four loads from one eight-wheeler load in order to get the bricks up to the top end of the site. The same applied to other materials, timber, cement, ballast, tiles etc: most of it was double-handled as a result. It was a very nice hospital after completion however and we were very sorry, many years later, when they went back to London and the hospital was dismantled.

Another development because of the war was the building of 'Witley Camp', to accommodate the large numbers of Canadian troops arriving in this country. It was built on the site of a previous camp for Canadian troops of the 1914-18 war, situated both sides of the A3 near Milford. When operational, the camp required several supplies, particularly coal and vegetables. I earlier mentioned coal from Milford Station. I shovelled many tons of coal from the railway to hospitals and the camp as a weekend job. There was a period when there was produced a large briquette, made from compressed coal dust and held together with some sort of chemical. We had to manhandle these blocks from the railway truck to the lorry, drive about 2½ miles and then hand-stack them at the hospital. Apart from crumbling apart, the blocks gave off a fine dust that attacked the eyes and created total non-vision. So much so, that my assistant and I together with another two from Witley, had to be rescued by my mother in her car and the job abandoned for a day or two. We cleared the consignment eventually but saw no more of them. Another job was the collection of vegetables - carrots, potatoes, cabbage etc., from the fields of the larger growers for the NAAFI at Aldershot, Bordon and Witley camps in order to feed the growing number of military personnel.

As we had been able to replace two of the vehicles, it was a great help to have hydraulic tipping mechanism on one and a carrying capacity increase from two to five tons on each of them. One job that occasionally came up from another haulier was delivery of household coal to private houses. Loading was not too bad because the sack was filled on the scales and then transferred to the lorry at platform height. The deliveries could be a long street of terraced houses with two or three steps at the front door. This always meant that this one hundred weight (50 kilos), black open-topped hard bag had to be carried through the house and out through the back door where one would find the coalbunker. I always found this more than difficult, yet some men did this job for years!

The next thing to affect our business was when the Heald Sack Company moved part of its business into Ockford Mill, a disused three-storey mill on the outskirts of Godalming. The original premises were retained, albeit much reduced, in Bermondsey Street near Tower Bridge in London. They manufactured sacks made from hessian, imported from India, which arrived in heavy dense bales. This does not sound very exciting but at the time, it was a very important factor in several different trades.

I will now embark on a mini history lesson but for those who would rather not bother, then turn the pages. However, it is a part of our business history and it is part of the ever-changing world. The London river, east of Tower Bridge, consisted or wharves, warehouses, then the docks and so on to the Thames estuary down to Tilbury. Various activities were under the control of the Port of London Authority who had the foresight to obtain possession of the waterfronts down to Tilbury many years before they would need them. Originally, shipping under sail would make its own way up river from the open sea, no doubt assisted in either direction by the tide. The tide obviously, would vary the depth of water underneath the ship at any one time. According to where and when they had planned to be on the riverside, they would establish loading or unloading wharves. Therefore the larger the ship, the less distance it could travel up the river and so it had to be loaded or unloaded further down the Estuary, nearer to Tilbury.

Tower Bridge is the last road bridge down river. As you know, it "opens up" lifting each half of its roadway up vertically, thus allowing ships with tall masts to pass through, gaining the length of water known as the Pool of London, up to London Bridge. To those interested, Tower Bridge is a brilliant piece of engineering and well worth a visit. During my lorry-driving years, this bridge held everybody up, including me, whilst a ship passed through. It is still operational. Further down river are Rotherhithe and Blackwall tunnels where, of course, the river is much wider.

Back to the history lesson. The larger ships would be off-loaded into barges and moored alongside the ship by river tugs. It was very labour-intensive. These barges would be tied together side-by-side and end to end making a "block" of perhaps six or eight barges being towed by one tug. The wharves and warehouses would be built with their own privately accessed water cul-de-sacs directly off the river - "herring bone fashion". These barges would be brought in singly and left there for unloading or loading. Once in position, they were unaffected by the tide until they were ready to be towed out to repeat the process. The tall electric cranes always in the centre of the yard of the wharf/warehouse could, by design, reach the barge in question and each floor of their three or four storey warehouse. These barge movements would be handled by lightermen or river men, not dockers, because of tidal movements requiring them to work difficult hours. The docks "proper" were further downstream and were really large water basins, the water levels being controlled by lock gates, as on canals. Ships up to a certain size could therefore move up or down river at high tide and be "contained" by these basins, as they would not dry out, so the barge traffic could be eliminated. Dock labour would then load or unload these ships, into or from the adjacent warehouses for storage or onward transit. The predominant method of road transport of goods would be by horse and wagon, as this traffic originally at least, was predominantly London-based, not long distance. But of course this was changing as well.

Due to the spectacular change in mechanical handling engineering, much of it because of the rapid development of hydraulic power, the need to bring merchandise in and out of London was diminishing. A large deep-sea vessel, docking at Tilbury, would be attacked by a massive fork-lift truck, which lifted two, not one, sealed containers straight off the boat and they were distributed from Tilbury by road or rail. The ships would be turned round in a matter of hours not days and the major need for the river traffic and wharves and warehouses had gone. I do not wish to give the impression that with the run-down of the wharves and docks commerce on the riverside from Tower Bridge to Tilbury is finished, far from it. There are many establishments still working on the riverside, names such as Rank, Hovis, McDougall, Thames Tunnel Mills, Tate & Lyle, B.O.C.M and many others who together are preparing and producing a vast quantity of human and cattle foodstuffs for use nationwide today. But change there has been. End of history lesson!

The Heald Sack Company's main function was the making of new sacks from the aforementioned bales of hessian from India. These bales were made from jute and came in two weights, 7½ ounce or 10 ounce fabric, the lighter material being a looser weave. The sacks were important because without them the cattle and poultry food manufacturers could not function. At that time it was by far the most usual means of packaging in order to distribute products. Potatoes were another product that used very large quantities of sacks. There were of course, many other applications using sacks, but animal and human foodstuffs were probably the most important. Papers sacks were only just coming onto the market and were very expensive, so did not initially compete with Hessian. Most of these new sacks were printed with the name of the producer and the name and grade of the product in the sack. Different colours of printing ink would be used which made for easier recognition of what was contained in the sack when filled, thus reducing mistakes with deliveries.

These mills and processing plants required a continuous supply of sacks for the products, so that a pattern of deliveries geographically established itself. This was only the start of the story. Heald Sack would buy used sacks from users. We would therefore collect used bags, usually on return journeys and bring them back to Godalming. There they would be inspected, cleaned by vacuum and repaired on heavy industrial sewing machines and we would deliver to users who could use second-hand sacks. After this there would be a residual amount of bags that were below standard condition to be repaired and these went to Poplar, London to Mr Lutovitch, who would buy them from Heald Sack. His female workers would process them, obviously to a lower standard than Heald's but for a market that would use them. In addition, the real "rubbish" sacks that were really finished, were loaded as "junk" and we took them to Plumstead, London. Here they were picked to pieces, washed and processed into felt and into flock for mattress making. In addition, a certain amount of cotton bags came through which were cleaned and went to a local flourmill. Another commodity that Healds bought was bacon wrappers. These were muslin wraps covering sides of pig. They were sold to a firm in Chadwell Heath where we delivered them. There they were washed and dried in a large field that had posts with drying wires across them. I think that they were sold for polishing cloths.

All of this traffic required the driver to manhandle and stack the goods as they came aboard. This was primarily to prevent them from falling off the vehicle and so to keep them safe. It was normal for the driver to work from his lorry deck both to load and unload and then to rope it securely. After that, it always required sheeting to keep it dry. I fear that with most modern day vehicles, drivers seldom need to do this and could well have lost the art. We took pride in making the load as square and neat as possible.

The area that we covered was Eastern Counties, Hertfordshire, Essex, East and Southeast London, Surrey, Sussex, Hampshire and down to Dorset and Somerset. We did obtain "Goods for Heald Sack Company, 150 miles from Elstead Post Office" on our 'B' licence.

The Heald Sack Business was a London company operating at 152 Bermondsey Street, which had obviously generated its work from Southeast and East London and then radiated outwards to the area as outlined above. It was quite amazing and very enlightening to learn the unexpected that went on in London in the sack trade. We did a lot of work for Heald Sack in London and could always load home, usually with bales of Hessian. The knowledge of London and experience that I gained about the job, about the people and the culture of the time some sixty years ago now, is something that I would not have missed. It came about because the war had driven part of Heald Sack Company out of London and down to Godalming. Before leaving the subject of London, I have written a few random memories of happenings during this time frame not in any particular order.

There was at Tower Hill a "Clearing House". Lorry drivers would report to the Clearing House Office on Tower Hill with the hope of obtaining a return load, toward their home base and would wait to be called. They were mainly regulars. It follows, that waiting for a load meant that the vehicles were empty and in those days they were usually flat beds. The railway horses pulled six tons with two horses and three tons with one. They would come from Lower Thames Street at the gallop, reigns loose, to gain maximum speed at the bottom of Tower Hill and got slower and slower as they struggled to the top. The lorry drivers were ready and would hear the wagons coming. They were already facing downhill and would rush down hill and then catch up with the horses by reversing up behind the wagon and assist it up to the top. Very nice to see.

There was at some time a specially-built but very small steam traction engine built by William Tasker of Andover for the R.S.P.C.A and retained at Tower Hill, where it spent its life helping the horses by hooking on a rope and helping pull the wagon up the hill. These horses and wagons were probably based at Royal Mint Street Station, which was near the top of Tower Hill. We used to deliver sacks there to put on rail, usually to go up north. The railway was above, being built on a series of large brick arches. It was in these arches that we would reverse to the loading bank. The horses with wagons would also be there alongside us and the space was very limited.

However close we got to the horses, they did not "turn a hair". From these arches or others nearby would be found at night the "down and outs" sleeping rough, but it was dry. It was from such a scene that Flanagan and Allen created and sang their famous song "Underneath the Arches". They became very successful but came from humble beginnings. Bud Flanagan lived at Thursley and we often had to collect him from or take him to, Milford Station. Several councils of Southeast London had built substantial horse drinking-troughs at the roadside. The horses knew where they were and ignored their drivers and pulled over to them of their own accord to take a good drink. On one occasion, an unattended horse and wagon took fright for some reason and it bolted along the street, a traffic light turned red and the horse stopped! Was it because of cross traffic or can they distinguish colours?

The breweries also delivered their products or some of them, by horse and wagon. These were usually very smart affairs and beautiful animals. It was a prestige exercise and helped to keep the horses in condition, they were also used in the annual Lord Mayor's Show. Both Whitbread's and Young's Breweries did this.

If on occasions there was a fairly long traffic trail back as a result of Tower Bridge being opened to shipping and we had an empty lorry, when the traffic started to move, a glance in the mirror would show that we had passengers. There would be a row of fingertips grasping the top of the tailboard and as we started to move, three or four kids would run out from the pavement and hang on to the rear of the lorry and then lift up their feet. It was quite a distance from one end of the approaches to Tower Bridge to the other and our passengers wanted a lift. When they wished to alight, they would lower their feet and pick up speed to that of the lorry and then let go. I never knew of a problem. Another hazard were the trams. These ran on tracks in the centre of the road in each direction. Therefore, every time they stopped we had to stop as the passengers joining or leaving the tram walked in front of us. It was a hazardous business because if we attempted to pass the stationary tram, we might meet one coming the other way and just hope that the gap between them was large enough. Another problem was when cyclists got their front tyres stuck in the tramlines and then fell off, it was not unusual.

I must mention the London smogs of those days. They were absolutely dreadful. Imagine if you can a tram, which was obviously on rails, being led back to its depot by a London Transport employee walking in front with a blazing hand held flare fed by paraffin, which only added to the problem. I remember once, following the kerb slowly with my one masked headlight, which led me into a housing estate and a dead end. The cause of the smog was the pollution from factory and domestic coal fires, mixing with the fog coming mainly from the river. Once out of London, the light was clearer and one could carefully follow the A3 southwards. It is absolutely incredible how much clean up has been achieved and what a contribution smokeless fuel has made. I must try to describe Mrs Bishop's 'restaurant' in Bermondsey Street.

Heald Sack in London closed for lunch. Ma Bishop's was a few doors up the street. It was not very large and became very full at lunchtime. It was quite pleasing to obtain any off-ration food and their speciality was homemade steak and kidney pudding. These were presented in small, scruffy, half-round metal moulds, which were tipped onto the plate then out would come the steamed cabbage and mashed spuds. It appeared that everything was steamed because the whole place was running with condensation.

Tea was brewed in a large two-handled flat-topped metal teapot. The front half-lid folded back flat to admit the spoonfuls of tealeaves. These would be a soggy mess stewing in the bottom of the teapot and occasionally Mr Bishop would add a spoonful of fresh tealeaves, rationed of course, to the brew and inject it with more steam. From this could be obtained a "large spesh". This was a large mug of very thick china, although what was spesh (or special) about it, I do not know. It resembled creosote in colour, texture and taste. This could be followed by a plate of baked rice with a dollop of jam, from a very large tin. Ma Bishop was nearly too wide to waddle up the gangway between a row of seats each side, like a Wesleyan Chapel, with a table in between each row of seats. She would serve and take the money. As customers we knew no different. To me it was wartime, the food was rationed, but it was good and I was glad of it. The Bishops were not making a fortune but they were doing a good job and they could not get out of London when the bombing started at night, I could.

One day, somewhere down the east end, I sensed that the place had become more or less deserted, then realised that the air raid warning had sounded - where to go for shelter? Then a terrific bang which shook the road and the lorry. A flying bomb had done its worst a few streets away. I finished my day in sombre mood.

There was one recurring problem from the wartime "pool" petrol. There was only one grade, called Pool. To improve its poor quality, it had excessive amounts of lead added or something similar. It caused the exhaust valves of the engine to burn out and literally split like a mushroom. I had to carry out most of my own repairs and maintenance, which often meant "midnight oil". When the valves burned out, the repair had to be carried out as a matter of urgency. There was no covered space available at the yard, so I would nose the vehicle under the veranda of the house, connect an electric lead light through an open window and start. This was almost always after a day's work with the lorry. Having removed the cylinder head, it would require cleaning up and then to fit new exhaust valves. Because of the burning of the valve seats it would require a lot of grinding in, by hand, to get the seats to an acceptable level. This was about two hours work on the bench. I then had to reassemble the engine, working a total of some six hours.

On one occasion I had gone through this process, filled the radiator with water and went for a short road test. I stopped after about two miles and looked into the radiator with a torch. No sign of any water. Pulled out the oil dip-stick to find a grey emulsified mess on it and this mess was way over the high mark for oil on the stick. This meant that the cylinder head had cracked, allowing water to run down into the oil sump. This was because the engine had been allowed to run for too long with burned valves and exhaust flame had burned across the valve seat and wrecked it. I discovered this delight at about 2 am. I returned slowly to the yard and then started to dismantle the engine again. My father came out with a cup of tea at about 6 am.

The next problem was to find a cylinder head, because this trouble was widespread and frequent and spares were often in short supply anyway and furthermore, it was not a cheap item so it could be a day or two before we got going again. Eventually a partial cure was found. New valves would be stellited. Stellite is a very hard material. A coating would be welded on to the seat of a new valve and then "turned" in a lathe to the original's dimension. This material did not burn and so the valve life would be considerably extended.

Carrier's licensing was suspended at the start of the war and defence permits were issued instead by the Ministry of War Transport, whereby they were effectively in control. Petrol rationing was no real problem because the Ministry locally knew what was going on at any one time and the petrol coupons were allocated according to the work to be done. It was therefore monitored to make sure that only essential work of national importance could be carried out. The Ministry would often ask us to carry out some work or, if we were doing something to a non-regular destination, we would advise them and they would arrange a back load for us or give us the number of the appropriate district manager to contact and thus avoid empty running.

It was fortunate that two of the vehicles had been renewed, thereby reducing dramatically the repair work that they required, but this valve trouble really was a difficult one. Another of the old tippers collapsed and we put in for another permit for a new vehicle that was granted. I think that I went up to Luton to collect it. We were very fortunate that three or four of our staff were over call up age and had been with us pre-war.

The business was trading from 1935 as May's Motors (Elstead) Ltd and the garage, repairs, the lorries and the "taxi" were all operated as one.

My mother did all of the bookwork and Bob Pearce ran the garage and repair workshop. Two others mainly drove lorries but turned their hand to whatever was required. My father was not academic or mechanically minded, but always doing something, including teaching the "ambulance drivers". Other employees, such as mechanics, drivers, trainees were progressively taken on through the years and then the outbreak of war changed all that. Everyone and everything from 1940 onwards was in a state of change and the unknown. It was a matter of getting on with whatever needed doing as it arose.

I was expecting to be called up at any time but Ministry of War Transport (Guildford) said that the work that we were doing was necessary and had to be carried out by someone. They said that they were going to hang on to me as long as possible. I was very mixed about this, but accepted the situation. In fact, it was 10th September 1946, when I was called for a medical at Kingston, Surrey, which I passed, but heard no more.

The direction of the war was changing from fear of invasion to the reverse, that we should invade mainland Europe. I am amazed that the evidence that we were about to invade did not leak out, thereby destroying the element of surprise. The evidence was everywhere. On my way to Christopher Hill Ltd, a large producer and processor of cattle foods at Poole in Dorset, I passed through the New Forest. There was no mistaking what was about to happen. The place was absolutely packed with vehicles, personnel and equipment of every kind. They were parked in the trees just off the road, waiting - but ready.

In the next few days, it became history and so eventually we emerged from wartime to peacetime. It took some time to realise that the war was truly over, that the bombing, the sinking of our ships and the killing of our airmen and troops had stopped. There was no doubt that the enemy felt exactly the same. To see pictures of the destruction that each wrought on the other, such as London, Coventry, Portsmouth, Dresden, Berlin, the Ruhr and so on and then the atom bombs on Japan. As I have said earlier, plenty has been written on this subject by others more eloquent and capable than I, but it is a source of wonderment that it was ever all sorted out afterwards, or was it ever sorted out? Immediately after the war, everything remained in short supply, most things were still rationed but there was great relief. Much of this is now just a happy memory, as it is so many years ago, but one thing sticks vividly in my mind, the lifting of the blackout and we could now use unmasked headlights, wonderful!

During 1945, the last of the old two-ton hand-operated tippers was replaced with a new Bedford non-tipper. All four of the old vehicles had now been replaced in turn. Each had to be paid for on delivery as there was no thought or suggestion of any credit, loan or hire purchase. It had to come out of revenue so each one took about one year to rebuild the bank balance before another could be purchased. We had therefore increased our carrying capacity from eight tons (4 x 2 tons) to twenty tons (4 x 5 tons).

By now, a five-tonner, be it a Bedford, Ford, Austin, Dodge or Commer perhaps, was the most popular size for the smaller operator and were the most popular makes. The additional carrying capacity, from two to five tons, enabled us to be competitive with our neighbouring operators. But of course we had to find more work, or more tons to carry. Despite this, the job being what it was and the industry being what it was, we all regularly carried overloads - probably up to seven tons on a five tonner, both tippers and non-tippers.

On 13th June 1944, we joined the 'Associated Road Operators' (ARO) and the fee was £4-15-6d. Its badge was green and showed an outline of the UK. The caption was "The Roads are yours, use them". Our joining enabled us to obtain an "RHD 20", which was an agreed schedule of rates. Agreed with Government, I presume for lorry hire. It was graded into time, mileage and carrying capacity.

I would emphasise that the great majority of operators with small businesses such as ours, would have had no financial or business training, me included. The accent was much more on the practical side of things, how to do it and how to keep it going. From this came experience but looking back, more knowledge of the financial aspects would have been very useful. I have no idea how my mother discovered Associated Road Operators or the RHD 20s but she did. The ARO, South Eastern area was administered from Chatham by Percy Woodhouse. The Associated Road Operators merged with the London Cartage Association in December 1944 to become "The Road Haulage Association", administered by Stanley Jardine in London. My first appearance at a Road Haulage Association meeting was 16th October 1946 at Guildford sub-area.

6. Passenger Transport

On 25th January 1949 I was elected as Honorary Secretary and Treasurer to the Guildford sub-area RHA. I was then actively engaged on many different committees throughout the years, including some five years or so on the National Executive Board. On 27th January 1993, I was elected an Honorary Member in "recognition of eminence in, and outstanding service to, the Road Haulage Industry and to the Road Haulage Association".

In 1945, a Labour government was elected. They decided that it was necessary to nationalise road and rail transport, although I do not recall any valid argument for doing so. No politician has so far to my knowledge ever solved the inherent problems belonging to either. They are good at spending taxpayers' money on a whim, but are not held responsible for the almost certain waste of that money.

The road haulage industry was to be nationalised in 1947. It was denationalised in 1953 and the next one was to be in 1970. This makes my point that all of this legislation, created by people who do not understand the subject and who do not consult or take notice of someone who might. This, over many years and from all parties. I would say, just look at the state of Road Traffic today. In particular, consider the state of the railway today - what a mess and there is still no answer to the problem, far from it! I digress, my apologies.

Back to 1945, with the threat of nationalisation of road haulage happening in 1947, the yardstick was apparently, in simple terms, 50% long distance in 1946 would qualify for nationalisation. This was defined as twenty-five miles radius of base or forty road miles from base. Although we were very small, we could be construed to be vulnerable. The two tippers were safe, transporting building and civil engineering materials thirty-five miles and other goods within twenty miles of Elstead Post Office. But the two non-tippers were both licensed "Furniture and Effects" to 150 miles but furniture removals were exempt and goods for Heald Sack Company within 150 miles of Elstead Post Office. The Heald Sack job could be the problem, other goods being within twenty-five miles of Elstead Post Office. I have over-simplified the thing but that was to be the essence of it. With the threat of nationalisation in 1947, we formed a separate company for the lorries, May's Motors (Transport) Ltd in November 1946, just in case.

We have now entered another phase of our story in common with most other people, that of the changing world of the post-war. We were very worried in that we believed that we could lose 50% of our transport business, which would have been a serious concern. There were those who could not escape being taken over, for instance, Harry Rackliffe of Guildford, a family business and contemporary of my parents. He was 'A' licensed and certainly over 50% long distance. He was very proud of the business that he had built up with his wife, amounting to ten vehicles.

The 1947 Act would take him "lock, stock and barrel", including his premises, at an agreed scale of compensation, which was way below its true value, Harry was not happy. Large companies could fight for themselves but the scale of compensation was "set in stone" and so, from this, British Road Services was born. In our case it could have been different, they would not have been interested in our garage business or our tippers, so they would not have bought us out. What could have happened was that we would have to stop anything over 25 miles except furniture removals and I assume, this without compensation, but I think that we could apply for a Permit to continue certain traffics. I do not recall how this worked out as so far, my parents had dealt with licensing affairs and I had no knowledge or experience of such matters at my then age.

The Heald Sack work was building up and was important to us, but probably not of much interest to the state. Maybe we were given permits to continue with the work or maybe we were using a "Contract A" licence, which might have solved the problem. Whatever, I do remember that we were allowed to continue with the work. Initially we were not to know this and there would have been no certainty of continuity for the future. On the other side of the coin, there were some operators who could not wait to be taken over. One such person had six vehicles, all working for one customer. He had no premises and parked them at various places. He was taken over and got himself the job of running the new depot that British Road Services set up locally. Another with about half a dozen lorries on "A" licence was happy to retire and live off the proceeds, as they also bought his premises, which they afterwards sold. In addition he managed to get the Traffic Manager's job at BRS for his son. All were well satisfied.

Coming back to our business as stated, we were very worried rightly or wrongly, so I decided that we should create an alternative activity and persuaded my parents that we should go in for operating one or two coaches as well as the existing activities. One of our drivers was discharged from the navy on medical grounds, not very serious if I remember, and this allowed me to reduce my driving from full time to relief work and begin to deal with the many other day-to-day items that constantly occurred. I did however put in for a schools contract locally and got it. However we had no passenger vehicle, so had to buy one.

I somehow came into contact with a very nice company in Tonbridge, 'Ashline', who had some Bedford buses for sale. During the war, buses and coaches became 'utility' as opposed to luxury. Government decided which manufacturers would build what, as many factories were turned over to tanks, aeroplanes etc. Bedford was one such manufacturer.

The vehicles, like the lorries, were allocated on permit. The wartime Bedford bus was 'utility' being fitted with basic bodywork and wooden slatted seats. The two that we bought from Ashline would have been post-war build, as they were not 'utility' but a better shape with upholstered seats and one or two other refinements and they were in good condition. Ashline could not part with them until after the school contract started, so they very kindly loaned us a twenty-seater Dodge coach for a few weeks, to enable us to commence operations.

In mid-1947, Peter Perry and I had been on a "Pub" coach outing to Brighton or some such place from Elstead. As with a "pub" outing, the beer consumption was "steady" throughout the day and we finished up at the local village dance in Elstead at about 9.30 pm. I spied a very attractive young lady and asked her for a dance. My dancing ability was and still is a non-professional foxtrot and waltz. During this dance I was boasting about the number of pints that we had consumed that day and the young lady was not impressed. I also asked her if she liked motorcycles, to which she replied "yes", so I arranged to meet her one evening in the coming week for a motorbike ride. I learned that she was working, together with her friend Eileen, as cooks at an agricultural camp at Oxenford Farm some two miles towards Milford. This had been built by the Surrey War Agricultural Executive Committee to accommodate German and Italian prisoners-of-war who were taken to local farms daily by lorry to carry out agricultural work. Surrey County Council took over, post-war and used it for volunteer workers for working holidays and the two girls did the feeding as permanent staff, paid by Surrey County Council. As arranged, I turned up with the motorbike but there was no sign of June Swanston, that I had learned, was her name. I asked someone to find her. I understand that he found her and said "there's a bloke out there with a motorbike who says that he's got a date with you"; June was not ready as she had been quite sure that I would not turn up! However, we were soon on our way with no goggles, no crash helmets, to the Devil's Punch Bowl at Hindhead, a local beauty spot. Neither knew what to say to the other, I suppose that I knew nothing about cooking and she knew nothing about lorries, a situation that has not changed, fifty-two years later!

Subsequently I had to overcome the opposition in the form of other staff members at the camp and the odd holiday worker. Then we lost touch. I have always thought that two words, faith and fate, have a great influence on one's life, one must have faith in something whatever that may be and fate plays its part anyway. I was driving a lorry between Milford and Elstead, on a "B" class road and I was following the Godalming to Farnham bus, an Aldershot and District Traction Co. Ltd vehicle, running on one of the original routes, which had been started by my parents. The bus stopped at Oxenford Farm and I also had to stop and wait behind it. It had stopped to drop a passenger. When it moved away, there stood a very smart young lady with long dark hair, "pageboy" fashion, fitted tweed topcoat, saucy little "Band Box" fur hat complete with matching fur muff - Miss June Swanston. That is what I mean by fate and it went on from there. This was mid-1947 and all a part of the "turning of the wheel".

Before we could enter or should I say, re-enter the passenger carrying business, I remembered having been told that we had signed an undertaking to not operate passenger vehicles for a period of so many years after our bus business was sold to Aldershot and District Traction Co. Ltd. Research showed that this period of time, five years or something like, had expired. So that was no problem. I said earlier that we had paid cash for the purchase of new lorries as it arose. We were now faced with the problem shared by so many similar private businesses of trying to generate capital out of revenue to pay for new equipment and to finance working money for what was, in fact, an expanding business. So, we had to borrow. Theory says that increased turnover and profit would well pay for the cost of borrowing. Well it is a nice theory.

One might ask, why buy two buses for one contract? The reason is that we had to provide our own cover for maintenance and risk of breakdown, as obviously, in the event of trouble, we could not leave young school children at the roadside. Therefore, we had to find sufficient other work to justify the second vehicle. It goes without saying that there were no guarantees. In the event the lorry work did not decrease, it increased and we had to create a new and completely different business alongside the existing, carriage of passengers as well as the carriage of goods. But we set out to achieve it.

We were not the only ones to think this way. Apart from Warner's Coaches at Milford, a long-established family business, we entered the field, as did Blackburn Brothers of Godalming (Haulage Contractors), and the aforementioned Harry Rackliffe of Guildford and Petrich of Farnham.

Initially and understandably, Warner's were not very thrilled with the opposition that we were setting up. In the coaching business, there appeared to be plenty of work at weekends, football matches, London theatres - usually on winter Saturday afternoons and evenings and coastal work on summer Saturdays and Sundays. We had known Warner's for many years and very quickly overcame all adverse feelings between us. This resulted in a great deal of inter-working between us with complete trust that we would not knowingly accept each other's work if offered.

Often on Saturday evenings, after a football match in the afternoon, then perhaps a London theatre in the evening followed by a midnight pick up from a local Dance Hall, meant running round the villages delivering passengers rather like a taxi. Together with the cleaning of the vehicle, inside and out, it was often a very long day.

I should explain that arising from the 1930 Road Traffic Act came licensing of passenger vehicles. Briefly it meant that we could not ply for hire from individual people or passengers. Buses can pick up passengers on their various routes and collect the appropriate fare as they go along. Bus and some coach operators have their own licensed routes and destinations in the same way. We could only take bookings from a collective organisation and were not allowed to collect separate fares. We would quote a price for the job - either a football club, a cricket club, pub social club, British Legion, Old Time Dance club. The person who organised the trip to wherever would pay us for the job and collect the money from his colleagues. If this involved theatre tickets for Wembley Ice Show, or the Palladium or whatever, the organiser would ask us to order the required tickets, we would add the total price together, and the organiser would sort it out. It was known as 'Private Hire' - company outings and the like, paid for by the company, quite in order.

We could not interchange our lorry drivers with our coach drivers unless the driver held a PSV Licence (Public Service Vehicle). A non-PSV driver could drive an unladen coach, such as a workshop mechanic. We had to make sure that we had PSV drivers available as required, so several of them passed the required driving test. When HGV (Heavy Goods Vehicle) driving licences came in, (following the Transport Act 1968) and by passing the appropriate test or tests, both licences could be held.

This private hire work appeared to be fairly buoyant as for years people had been unable to enjoy such activities and we were very lucky that one person, Bill Adams, started to organise parties to go on various outings including coastal trips in summer and London theatres, ice hockey or various shows in the winter. Our Bedfords were 28-seaters and not very comfortable. Bill Adams was actually a bus driver for "all the lot and risk it" as it had become known and drove one of the two buses that were based in our yard.

He suggested that improved comfort would be an advantage and that he would lend us the money for two sets of new seats. We therefore purchased from Duple Motor Bodies the seats and fitted them. We also obtained two pairs of heavy-duty shock absorbers, which considerably reduced the "bounce" at the rear of the vehicle. These actions were certainly improvements. Some of the old seats were used in the workshop mess room. The story of the coaches must be read within the context of the rest of the business. It was all going on as before and the coaches were really an additional activity requiring additional attention and energy and it went on for about six years possibly until circa 1954, so there is more to come as it unfolds.

The garage side of things was progressing steadily. We still had an Austin Agency, which became BMC and there were plans to demolish a shed adjacent to the original workshop building and erect a new structure. This is where the Aldershot and District Buses had "lived". We had therefore built a replacement garage for the buses on the other side of the property. This was the start of what became the transport yard. It also gave access to the rear of the site from which my parents had dug out the aggregates as mentioned earlier. The tippers were fully occupied with a substantial throughput of sand and ballast on a supply-and-deliver basis. I remember one job, involving up to twelve loads per day (sixty cubic yards). The pit was at Ash near Aldershot and delivery to a new council estate to Denmark Square, Aldershot.

Other work was for Surrey County Council and other operators. The non-tippers were also busy, partly because the Heald Sack work out of Godalming had increased considerably. To handle the removals trade we had bought a secondhand furniture van, a proper vehicle for the job. I spent many hours working with that on removals, the "walk in" tailboard was a great improvement. The coaches brought work from local cricket clubs, Saturdays or Sundays, short distance work. This could tie up a coach at the expense of a London or coastal job. We used the furniture van for Puttenham Cricket Club; with "village hall" benches each side for seating if we had no coach available. They were delighted with this arrangement and it went on for several years.

Imagine how the "Law" would view such an operation today - the "village hall" seats that we used were not even fixed! Another weekend job with the van was the Normandy (near Guildford) Motorcycle Club. They would prepare motorbikes for scrambles or trials, not road use and these bikes, together with all the gear and the riders and club members, would load up and away we would go.

Most of these clubs and some of the other lorry customers, would have a social side having at least one summer and one winter outing, often involving two coaches, so one thing led to another. Boy Scouts' or Girl Guides' summer camps would involve the van for equipment and a coach for the members. The one and constant problem, was the shortage of money. We never had any because every penny that we earned was ploughed back into the business. Vehicles, workshops, equipment and particularly the money to pay the aggregate pits for materials that we drew, before we could invoice the customers and then give a month's credit, was a strain. To a lesser degree in the winter, money up front for theatre tickets, often months ahead of the date of the show, could come to quite a sum. In other words, working capital or lack of it was always a problem for us.

I have already said that my mother was the driving force of the business, or the brains of the outfit and she was very forward-looking. As we had no money, there was always the possibility of failure though not for lack of trying. With this thought at the back of her mind, she considered that I should broaden my technical knowledge and get some qualification as a fall-back should it ever be required. I was not at all keen on this but under extreme pressure from her, I enrolled at Guildford Technical College for a Higher National Certificate in Mechanical Engineering. This was a one-day release course from 9 am to 9 pm plus one other evening each week. It must have been toward the end of the war, 1945, for three years.

Certainly our labour situation was easier, so that I did not have to do so much driving but with everything else as outlined, it was not easy because it also involved homework. I really had to push myself to do it. Despite failing and having to retake a part of it, I did come out with a Higher National Certificate in Mechanical Engineering plus Section C Industrial Administration. I could never do that again! This did give me initial access to the Institute of Road Transport Engineers and the Institute of Transport. I am still a retired member of these two organisations and fortunately, the prime reason for taking the course never arose.

Our Bedford buses were doing a good job but twenty eight seats instead of thirty three was proving to be an obstacle and the lack of a luggage compartment and the "dating" of the body work was costing us work.

The two 1945 Bedford OWB 28-seater buses HKJ 531/3 with their replacements, the two Crossley 33-seaters TMK 215/6 purchased from Fountain Coaches of Twickenham. The Bedfords were then sold to a local Bedford dealer. The drivers are (left to right) John Robinson, George Taylor, Peter May and Reg Mitchell.

The next move was the purchase of two Crossley luxury coaches, second-hand, from Fountain Coaches of Twickenham. With this came quite a bit of work on hire to Fountain, when we had availability; there was a penalty of about 25 dead miles each way, however it was a revenue. These vehicles were a great improvement.

Before we leave the Bedfords, there were one or two happenings that come to mind. Firstly having been involved with Witley Camp for the Canadians, with coal and vegetables, we were subsequently involved with its demolition with the tippers, our retail workshop and the coaches. We had to collect workmen from Petworth, Sussex, five mornings weekly and return them late afternoon. This meant leaving the yard at 5.45 am each weekday morning regardless of the time that I finished the night before and I was usually the one to do it. It did, however, fit very nicely with the school run both night and morning. Aunt Ethel who now lived with us would usually get me up in the mornings.

Another memory is the International Help for Children. This charity based in London, had or hired a large property, ex-school or nursing home type of premises at Grange Road, Tilford, Surrey, quite near us. They at the time were providing convalescence and some comfort, a holiday, for damaged or orphaned Greek children. My history was never very good but it must have been resultant on some sort of civil war or disaster in Greece at the time. Anyway, these poor little children were brought over by plane, usually to Manston Airport in Kent and then changed over for another batch and so on, for as long as possible.

More than once, it meant going to Manston with a coach to find that the trip had been postponed. On one occasion, I got back to the yard accompanied by the Secretary to the Nursing Home, to turn around and go straight back. This time they arrived. I suppose that as one grows older one hardens to the world, but then, many years ago, when those children arrived at Manston and we came face to face with some twenty-five of them, it was a shock of some magnitude! Some were minus a leg or an arm or had some visible injury - one even had a foot back to front, some on crutches and some limping. They were tired, bewildered, excited but marvellously happy.

The Bedfords had an access door at the front and the driver was not separated from the passengers. We subsequently had to take the children on various outings that had been arranged and it was amazing how quickly, on boarding the coach, they recognised us as having collected them originally and would come up and smile or touch us, before going to their seat. Upon reaching our destination we would assist the carers with the children before returning to the coach.

What came through strongly to us at the time was how much effect a little "fussing" and affection would have on the children who had been so deprived but who rewarded us immediately by being so happy. There was one lad, Nicholas, who was about fourteen. We think that he must have been recruited. He was a lovely cheerful lad, good looking with black curly hair. He acted as an interpreter as he could cope with English and was invaluable to the staff. He was there throughout the time that the children visited.

Whenever June was available, she would come with me on these trips and being a "natural" with such matters, was kept very busy the whole time. The principal people involved were a Mr John Barclay and Miss "someone" in London and James and Mrs Joyce who ran the Nursing Home at Tilford. They were wonderful people, all of them. How could we charge such people when we had a dead trip or two to and from Manston? We couldn't it would be our contribution. June's job at Oxenford Farm came to an end as Surrey County Council closed the camp and she got a job as a cook at Farnham Hospital, living in. I would visit as often as I could.

During the war, my sister had joined the army, the ATS. She became a Staff Car Driver, stationed at Aldershot. There was in Elstead, a retired Colonel Braithwaite who must have been on the army reserve because he was quite old. Presumably he was called up and as a customer of ours, he knew my sister. Surprise, surprise, he claimed Christine as his driver, so for a year or two, that was a cosy arrangement. She was subsequently posted to near Chertsey, still not far from home. From the army she met and married Alexander McDonald Doughty. He apparently had been loaned from the Black Watch to Wingate's Chindits. The Chindits were operating in Burma against the Japanese and were as history relates, a bunch of "wild men". A much respected and feared force in the jungle. Alex told me that one of their favourite activities was to sneak up and surround the mess huts where the Japs were feeding. These had openings, but no fitted windows, just square holes. At a given signal, they would pull the pins and lob hand grenades through these openings, smartly melting away into the jungle. He said that the Japanese had no idea that the Chindits were anywhere near and concluded that they were high level bombing attacks.

As the reader will gather, there was quite a lot going on business-wise and the coach work had certainly filled in many hours of work, from early morning to late at night. I had started attending Road Haulage Association, Guildford Sub-Area meetings. At the same time, in the interest of our retail garage side, I started attending Motor Trade Association meetings at Farnham. Each of these were necessary, enabling me to meet fellow transport operators and fellow motor traders and to gain much more knowledge of each subject. This was extremely valuable, coupled with the bonus of making many friends.

One Sunday evening, Peter Perry, June and I had been to evening service at Elstead Church, June reminded me that I had been asked to read the lesson. On walking past our premises on the way back, I nipped indoors for something. June asked Perry why had I gone in there and he replied "he lives there". This was the very first time that June learned that I was the son of the "Boss", not just an employee. I came back out and Perry and I took June in to meet mother and father. I learned afterwards that June was petrified! She was certainly very quiet, but there was no problem. A little family background is now necessary. My parents started the business. They both worked very hard and long and they undoubtedly made progress, as is evident from what I have written.

A close-up of one of the Crossley 33-seaters, TMK 215. The photograph was taken at the time of purchase from Fountain Coaches of Twickenham. They had an 8.6 litre Crossley diesel engine, a four-speed "crash" gearbox and servo-assisted vacuum brakes and were fitted with Santus coachwork.

I have also made it clear that mother was more forward thinking and that the old man, could quite easily get "steamed up". Furthermore, after the event he would clear off and completely forget it. With June changing her job, she had lesser hours to work than previously so she came from Farnham whenever possible by bus, to our home and made herself generally useful. Whenever possible, she came with me according to what was going on at the time. I had always got on well with my parents but there was a disagreement building up. My mother was adamant that my future lay with the business and that I should be "married" to the business as a first consideration. I argued with her that whilst I was also dedicated to the business, I did not want a businesswoman, I wanted a wife and a mother and there the discussion rested. More on this subject later.

My granny died sometime in 1947, shortly before I met June, leaving aunt Ethel, mother's sister alone in the home next door. It must have been shortly after this that my sister got married. Also around this time, my mother became ill and was confined to her bed for a week or two. This meant that all of the office work ceased. Petrol rationing was still in force, but our petrol pumps, now four, had been released. Each delivery to us required the supporting coupons to be ready for the delivery driver and the cheque for the petrol. Some of these coupons were for half a gallon for motorcycles, they were small and fiddly and torn out of ration books. They all had to be counted and recorded and put into a special envelope.

I got June involved in this all from the front room, which was the Office; its original intention was that of dining room. I had to tackle some of the office work mainly evenings, but had no clue really about what I was doing. I cannot remember who made up the wages or how they were paid, but they must have been. This episode, I now realise, subconsciously left a warning that the subject of accountancy and staff to operate same would have to be addressed, perhaps shortly.

We did soon after take on a full-time girl to assist my mother, Joan Sharland, which was a start. Another development a year or so later, was that we decided that we needed a third coach. I found an excellent 9.6 litre AEC Duple-bodied, thirty-three seater from Lily Coaches in North London who were closing down. But how to pay for it? The two Bedfords had been sold, the AEC would bring the fleet up to three thirty-three seaters. My parents had a small saving of about £2,000 for retirement and they gave me this toward the coach, the balance being found by hire purchase. They had nothing else except for whatever equity there was in the property, but this was not available to cash in as we were using the property. Nevertheless, they put this money into the company and I collected the AEC. I remember vividly and suddenly realised, that it would fall on me to provide for my parents. They did not ask for this but I knew that this was my responsibility and that the only way was to expand the business and get on with it. It was a conscious decision.

The acquisition of the AEC meant that our coaches were of good quality, all very comfortable and all thirty-three seaters. That was the usual seating capacity at the time, therefore the vehicles were completely interchangeable work-wise and we were able to obtain work more readily from other operators when we had availability, and so it proved to be. Heald Sack Company mentioned earlier as transport customers, had an employee who organised outings for her fellow workmates, her family relations and friends in Godalming. Among her relatives were a married couple that were both profoundly deaf. They had other friends and associates with the same problem and they joined together for their own social occasions. We all learn to speak by hearing and then copying by imitation as a child, thereby increasing the ability to speak as we learn more from our hearing. If we cannot hear from birth, then learning to speak must be almost impossible. Furthermore, if one is stone deaf, one cannot hear one's self speak either. Through Heald Sack Company, we came into quite frequent contact with these people.

Whenever possible, when carrying passengers from our local area who were our regulars, on Saturday summer coastal trips, we would have found a pub off the main road, about halfway between the coast and the Elstead/Godalming area. Most of the pubs that catered for coaches would be packed, as everybody moved at the same time in the mornings and evenings. A few miles diversion, into the countryside of Sussex or Surrey, was extremely popular. We would have alerted the publican by telephone a day or two earlier.

We would assist the trip organisers and the non-deaf among them to obtain the refreshments required and it was very successful, had the full co-operation of the publican and totally removed any embarrassment that could have been. They went on winter trips to various shows going on and did not allow their disability to interfere with their enjoyment. Once more, we found that people such as these with such problems were always laughing and happy and very appreciative of any assistance that we could give them.

When permission was given to build Witley Camp for the Canadians, it was on condition that the site was returned to common land, as it was before the war. Messrs Charles Griffiths of Barking, East London, had the contract for demolition. We were collecting some of the workforce from Petworth with a coach, as previously mentioned. We were buying materials, particularly brick rubble for re-sale, using our tippers. Griffiths had several large American-built International flat trucks and tippers, several Bedford tippers, several vans and cars. Our retail garage was handling servicing and maintenance for these vehicles, although we could only get the front end of their large lorries into the then workshop. At the end of the job, we supplied and delivered many tons of topsoil, which was stripped off the top of Runfold Sandpits. Also, as the job closed down, we gained two good drivers, Ernie Chaplin and Jock Smollett, both of whom stayed with us for many years until their own retirement.

In 1949, June and I became engaged. She was not very happy at Farnham Hospital. We had a spare bedroom in mother's house and it was agreed that she would have the room for thirty shillings per week full board. June obtained a telephonist's job at Godalming Telephone Exchange, we think that the old man knew someone, but we never found out. Away she would go, on an old "sit up and beg" bicycle, scarf flying, past Oxenford Farm where she used to work and arrive in Godalming anywhere between 8 am and 3 minutes past. The postmaster would impose a fine for every minute late. Sometimes she would have to cycle to Witley on relief work, this was almost exactly opposite King Edward's School where my grandparents and Winifred and Ethel had lived. Aunt Ethel gave us a very nice tiepin, which had belonged to my grandfather. It had a sizeable turquoise central stone, surrounded by four small diamonds, set in gold. We had it turned into an engagement ring and it has been worn continuously every since. It is still as good as new and certainly quite unique.

Probably the worst of the coach experiences were the darts matches. There was one particular Working Men's Club outfit where the Honorary Secretary was full of his own importance. He would get his wife to ring and say, "Tell Peter that Charlie wants to see him"; this meant my going to the club in the evening to see Charlie. On my arrival, the four or five members sitting at the bar would one by one, drain their pint glasses and put them down onto the counter. This was the signal for me to order drinks for both myself and them. Charlie would then tell me that they wanted a coach for Friday week, for a darts match to be held in a pub or another club a few miles away. This was the business completed. Of course it could and should have been dealt with over the phone. The usual price was £1-10-0. The customers would get to the club for 7 pm by their own efforts. But late on, after turn out time, the return journey would be a circuit of four or five villages. I know that prices today are relative, but we were well out of pocket before we started and the Honorary Secretary still thought that he was our star customer! As this was before coaches were fitted with heaters, we bought fifty travelling rugs. June was always handy with needle and sewing machine and made two small rugs out of each one. We had ninety-nine rugs, one for each passenger.

June in 'pensive mood' at Elstead in 1953.

After June had moved to Elstead, note separate rooms, it was not unusual, on hearing my late arrival back to the yard after an early start, for her to get up and clean out the coach whilst I got some sleep. Unfortunately, after some of these pub or club dart matches, some of the mess that she was confronted with was extremely unpleasant. After one such job for a pub some eight miles away, June discovered that nearly all of her thirty-three rugs were missing. Not surprisingly, because there was no doubt about when they went missing and because I was at the pub the next morning in a very firm frame of mind, the landlord succeeded in getting them all back.

Quite a lot of work came from the Telephone Exchange, as one of the girls organised many outings and trips, supported by her colleagues. Whilst at the Exchange, June was repeatedly pressed to join the Union but she steadfastly refused, as she did not agree. She also felt it immoral to listen in to telephone conversations, but she was in the minority.

June and I had been looking for a house and had managed, we thought, to get a small bungalow down the Milford Road, opposite the Star Pub. We had got so far as to buy some furniture from Ron Ford's brother, Ron being one of our mates, and his brother was going to Canada. We had put these items in the bungalow for storage thinking that we were on our way. However, it dragged on and on and we never did purchase it. Neither of us can remember what or why this happened. Perhaps fate took a hand, because in the event, we did much better. However at the time, we were absolutely fed up about not getting anywhere regarding housing.

Our first home - the caravan "Raven Cottage" with my mother in the doorway, on the lawn behind her house. The firm's accountant, Albert Bunting, is standing in the other doorway.

I have spoken about Reg Adams, one of our drivers who had come to us from the Aldershot bus company as previously mentioned. Funnily enough, he was working on the buses as a conductor with his then driver, Bill Adams, to whom I referred as the organiser of coach trips many years later, same name, no relation. As a schoolboy I would go with Reg on the lorries as often as possible and several times, went with him and his wife on his yearly holiday to Eastbourne. Over a few years, this had become an annual pilgrimage to a typical guesthouse, not in Blackpool, but in Eastbourne. I used to think it wonderful!

Time was moving on and June and I appeared to be getting no nearer to getting married. In the end, we make a positive move. We bought a new caravan, called a "Raven Cottage". It cost £300 and we borrowed the money from Reg Adams. We set up a weekly "Rent Book" and started paying regularly. The next thing was, where to site it? I decided that we had plenty of room in the yard and unused bits of Glebe Meadow and that we could go from there. The caravan arrived, one Saturday morning, sparkling new. The balloon went up. My mother said "no son of hers would live in that, in the yard". We were both feeling pretty down by that pronouncement but I told my mother that she could at least come and look at it. I think that she had always considered that it would not happen, but it did and there it was. She came in, looked around, sat down and said, "It can't stop here in the yard, it must go on the lawn". Behind her house was a sizeable lawn.

It was not overlooked, as one side was bounded by the cemetery, so our neighbours would be quiet enough. Various things were discussed, at the end of which it had all been sorted out, including setting a date for the wedding, 16th March 1952, five weeks later. This was literally a turning point. We could not believe what we were hearing. We kept thinking that it would not be, that it would all be reversed. We were wrong. From that moment onward, there was no problem.

My sister's small son Mark, 4 years old, had arrived to inspect. June was so upset that she was in her room trying to pack. I said to Mark, "go and ask Auntie June to come over" and this he did. June listened speechless to the news. When later we moved the caravan into position, we dug a trench across the lawn for a water supply. There was an electric water heater over the sink. We ran an electric cable from the house and installed our own meter and paid my mother for our electricity. As I was on night call for the business, I ran a telephone cable along the cemetery fence. The caravan had a small coal fire, above which was an airing cupboard, and we could use my mother's bathroom - very cosy and rent-free.

This period of 1947-53 whilst nationalisation was in progress prevented any real development of the transport business. We had kept the lorries busy and in 1946 we had actually added one further tipper. As explained, the workshop and garage was busy and the coaches had filled quite a gap. As time went by and governments changed, the possibility of denationalisation was emerging. In 1953, it happened.

Tickets for the various London shows, events at Wembley and Haringey Stadiums, Royal Tournament, Earls Court, all non-summer activities etc. would almost always require ordering very early in order to get them so we were buying and hoping to sell them nearer the date. We would let our regular organisers know that we had them, but it often required June to get on her bicycle and go round the village and spread the word. If we had a spare Saturday or Sunday afternoon, we would put on a mystery tour. These never failed, especially with the older people. There are plenty of lovely rural runs around Surrey, Sussex and Hampshire, three to four hours, including a stop for tea. Strictly speaking, we were breaking the law by dealing with people individually, but we could always find an "organiser". We were always full up.

It was in 1953 that another momentous and infrequent event took place, the Coronation of Queen Elizabeth II. London was decorated as never before. There was a "Coronation route" throughout the West End of several miles, along which the entire procession had passed. All along the route were displays and decorations of all kinds, shop windows with their own exhibits and so on. This was a once-in-a-lifetime spectacular and everyone wanted to see it.

After dark, it needed seeing again, as the illuminations were something else. The schools all wanted to go, often two or three different days for different classes and other organisations clamouring for a booking. This was for a daylight run. It was followed by a different set of people for the evening run. We did this for fifteen days and nights without a break, usually two coaches at a time. It was so congested that it was hours of concentration - stop, start all of the time.

On several occasions I was dropping off the daytime passengers and picking up the evening customers at the same time. June would arrange for someone to meet me with a packet of sandwiches at some convenient rendezvous. We took some useful money but we well earned it.

We had taken on a full-time bookkeeper in around 1951. This eased my mother quite a bit but it did not tell us quickly enough what was going on financially. Figures were always roughly two months later, after the event.

Then the twelve months' figures went to auditors who took another couple of months before turning up for the ritual annual inquest. This performance was never very inspiring or encouraging, we could not understand what they were talking about and they could not understand why we kept on doing it.

We had however, to make some far-reaching decisions as in 1953, the Conservatives de-nationalised. They were in effect, offering British Road Services for sale. With an ex-BRS vehicle went a special 'A' licence. That was all I wanted, an entry into an 'A' licence. I put in a tender for one articulated vehicle, it was accepted and it was an ex-Pickfords machine with the scruffiest, most battered looking box-trailer. But it had an 'A' licence. So the decision was to give up coaches and concentrate on lorries. June had been pushing me to do this for some time. We had in the office, sixty-six tickets for the Wembley Ice Show to be held on Boxing Day in 1953 and we had no takers. We decided that, rather than waste them, we would give them to the local Doctor Barnardo's Home at Shackleford. We had worked for Barnardos and were friendly with Bill and Jean Jollife, another couple who were dedicated to their cause. We duly took the children to Wembley on Boxing Day, totally without charge and felt the better for it.

This was the end of our coaching history or nearly. In order to honour the forward work that we had undertaken, I had arranged with Warner's to take it on. There was one job on a Saturday in March not covered. I could not hire anyone, the AEC was the only coach remaining, and its road tax had expired. I used the AEC to cover the job myself. So ended our coaching operation.

A line-up of Bedfords with the 1938 Bedford pantechnican on the far right with seven Bedford OW 5-tonners - note the two with *Guildcrete* headboards.

7. Building a Business and a House

We were married in Elstead Church on Sunday 16th March 1952. The reception was at 'Glebe Meadow', on the lawn where our caravan stood. We set out on our honeymoon for Cornwall at about 3.30 pm. Our first stop was in the New Forest, where we combed out confetti from June's hair. Our next stop was Lyme Regis, then Hope Cove in Devon and on to 'Tye Rock Hotel' in Porthleven, South Cornwall.

My first visit to Porthleven was because Pete Perry, who worked at the Royal Aircraft Establishment (R.A.E.), at Farnborough and who was a bit of a "boffin", had met two Cornish fishermen, Wallace and Norman. During the war they had been commissioned by the RAE to work on the reservoirs in North Wales with small open boats similar to their Cornish fishing vessels and to use their skills with their fishing nets. They would set out their nets, stretched crosswise on the lakes, like a large curtain on a window, fixed vertically from the surface in the shape of a large rectangle of net. They would then repeat the operation some prescribed distance further down the lake.

They would go on doing this for a considerable distance and, as they proceeded, they would set the nets progressively deeper until there was a large area of the lake with rows of parallel nets going deeper and deeper. When this was set up, it would be handed over to the RAF. A single plane with one non-explosive bomb on board would fly in low, approaching the nets on a line from the shallow nets, toward the deep ones. The bomb would pass through all of the nets from which was plotted its course by lifting the nets one by one and measuring the holes, this also established its under water projection. By altering the design of the bomb and 'trying again', the course that the bomb took could be influenced until, within limits, they could make it go more or less to where they wanted.

In between 'shots', the Cornishmen would be busy mending the holes in the nets ready for the next trial. It was several years later before I learned anything about this and my knowledge is still very limited. It was only fairly recently, perhaps over the last five years, that I had the thoughts that I now relate and these were prompted by a visit to Porthleven and reference being made to Guy Gibson, a native of Porthleven.

My thoughts turned to Sir Barnes Wallis and his 'bouncing bomb' about which plenty has been written. His genius required the thing to bounce along the surface of the water for a pre-determined distance and then take an angled dive from the surface of the water down to the base of a concrete dam and then explode, and it did. Complementary to this, Guy Gibson led the team with equal brilliance to drop the bombs at the required destinations in Germany, as history relates. I must emphasise that all of this is pure guesswork on my part and must not be accepted as fact, but it could have all started with the Cornishmen working in Wales. As a result of that, Perry and I visited Wallis in 1947 and stayed, bed and breakfast, at his house in Cliff Road. Subsequently we visited Porthleven as bed and breakfasters, campers and in caravans or hotels, usually in gangs of six or eight or us, and then as a couple of honeymooners.

Much later, around 1958, we had converted an ex-Odiham Motor Services 28-seater Bedford utility bus, into a mobile caravan. Our petrol pump attendant, Vic Debenham, converted this bus. Vic was also a very competent carpenter and he worked on the bus during evenings after work. June then fitted it out with handmade curtains and bedspreads etc and by then, with our three young children, it was ideal for travelling and holidays. It was much used both by ourselves and our staff all of who were experienced drivers and we often left it in Cornwall on site by the Atlantic for my parents and others to use and then collect later on. It was so successful, that it prompted another conversion, this time a 29-seater Duple-bodied coach, again a Bedford.

The first caravan conversion, a Bedford OWB bus purchased from Odiham Motor Services, converted to a caravan and sited at Porthleven.

With lessons learned from the first bus, this was certainly an "up market version". It had the advantage of a sliding door and a spacious rear luggage compartment and by the time that June had finished with the interior, it looked, and was, very comfortable. We then undertook a brave adventure of a trip to Sweden to which the drivers' comments of "you'll be bloody lucky to get to Dover, let alone Sweden" were taken in good humour. June had two married sisters both with young families whom we intended to visit, one in the Stockholm area and the other in Hudiksvaal. We had a wonderful trip and because we had a large vehicle, we were always placed in the lorry queue for the ferries, often bypassing long lines of waiting cars. The further toward the north of Sweden that we went, the better it became. We always made sure toward evening time that we had petrol, water and a pint of milk and our trip proceeded with absolutely no problems.

The buses had a hard and full working life. We bought them as worn out and we were not concerned about internal condition as we could put that right and the seats were to be scrapped anyway. Between us, we made sure that they were brought up to top mechanical condition and safety and we had plenty of Bedford spares available so that neither of them cost much money in real terms, but we certainly had our money's worth out of them.

The second caravan conversion, this time based on Bedford OB/Duple coach registration EMW 96. It had the advantage of a sliding door, a full-width rear seat, with a large rear boot. Both of the conversions had 28 h.p. petrol engines with four-speed constant-mesh gearbox and servo-assisted hydraulic brakes. This took us to Sweden and other destinations.

These were the years when Porthleven had its own fishing fleet, mainly for pilchards. We would watch them set sail in the evening and later, could see lines of mast head lights on the horizon. These fishermen had no navigational aids other than a compass and a watch and much of the fishing was carried out during the night. Norman tried to explain how they would navigate by 'Dead Reckoning'. The dictionary describes this as "a method of establishing one's position, using the direction and distance travelled rather than astronomical observations". They would travel on a certain course, for a certain time at a fixed speed. Presumably they would sail roughly parallel to the coast, for an example - one hour at five knots (one mile and one eighth). So that in one hour, they would be 5 x 1¼ miles or approximately 6¼ miles along the coast towards Porthleven, then at that point, change course or bearing for another period of time and so on.

"After the washing up" at Porthleven. Note Judith beaming through the window.

If the weather was clear, they would look for the landmark of Breage Church, a distinctive square tower on the skyline, which could be seen from many miles when out at sea. On approaching Porthleven, they would line up on two green harbour lights and Breage Church, giving a straight run in. If the weather was rough and they were perhaps thirty or forty miles out, they would have to allow for the effects of wind and tide and correct their course accordingly. If the harbour was closed because of rough weather, the two approach lights would be red. They would then have to anchor in the outer harbour or go on to Penzance Newlyn. In foggy weather it would have been extremely hazardous with such a rocky dangerous coast. They had no ship-to-shore telephone, no radio, no radar and no GPS or navigational aid. They had a lot of courage and a great deal of experience and certainly earned their money.

It was not unusual for June and me to go down to the Harbour between 4.00 and 5.00 am armed with an empty bucket and have the bucket filled with pilchards, plus possibly a few mackerel as well. June being the only one of the gang who could fillet them, would then prepare a wonderful breakfast for us all. Payment would be on Saturday evenings in the harbour pub by buying the fishermen a few pints. Between 9 and 10 pm, there would always be spontaneous singing of the then popular hymns when one would appreciate the natural ability of the Cornish Male Voice Choirs.

This 1959 view shows June standing on the site in Porthleven, part of the wonderful coastline of Mount's Bay is visible.

Wallis would sit quite happily in the smoky old pub with his pals and our gang would be with them, feeling like natives of the place. Sometimes, not often, Wallace would burst into song, all on his own as follows:

I was passing through the graveyard in the City,
When I saw a beggar old and grey.
With his arms outstretched, he asked of me for pity,
And this is what I heard him say,

Oh I wonder, yes, I wonder, with the angels way up yonder
will the angels play their harps for me?
For a million miles I've travelled, and a million sites I've seen,
and I'm waiting for the glory soon to be,
and I wonder, yes, I wonder, will the angels way up yonder,
Will the angels play their harps for me?

As I ride up to those pearly gates of glory,
In my chariot of burnished gold,
And I see the folks that went up there before me,
And are safely gathered in the fold,
And I wonder, yes, I wonder, will the angels way up yonder,
Will the angels play their harps for me?

Memories of some wonderful evenings!

Jan, Judith, an unhappy Andrew and Sandra Thomas from the farm. Porthleven 1961.

I have mentioned that with de-nationalisation in 1953, I had succeeded in buying a special 'A' licence from the government. I also mentioned my realisation that to survive, I had to enlarge the operations of both 'May's Motors (Elstead) Ltd' and 'May's Motors (Transport) Ltd'. I suppose 1953 actively started that process, the transport company had followed its early pattern of being a 50/50 split of two vehicles being non-tipper and two vehicles being tippers. There was so much that happened over the next forty or so years, that I cannot accurately or chronologically recall it all.

My sister and brother in law, recently married, were living somewhere in Farnham, Alex being still in the army at Aldershot. He came out of the army and my father decreed that I would give him a job. I remember his income at the time, 10/6d per week! For a while, Alex worked on the petrol pumps and general mucking about in the garage. Having only experienced the army, including wartime service, he was like a fish out of water but over a period he was able to take over the tipper operation. Alex didn't have an HGV Driving Licence and the tippers were engaged more and more in the supply and delivery of clinker or ashes.

Alex and Christine Doughty, brother-in-law and sister.

Collecting this product from various sources over quite a large area required a mobile loading shovel. This was a machine, based on an agricultural tractor and fitted up with a manually operated winch, which would lift a 'bucket', travel to the lorry side on, and pull a cable and the bucket tipped its contents into the lorry. It was very heavy to steer having no power steering, had very poor brakes and was quite hard work. 'Chaseside Engineering Company' built this machine. There were other makes as it was a developing commodity. However we were very pleased with it as it moved quite a way from a man on the end of a shovel.

The first Chaseside Shovel, cable-operated. This machine was built on a Fordson industrial tractor and the early ones were fitted with a Fordson petrol/paraffin engine but ours had a Perkins P6 diesel engine and was really over-powered. It was fitted with a chain-driven winch from the gearbox power take-off that was engaged by pulling a heavy lever. This brought friction rollers onto the cable-winding drum. The bucket was released by a sharp pull on the wire cable, and had a free fall discharge. Also visible in the photograph are Bedfords JPK 901 and KPA 331 and Bedford artic FYV 767.

Alex Doughty became the operator but he needed a licence to drive it on the road, so up went the "L" plates. This meant that the driving examiner had to come to the machine, being really an item of 'plant', rather than a vehicle and so on the due date he came to our yard. I will always remember the scene. A man in a suit, with a clipboard, literally clinging to the rear of the machine and not looking very happy, and certainly not comfortable, as the contraption proceeded up the Thursley Road. It could have been predicted that it would not be gone for very long, it wasn't. Alex was awarded a pass for his driving licence and we afterwards discovered that it covered driving a lorry as well. As the years went by and the age of hydraulics took over, our loading shovels became more and more sophisticated, much easier to drive and much more productive. To look at a photograph of those early cable operated machines, then a photograph of its modern counterpart, makes one marvel at the difference. We had several of these machines through the years, usually operating at least two at any one time. The other sad fact is that I could and did regularly drive these old things. Perhaps today there are not many people left who can; equally, today for me to sit in a modern JCB or similar would be as foolhardy as trying to fly a 747. These machines enabled us to undertake a certain amount of earth-moving which created tipper work as well. I once dug out a factory site area for one of our customers, F. Milton Ltd, on which they built a new factory for Paine's Knitwear of Godalming. Paine's were well known as a long-established company producing very high quality woollen garments. Both F. Milton Ltd and Paine's Knitwear have long since passed into Godalming history.

With the arrival of the hydraulic version of the Chaseside Shovel, we had a small, easily moved lever that operated the jib and another to control the bucket. This gave a beautifully controlled loading and emptying function of the bucket. In addition, the bucket was wider than the front wheels allowing the job to be "cleaned up" as we worked. It had an enclosed cab, and most important, power steering while the engine was the excellent Fordson 4D diesel, with its three-speed tractor gearbox with a high and low ratio lever.

On the 'non-tipping' or long wheelbase 50% of the operation, work was building up with two main customers, 'Heald Sack Company' as described earlier and 'Guildway', Guildway obviously from Guildford. They started making wooden structures of all sorts for the poultry industry. This soon changed from Guildwood Ltd to Guildcrete Ltd, making agricultural buildings in concrete and we started carrying for them. This eventually changed into Guildway Limited, making prefabricated timber-framed housing and for many years, we delivered all over the UK and later into mainland Europe.

May's Motors (Elstead) Ltd who owned our premises, were continuing to make progress and this, despite the reign of Stokes and Red "Robbo" Robinson. Austin and Morris became British Motor Corporation (BMC) and after that, British Leyland Motor Corporation (BLMC). Stokes, who became Lord Stokes, philosophy was "the bigger you make it, the better it must be", which was not true and this, coupled with the trade union activist, 'Red Robinson', between them destroyed the company, driving the work abroad. Bad management and bad labour.

Recipe for disaster? Surprise, surprise! As BMC dealers, the attitude from the factory, through the distributor to us the dealer, was quite appalling. The absolute last thing that mattered was the customer who had ordered the car to his specification, including his required colour, from the brochure. He only paid the money but he did not matter. One of the reasons for our joining the Motor Traders Association (MTA), which later became the Motor Agents Association (MAA), was to try to combat some of this negative attitude from above. Most of these traders were family businesses. Intermingled were the 'distributors' who were usually much larger companies. To a young man, totally unused to such fascinating people and feeling very much the "new boy", it was a most interesting and educational experience.

We were joined to the Farnham section of the South East Division of the MTA. Therefore we were all local and mostly knew of each other's existence, albeit vaguely. To meet them was an experience and of course, several of them were some real characters. From this I learned much about debate and, particularly valuable, the correct way to run a committee. There were always one or two in attendance, who were waiting to pounce on a Chairman, who slipped up on a point of order. This training was equally valuable to me and exactly the same was applied from the Road Haulage Association. These rules for committee working are well established and are fundamental. I feel that many of today's political and social problems would be very much less, if these 'rules' were observed and adhered to. One can but hope.

The caravan on the lawn was a great success. In June 1953 our first-born, Jan, was born in Mount Alvernia in Godalming, run by the nuns who were a most dedicated set of people, the birth was also attended by our own Elstead Doctor, W. Lascelles, ex-Royal Navy. He was another of life's characters. The entire village greatly respected him and his 'doctoring', which he carried out in his own way and he was held in great affection. Jan came home to the caravan and I managed to buy our first washing machine on hire purchase. This was a top-loading machine, with a detachable lid that looked like a saucepan. Inside was a paddle, which oscillated to and fro and it heated its own water, which was filled by hosepipe. Fixed to the top was a hand wringer and at the bottom, was a tap to drain away the soapy water. This stood on the lawn outside the caravan and we put it away in the shed after use and thought that it was wonderful. We had plenty of visitors, friends and small parties in the caravan and no matter what the noise, Jan slept through the lot. Our second child Judith came home in January 1955 but not to the caravan.

Our new house in 1954 built onto mother's house.

Mother had given us the land adjoining her house on which we built a three-bedroom house on to the side of mother's house. She had four bedrooms and we had three but we could walk through upstairs either way. We therefore had a built-in baby sitter! We still had no cash, therefore we built in every shelf, cupboard, wardrobe and storage place that we could to save buying furniture and to get as much as possible on the mortgage. George Taylor's uncle who was a gardener but who also made furniture for a hobby, made our bed. This was a solid hardwood base, with bolt-on legs. Our mattress was Dunlopillo, obtained at a discount from the Dunlop Tyre rep, as we were customers of Dunlop's for car and lorry tyres.

Whilst June was away, Jan was installed in granny's room next door. Granny so enjoyed this period that she delayed Jan's return as long as possible to "enable June to get some rest". And so the caravan was sold and drawn away to another site. June was in tears but her mother, who was there at the time said "I cannot understand you, with such a lovely new home, why be upset?" We were both somewhat sentimental about it, understandably. When June arrived home with Judith, unbeknown to her, I had managed to get a new red hair-cord carpet fitted to our bedroom but there were several bare boards in the other rooms yet to be covered.

At the same time as the new house, we replaced the 'bus shed' with a new Guildcrete building, adding two bays and a body and paint shop to the original building. One of the two new bays became the M.O.T. car-testing bay. On the transport side we spent a period of several years expanding the fleet to include an increasing number of seven tonners. Having obtained one vehicle on 'A' licence from de-nationalisation, we purchased Frank's Transport (Farnborough) Ltd. This company had two vehicles on 'A' licence and we simply bought its shares and changed the vehicles as authorised for two new ones. Similarly we did the same to Goulding Carriers' vehicle and two vehicles licensed to F.C. Bonner (Chiddingfold) Ltd.

We operated this lot as separate operations for a period and then May's Motors (Transport) Ltd officially applied to take over the licences to these companies. We had now added five vehicles to our own licence, which now included six 'A' licensed vehicles. From now on we could apply for additional vehicles in our own right through the traffic courts.

In 1955, our fleet was 15 vehicles, which meant its carrying capacity became 98 tons and by 1958 we owned 19 vehicles and held a carrying capacity of 124 tons. I heard about Frank's Transport from a vehicle salesman, it was not actually operating and the two vehicles were not actually 'alive', therefore we operated it for a while, feeding it with our own work, using our own vehicles and then taking it over.

A similar situation applied with F.C. Bonner. Frank Bonner was a member of the Haulage Association, Guildford sub-area. He was one of the "old school" and was now very old and only actually operating one small lorry. I understand that, in his early days he would travel the country as required and often, literally sleep under his lorry, oil drips and all. He found difficulty in coping with the increasing regulations and paper work such as keeping log sheets etc. He told me that if he was checked and asked for his log sheet, he claimed that he could not read or write. "Then how can you find the place that you are delivering to?" "Well sir, I just look at the bit of paper with the address on that they gived me, and I goes on until I sees the same letters on the sign post and I goes down there."

Soon after his wife died, he came into our house one morning, sat on the bottom step of the stairs and sobbed his heart out, despite having two sons and one daughter; somewhat predictably, he died soon after.

I earlier mentioned the supply and delivery of clinker or ashes. We all know from the use of coal fires, that after burning coal, the ashes need cleaning out from under the grate. In large furnaces, some of these ashes fuse into larger lumps called clinker. Most factories, village halls, hotels, hospitals, warehouses, churches and so on were heated by coal- or coke-burning boilers. I said earlier that I shovelled tons of coal from railway trucks into lorries and delivered to hospitals and companies locally. All of these boilers produced considerable quantities of ashes or clinker. It was used for making up farm tracks, over rubble on new house sites and on new roads etc.

The boiler man would wheelbarrow his coal into the boiler room and wheelbarrow the ashes on to a heap outside which eventually had to be cleared. Together with the supply and delivery of sand and aggregates, we had a market, although limited, for this commodity to builders and road-making contractors. We would probably have to hand-shovel it on to the lorry, perhaps be paid a small amount to do this and get the ashes for nothing to sell on to the builders etc. The larger users of coal might have large hoppers for the ashes, whereby we could reverse under and pull a lever and be loaded by gravity. For these larger amounts of ashes, we would have to pay.

Of course, times were changing; coal produced smoke (remember the London smog?). The electricity industry was generating ever-larger amounts of electrical power distributed through the national grid, local gas works that had produced town gas were closing due to the influence of natural gas. Oil was taking more and more of the market and nuclear power was becoming another factor. Factories, which had generated their own electricity, changed over to a supply from the grid and hospitals went over to oil. Therefore our supplies of local clinker often dried up, so we went looking for it. There was another market for a different type of ash, which was called breeze and used for making breezeblocks. These blocks were much lighter than concrete blocks and much better for insulation, what's more, they were made from what was really a waste product, therefore were relatively cheap.

In an effort to reduce smoke and pollution, the coal-fired power stations would crush the coal to a small consistent size, about the size of a garden pea. This gave much more complete combustion and therefore minimal contamination of the atmosphere and use of a cheaper grade of coal. The resultant ash was ideal for breezeblock making.

June and I going to a wedding.

Alex Doughty would go round from time to time looking for clinker or ashes and negotiating contracts. Two in particular come to mind; Guildford Electricity Works generated in winter to supplement the grid. The clinker was stored in a large concrete hopper under which we could reverse. If necessary we would have to run seven days a week to keep it clear. This exceeded the requirements of the breezeblock makers so we had to store, which we did in one of the Runfold sand pits. This would build up stock during the winter and we would draw on it in the summer.

The other good one was the Aldershot Military Power Station, which supplied power for the Aldershot garrison, including the Cambridge Hospital. Although it ran all the year round, it produced more breeze during the winter. Here we needed to use a loading shovel. We had regular outlets for this material from several block makers and, of course, had one or two non-tipper vehicles delivering the finished blocks to site. Another source of clinker, mainly of a much coarser variety, was from the Metropolitan Water Board. They had several water-storage and filtering plants around outer southern London, using mainly steam-driven pumps from coal-fired boilers. Some had storage hoppers and some required a loading shovel.

There were other supplies as well that Alex unearthed and we had a consistent demand for these products. There was a considerable tonnage coming out of London itself as well as from the Home Counties.

The long wheelbase or non-tipping lorries were busy with primarily two main customers, Heald Sack Company and Guildcrete. Again the traffic was consistently 50% tipping and 50% non-tipping work in 1958 with nine vehicles working on each. We also had a contract to supply four vans of 1½ ton capacity for Haslemere Laundry, painted in their colours and with their own drivers, bringing the fleet to some 22 vehicles. By now we also had full time accounting staff and a growing number of maintenance staff for our own vehicles, in addition to the retail garage staff, therefore space was becoming a problem.

In January 1949, I was elected Secretary and Treasurer of Guildford Sub-Area Road Haulage Association, a post that I held continuously until the Area Office in the region of March 1984 undertook the job. Originally, the Sub-Area had a list of 61 members and on my going through that list in March 2005, I could only find five of the original names still operating, of which only two were under their original ownership.

I was still attending MAA local evening meetings and was elected Chairman of the Farnham section during 1959 - 60. Before this, June and I had attended one of the annual conferences at Torquay, which was an excuse for a few days off at the firm's expense. We had bought tickets for the Dinner Dance, one of the social functions and had presented ourselves at the Winter Gardens, or wherever, with June looking very nice in a pretty summer dress and me in my one and only best suit, to be refused entry! The tickets had stated 'black ties' and unfortunately, we had not read this and did not understand what it meant anyway. We were standing there somewhat bewildered when along came Len Heath and his wife who were old hands at the game. He had achieved fame in the motorcycle racing world and had a substantial business with motor cycles in Farnham and Frensham. They were a lovely couple who made us feel so welcome and relaxed and they promptly said "never mind the dance, let's all go for a walk along the sea front" and this we did. It was very much part of a learning curve, a valuable experience and very much part of my ever-changing world and another part turn of the wheel.

With the duties of Office, both for MAA and RHA, went the requirement to attend the next stage up, area RHA meetings in London and divisional meetings as a delegate for the MAA in London. These were usually monthly with one being held at Oxford Street and the other at Great Portland Street.

From 1942, we bought Bedfords for many years and this 1950s photograph shows the fleet in size order, with our Bedford CA van on the left, then five Bedford OWL long-wheelbase five-tonners with S-types visible on the right. On the extreme right is the second-hand 1938 Bedford 27 h.p. furniture van.

Looking back over the business makes one realise how much was achieved and how rapidly the years passed in achieving it. Everyone worked extremely hard and long. It is that sort of industry, not an easy industry and it is the sort of job where one expects and accepts that you are the one who must and will sort it out. I am sure that everyone of us feels the same way about their own occupation, whatever it is or was. I would take this opportunity to pay tribute to the many people, employed by our Companies throughout the years, for the dedication and determination that they displayed in helping us to succeed and making it work. Furthermore, again looking back, one can recognise just how skilled they all were in their various ways. It was not unusual, in fact the opposite, to find that a problem had arisen and had been solved before I had heard about it.

Of course, we did not always succeed and we would not have been normal if we had, but we did enjoy great loyalty from a very good-tempered workforce. Because of this, we tend to forget very easily, the troubles that we inevitably did have. It would be very remiss of me at this juncture therefore to fail to mention my wife June as we approach our fifty third wedding anniversary. I recall my early disagreement with my mother before our marriage and my words to her at the time that "I do not need a business woman, I want a wife and mother", and that is what I have. For the record I must also say that once my mother accepted the situation, no one could have been more helpful and there was no longer a problem with the subject.

Jan and Judith, with cousin Mark Doughty in 1957.

In the process of building up a business, of necessity, domestic matters more often than not took second place. I am the first to admit that the process of bringing up four children and the domestic scene fell heavily on June and she is very capable. Fortunately, we are completely different but are very compatible. She has given me every support in all of my efforts through all the years. Sometimes we are not very complimentary to each other but we are complementary to each other, and had June's side of things been left to me, I would not have been anything like as well fed and watered as I have been. There is no doubt that the stresses and strains of business can be very much eased when there are no stresses and strains on one's domestic life, particularly when the opposite applies in the form of support and encouragement and for this I am more than grateful. I am very proud to comment that we had a good name as both an employer and as an operator of well conditioned vehicles.

With our increased fleet and an increase in the retail commercial vehicle servicing and repair activity and of course the new body and spray workshop activities, conscious thought about space was required.

Our first articulated vehicle, Bedford OW FYV 767 with its battered trailer, bought from Pickfords. It operated on a special 'A' licence.

8. Continuing to Build a Business

Behind and adjoining the cemetery next door, was a large area reserved for the ultimate extension of the cemetery, all part of the church land from which my parents had purchased the Glebe Meadow originally. The land in question was very rough and had a small pond in the centre. The Parochial Church Council (PCC) decided in their wisdom that as the land would have to be made up and levelled with soil needing to be brought in, it was unsuitable for burial purposes. It had no access other than through the existing cemetery and the PCC then decided to establish a new cemetery at the top end of the village at Cock Hill.

We offered to lease the abandoned land from our local church. The due process of de-consecration and planning consent was eventually effected and we had a twenty-one year lease in our possession. Whilst this land adjoined our own, our lower boundary did not quite reach far enough to put an access road into the lease from our existing property. We could have managed it but it would have been very difficult. However, alongside our lower boundary was a piece of land belonging to Mrs Bentley from the Elstead Mill. If I could persuade her to sell it would solve the problem.

Negotiations took place and providing that there was no visible intrusion, i.e. no buildings, a deal could be agreed and it was. This exposed another rectangle of land also belonging to Mrs Bentley that was very wet and now completely isolated so another deal with the same conditions was eventually agreed and carried out. Twenty one years later, we bought the leased land from the Church thus joining up with the two parcels of land that we had purchased from Mrs Bentley and with our original property.

There was so much happening in both companies during the 1950s, 1960s and 1970s that I can only generalise and pick out various highlights as they come to mind. We were too busy to write diaries and therefore, I cannot accurately quote many dates but it is unimportant anyway.

By comparison, a much later Volvo shovel from 1976. It was "back to front" allowing the driver to see his work and with rear steering. It had a fluid drive, no clutch pedal and just one lever for forward and reverse and an automatic gearbox, plus the luxury of a cab heater. It was a very good machine.

Returning to the clinker operations, Alex had discovered a large quantity of mixed clinker and ashes near at hand in Farnham. It was not visible from any road and was to be found in a disused sand pit, which had had its sand excavated and had been filled to the top with railway ashes. It belonged to British Rail and was only accessible by a rail siding off the main line, just outside Farnham Station. We understand that the coarser ashes had come from the working railway steam locomotives based at various locations in London. The ashes would have been loaded into railway trucks and trainloads, brought down to Farnham (Weydon Pit) and unloaded into the sand pit. We also understand that a much larger quantity of fine ash in the pit had come from Lott's Road Power Station.

This provided the electric power for the underground trains in London for several years - what a find! There was a lot of it and Alex negotiated with British Rail at Wimbledon to buy this material and pay monthly for the quantity drawn, which was measured by the cubic yard (cubic metre today), as there was no weighbridge. All of the vehicles were calibrated and stamped with their cubic capacity and our sales were by cubic measure. British Rail wanted a guarantee of fifty thousand pounds minimum for the contents of the pit. The actual quantity was unknown so there was a lot of hope and guesswork.

Bought new in December 1954, this Bedford S 7-tonner had a petrol engine, Telehoist body and tipping gear.

Obviously a firm of our size could not risk such a guarantee, it might have been suicidal. However, Alex managed to obtain the backing for £50,000 from William Cory Ltd, a coal factoring company belonging to Shell-Mex. They paid British Rail the rate per cubic yard that Alex had agreed and we paid William Cory the same rate plus an agreed amount per cubic yard on quantities drawn per month. Over a period of a few years, we emptied the pit.

Alex had obtained a temporary road access point on to the road, renewed yearly with Farnham Council. We discovered in the bottom of the pit that the sand had not been fully dug leaving hefty ridges of un-dug sand all over the area. We measured the volume of this residual sand in cubic yards and claimed that this, converted into money at the agreed rate, should come off the £50,000 guarantee. The estimate that we had set out initially must have been pretty good because I do not recall any major amount of money being paid or claimed. And so for reasons already given in oil, gas etc the clinker supply was dying out and the Weydon Pit was nearly empty. However it was not the end of the Weydon Pit as British Rail started to fill it again but not with clinker and ashes - more on that later.

The non-tipping or long wheelbase part of the business was, during this period, working for an ever-widening base of customers and it will be remembered that we were able to purchase an 'A' licensed vehicle from the government on de-nationalisation in 1953 and this was articulated. This meant that it was in two parts, the tractor unit and a semi-trailer, which could be disconnected very easily from the tractor and another hooked on equally easily.

The Bedford artic FYV 767 at work with a flat trailer. It had a 28 h.p. petrol engine, four-speed crash gearbox and servo-assisted hydraulic brakes, but on the tractor only. The trailer had a cable-operated brake. Rated at 10 tons payload made it work very hard with a low ratio rear axle and 34 x 7 rear tyres.

A non-articulated lorry is called a rigid lorry but it was this 'articulation' that revolutionised the road transport business which really got going with the replacement of the railway cartage horses as described earlier. Two horses were needed to pull a six-ton load and one for a three-ton load. These horses were progressively replaced by a very clever design of vehicle called a 'mechanical horse' made by Scammell Lorries of Watford. Naturally, one version was a three-tonner and the other a six-tonner but it was quite a small machine that only had three wheels. The single front wheel could turn through 180° left to right and right to left. This made it very manoeuvrable, particularly backwards.

The trailers were really replicas of the horse-drawn wagons but with pneumatic tyres and a quick release mechanism controlled from the cab by pulling a lever. It was very low which meant it could be stepped into easily from either side. There were no doors, only a front end-fixed canvas 'door', which hooked on to the bodywork. They were ideal for short distance work. The crew on the railway vehicles usually consisted of a male driver and a female assistant. Whilst these were designed and operated as described mainly on railway cartage, they spread throughout the cities. There were a few designs of articulated lorries in earlier years that were very heavy and cumbersome. Scammell exploited the principle and developed their vehicles for a specific market.

Bedford S MLF 291 was the replacement for the ex-Pickfords Bedford FYV 767. Bought second-hand, with a Bedford petrol engine, it was photographed fresh from overhaul in our workshop, about to leave on its "maiden voyage" for May's Motors.

They were already building large, heavy four-wheeled tractors for general haulage and the older ones among us will remember these early machines with their wooden cabs and chain drive, dragging very large but immaculate milk tankers which were painted in orange livery. They were to be found at about hourly intervals running each way along the A30 and A303 to and from the West Country and London. There was a large milk depot at Vauxhall in London and in those days, they carried the logo of United Dairies and were limited by law to 20 mph. They were probably capable of about 30 mph but at that speed, stopping them became a major issue!

Bedford eventually got together with Scammell to produce a "Bedford Scammell" which was basically a modified four-wheeled tipper chassis. It was one of these machines that we bought from the government with its 'A' licence and which was marketed as a ten-tonner although it struggled a bit when loaded. However, it was quite a step forward as it extended the carrying capacity and the platform length and by using different types of trailer, the versatility of the vehicle.

Another important development during this period was the purchase of Rushmoor Garage at Rushmoor, Tilford by May's Motors (Elstead) Ltd. This was a very well built showroom with a spacious flat above, a petrol forecourt, a substantial workshop and a cottage with ample parking space. My thoughts were that it would link up with May's Elstead as a customer catchment area, it was approximately six miles away and if we could obtain another car agency, it would all fit together nicely. There was the little matter of how to pay for it. Lloyds Bank, with whom we had been since the start, would not finance it, so our solicitor, Reg Spalding, who was a man who did not mince his words, said to me "if you are determined to have this bloody place", and I said "yes I am", he said, "then I will get it for you but you will have to change banks. I've put a lot of money through Barclays Bank so they will have to do it for me if I say so". I said "OK" and we proceeded to purchase the garage from Mr W.N. Stiff, a man I had known for years through Farnham section MAA.

He was a great 'hoarder' and above the workshop was a useful 'attic' that was full of junk. Flat ex-cigarette tins that were full of burnt-out car fuses, old and scrapped car shock absorbers, worn out auto-mower parts (he was a bit of a specialist), old spark plugs and so on. In his younger days, he had been quite a clever motor mechanic but he was now quite old and not very well.

At Elstead, John Meade was manager including the commercial vehicle repair shop and the bodyshop. He joined us originally as a mechanic. Robbie Morgan was also a mechanic and his wife Edna, was the bookkeeper at Elstead. Robbie and Edna took over Rushmoor Garage as manager and bookkeeper. We were granted a Rover and Land Rover agency because Rover wanted Land Rover in that area due to its rural and farming nature. In the event, we could never get enough Land Rovers out of them and they eventually said that we were too small so we lost or gave up the agency. We then got a Volvo agency and this lasted for many years, very successfully until again, they wanted bigger premises in Farnham. Both John Meade and Robbie Morgan stayed with us up to retirement. Rushmoor Garage had been turned into a Limited Company and we sold it when Robbie retired in 1984.

This was a period of great activity for both companies. May's Motors (Elstead) Ltd and May's Motors (Transport) Ltd followed by Rushmoor Garage. I was on a 'mission' to build up the business through both necessity and desire. Therefore naturally, it was ongoing and took many years, years that passed like a hurricane.

We were permanently in a position of no money. Many readers will have been in this position or still are, in trying to build and operate a business. It was to me, really quite simple, probably over-simple. The situation was almost certain to be one of two things:-

(1) A public company can obtain capital from its shareholders, assuming that the shareholders are convinced that it is a good thing to do. The shareholders then obtain a return from dividends out of profits or increased share value or, if the company fails, they lose their money. The point is, that the capital is not repayable and no interest is payable on it by the operating company concerned.

(2) A private company has to create its own capital out of revenue as well as that revenue required to finance the operation of the business. The inevitable outcome for most people is to borrow. Theoretically therefore profits from the operation of the business should provide money both for replacements and expansion. "Theoretically" is the operative word but usually quite different in practice.

I have stated earlier that I had no financial training and had to learn the hard way.

Another factor common to us all was recession and inflation. I remember that we went through each one twice over the years and just had to survive it, but this we did. We had come some way from the days of paying cash for new Bedfords one by one and by the late fifties, early sixties, had expanded to a fleet of some eighteen or so vehicles, still working roughly 50/50 tippers and long wheelbase. Not only had we increased the fleet but the majority of the replacements were of increased capacity. It followed therefore, that we needed an ever-increasing amount of work and we seemed to find it. During the same period, a certain Geoff Wigley appeared on the scene as a sales rep for Guy Motors of Wolverhampton. We had a couple of Guy buses from approximately 1924 era. Geoff lived in London but wanted to move to Elstead. We knew of a house for sale and we were able to point him in the right direction. We became very firm friends until his untimely death in 1993. His widow Joan still lives in the same house, Myrtle Cottage.

Geoff and Joan Wigley became very firm friends and so did our dogs - "Bryn" and their dog "Kim" (right) as the picture shows!

May's Motors (Elstead) Ltd took the Guy Agency for commercial vehicles and over several years sold a significant number of Guys, including several to May's Motors (Transport) Ltd. After Guy Motors closed down, we took an agency for Dodge Trucks that were built at Kew in Surrey. By this time, John Robinson joined us. John was at the time living in Guildford and working in London for the South Eastern Traffic Area Licensing Authority through which I got to know him. Our own licensing affairs had by now become quite involved and to find someone who knew the system was a Godsend. The outcome was that he came to work for May's Motors (Elstead) Ltd. He did the licensing paperwork for us and he also set up a licensing consultancy for local operators under May's Motors (Elstead) Ltd and sold quite a number of new and used lorries until his retirement when he went back to his wife's roots in Crackington Haven, Cornwall.

We now had John Meade managing May's Motors (Elstead) Ltd, Robbie Morgan managing Rushmoor Garage Ltd and Ray Mitchell, an ex-driver who therefore knew the job, running the fleet of May's Motors (Transport) Ltd. Albert Bunting was the accountant.

The old man used to pop down to the local, the "Golden Fleece" most lunchtimes for "a couple of jars" usually using an old bicycle. He was most annoyed one day when he reported that someone had pinched the old thing. Four days later, the pub landlord said "is that your bike outside Dickie? It's been there for four days". He had ridden down and walked home! A couple of years on, his car also went missing. I asked one of our staff to have a walk down to "the Fleece". There it was, keys and all. This time it had only been there for two days!

Having said that, we were always without money, it was because we ploughed all that we could back into the business and this was not unwise. However, we did bring up four children and on reflection, we did have a pretty good selection of holidays. Several of these holidays were linked with Road Haulage Association activities as I had become very involved with the Association Committees. I have decided that it will be easier to devote a special chapter to that subject, which spreads over many years.

With the passing of time, several things had happened. My sister and Alex had been left the house next door as my grandmother had died, as did subsequently mother's sister, "aunt Ethel".

Jan and friend Glenda rubbing down a Bedford OW 5-ton tipper DHR 20 for repaint. Livery was Brunswick green bodywork with black chassis, wing and radiator grill.

Our companies had started a staff pension scheme, another John Robinson activity. Everyone was in this scheme except we Directors, who by law were not allowed to be in it. When the law was changed to allow Directors into the scheme, we could never afford the premiums required to catch up. Another development was that some of the drivers would realise they were building up some cash after a few years in the scheme and as with all of us, some of them became very hard up. They would leave our employ and be paid out their accumulated money. After the paper work had been completed and their money had come through then a couple of weeks later they would be back asking for their old job back. The pension scheme was a great help to a number of our employees in retirement. Unfortunately, many years later we experienced that the ever-increasing cost to the company was non-sustainable and eventually, we had to close the scheme to new entrants. We were however able to maintain the premiums right up to retirement for all of those employees already in the scheme, indeed two or three are still going strong.

In 1963 the Aldershot and District Traction Company gave up parking at our yard. My father had a habit of doing a whistle stop tour of the premises on most mornings clutching his little black notebook and pencil in order to "sort a few people out". This accomplished, off he went oblivious of any upset that he had caused. In fact, whenever we returned from holiday, we used to ask the question "who has he sacked whilst we've been away?" The staff used to not argue but just lie low until my return and things reverted to normal, as father had already forgotten the incident anyway.

One particular driver and one particular conductor, a two-man team on one of the two buses that parked with us, would be ready and waiting to leave the yard at 8.30 am. It was an unusual situation that driver Jack was a staunch Tory, while the conductor Jim, was an equally staunch Labour supporter. It was the old man's delight to come over to the yard at about 8.15 am and start a political argument, which set these two characters Jack and Jim at loggerheads and it would take several hours of their working day before speaking to each other resumed. This was great entertainment for my father and quite deliberate on his part.

The next development with the departure of the parked buses was to demolish the garage that had been erected for the buses and to erect a new commercial repair workshop. This was 100 feet by 40 feet with 16 feet to the eaves and easy access to all bays with two 30-foot inspection pits. We also installed a commercial brake roller-tester. The building had plenty of light and was the envy of the area. From this, Mays Motors (Elstead) Ltd developed a significant retail repair operation. My cousin Bob May, ran this for us until his retirement. He is the most capable hands-on engineer that I have ever known, a mechanic, electrician, welder, fabricator, someone who could recover disabled or damaged lorries, a builder and a superb gardener, Bob is very clever.

One third of the building was used by May's Motors (Transport) Ltd for maintaining it's own fleet and this was run by George Taylor, the same who started Ron Tracey's concrete mixer at ten o' clock at night and whose grandfather, George Chandler chopped his brakeless bicycle into two pieces as related earlier. Again, George could make a vehicle engine 'talk'. It was usual then to rebuild our own engines, gearboxes and rear axles etc before the more usual practice later on of exchanging units. George would start with a stripped chassis frame, stood on four old oil drums, and rebuild the complete machine, including the engine. It was stood in a sawn-off front end chassis of a scrapped lorry, fixed up with a radiator, fuel tank, exhaust pipe, gauges etc and George would have it quietly running for days.

This ex-Army Bedford QL reregistered 834 MPK started life as a gun tractor. We purchased it from Government surplus and fitted it with a Harvey Frost lifting crane. It had the usual 28 h.p. petrol engine and four-speed "crash" gearbox. It had a two-speed transfer box to give four-wheel drive and a substantial towing winch. It gave wonderful service. This 1962 view shows Andrew waiting for a ride on it.

It would be checked over, adjusted and ready for reinstalling to go straight to work. We would only apply this total rebuild to Bedfords but they would emerge from the workshop like new. Later on, we moved on to heavier, more robust trucks. Cecil Beaven who was the person who used to straighten buckled bicycle wheels and who had been with the company since before the war assisted George and drove the taxi, the lorries and worked in the workshop. Like my cousin Bob May, Cecil was an excellent gardener, a great countryman and naturalist who was very knowledgeable about wildlife, plants and trees. He could also predict the weather most accurately. Cecil was very hard working, willing and non-complaining and stayed with us until his retirement. Unfortunately, George Taylor died from cancer before retirement and so Cecil's son, Alfred who had initially been a driver, became the replacement for George and became the fleet engineer. Again, there was not much that Alfred could not do and so it was very rare that a vehicle was not ready for service when promised and it was not often that they failed for lack of attention. Again, Alfred was also a first class gardener.

Nevertheless, with any mechanical contraption, one gets problems and failures and we had our share. The haulage business was very busy. The nine tippers were going full steam on clinker, aggregates etc and the nine non-tippers were also fully employed. Two principle customers, Heald Sack Company and Guildcrete Ltd., took up at least six of the lorries and the customer list was expanding. We had five 1½-ton vans on Haslemere Laundry. These were painted in their livery and lived at the laundry, using their drivers and their own fuel.

It was at that time, in late 1960, that June and I went to Oslo via Newcastle, up to Trondeheim and then on a small coaster delivering and collecting goods round the Lofoten Islands. The coaster the "Nordvaer" took ten passengers only during the non-winter period although passengers were secondary to their main occupation of goods-carrying. It was a wonderful experience and the built-in babysitter, my mother, was also very useful!

With the new commercial workshop and our own increased fleet, the requirement for mechanics was ever growing. Up to now, we had only operated Bedfords, apart from the five laundry vans. We had one articulated vehicle with two trailers in the fleet. On one occasion, this one vehicle had engine failure at Grantham while returning loaded from the North of England. I was the only person available so I loaded up the car with a tool box and anything else that I could think of and journeyed up to Grantham. I found the vehicle and driver in a lay by alongside the A1 (there was no M1 at that time).

We went in the car, down the road and had some lunch then returned to the artic. As John the driver had been away from home for several days, I sent him home with the car as I reckoned to get the lorry going and bring it home without too much delay. I cannot remember the exact problem but I do remember removing the oil sump from the engine. As I had no new oil with me and had nowhere to tip away the old oil that was in the sump, I had to remove it whilst still full. I can still think of no logical reason for doing this, maybe I was trying to withdraw one piston from the bottom, or maybe I got one out and thought that I could isolate one cylinder and travel home on five. I had to try. To see if whatever I was doing was going to work, I had to refit the sump complete with its very black oil. There I was, flat on my back under the lorry, being showered with grit and road dust from continuous speeding traffic inches from my feet.

I was trying to lift the thing and it was quite heavy above and over the front axle, to then prop it on one knee and to reach up to locate a securing screw into each corner before I could take a rest for my aching arms and knee. The amazing thing is that I managed to achieve it. I then started the engine. The noise and thumping and the smoke that ensued, was horrific. I was tired, hungry and filthy and had no means of travel so I slept in the passenger seat. The next morning I found a telephone box and I telephoned June and asked her to arrange to dispatch George and Cecil to rescue both me and the lorry.

Because it was articulated, we could not tow the broken-down outfit with its loaded trailer, however, we had in the yard, an old, unlicensed Bedford tractor unit that we used to move trailers in the yard and in and out of the workshop. This machine would have to come to Grantham to bring home the loaded trailer. Really, its days for such journeys were long over and its appearance reflected this. George eventually arrived with our breakdown vehicle followed by Cecil with this poor old tractor unit. We pulled off the dead tractor and George with Cecil in tow took it away. I coupled up the trailer and set off. I had to stop to refuel and lost sight of the other two. I managed to get as far as just past Esher on the A3, which is about twenty miles from home when I was pulled over by the police. "What was I carrying", asked the policeman and I responded "I don't know", the next question "Where was it loaded?" again my response "I don't know". More questions and response "where is your paperwork?" "I haven't got any, it's in the broken-down vehicle". "This vehicle is on trade plates" "yes, because it isn't taxed". "It is incorrect use of trade plates" "I know, but what else can I do?" By now I was at zero tolerance and I let the policeman know it. He said "hold on boy, we know your company" (the name of the company was on the trade plate licence), "We've had reports of stolen loads and are just checking, get off home!" I apologised for being wound up and went home gratefully. Thinking back on the episode, it is surprising that I was not stopped earlier, considering the appearance of the outfit and its filthy unshaven driver!

Guildcrete had started to make timber-framed houses, naming the new company "Cedar Homes Limited". This developed and the Guildcrete activity decreased and eventually ceased altogether. They then changed the name from Cedar Homes Ltd to Guildway Ltd. This required that we must introduce a much-increased concentration of articulated vehicles. We had four step-frame semi-trailers built by Taskers of Andover. These were longer and lower than rigid vehicles and were required because the Guildway package was much larger and lighter than their previous concrete product.

We had originally only the ex-special 'A' licence battered box-trailer, which we soon scrapped, and only one flat trailer that had been extended from 20-foot platform to 22 feet. We now needed additional tractor units to pull the new trailers. As a result of the 'Guy Agency' of May's Motors (Elstead) Ltd, we took in part exchange two used Guy tractors which were sold to May's Motors (Transport) Ltd. These were designed to work at a maximum of 24 tons gross. A further six step-frame trailers were acquired, making a total of ten. This enabled Guildway to pre-load trailers as the panels came off the production line for next day delivery to site.

Delivering for Guildway. A consignment after arrival at Windermere in Cumbria.

All deliveries were arranged for 8 am anywhere in the country. Therefore, dependant on the distance of the site from Guildford, the day and time of departure would be established. In those early days of Guildway's development, all of us involved including some of Guildway's Directors could often be found helping to finish off loading a trailer, which then had to be sheeted, roped and pulled out of the loading bay ready for a driver to couple up and leave often during the night.

Their initial product was Cedar framed bungalows. They worked hard to develop an insulated "party wall" which became accepted by local authorities to use as a partition wall for semi-detached, two-storey council housing. This opened up an entirely new field. They also purchased a special jig machine, which enabled them to manufacture their own roof trusses, by cutting timber components to varying angles for varying roof pitches. This became useful for subsequent application for the high pitched roofs to be found in Holland, Belgium etc. Therefore Messrs Guildway Ltd became an important factor in our development. We were still using some rigid lorries on this and other work, but more and more we were turning to more and heavier 'artics'.

It was an extremely complex traffic to organise. This was because it could be one small bungalow to the north of Scotland, which would all go on to a rigid lorry or a large bungalow for a site in Surrey or the Midlands perhaps, which might require two artics to deliver the order. Trusses were particularly difficult as they were bulky, usually 28 feet 6 inches long and maybe 9 feet wide.

They had to lie flat on the top of the load and of course, the larger the building, perhaps a village hall or similar, the greater the number of trusses. They were loaded at Guildford, where the trailer was reversed into a sunken loading bay, bringing the trailer floor to factory floor height. At site, most times, everything was manhandled off. Life was much easier when Guildway secured a contract for twenty or thirty bungalows or Local Authority Housing, when we could plan repeat and timed deliveries.

One good example was in Pontypool, South Wales, when we had to deliver a substantial number of local authority two-storey housing. The return journey could be achieved within the then legal driving hours. With the statutory break or rest period taken on site and doing nothing else but driving, we couldn't afford any hold-ups. We would arrange for driver accommodation on a weekly basis at Pontypool. The first load went to Pontypool where it was unloaded and trailer sheets and ropes were folded and secured. The trailer was parked on site ready to be picked up the next day and the driver and tractor unit went to the "digs".

The next day another unit with loaded trailer would leave early to arrive at Pontypool during the morning. It would drop its loaded trailer and the driver would have his break. He would then pick up yesterday's empty trailer, return to Guildford and then the driver would finish work. On the same day, another unit and loaded trailer would leave Guildford at about 10 am, arriving in Pontypool mid-afternoon, repeat the performance, drop the loaded trailer and collect the now empty morning trailer and return to Guildford at approximately 8.00 or 9.00 pm. We organised it so that a driver and unit would be on site from Monday morning to undertake all of the shunting, trailer positioning and sheet folding etc. They would return home on Friday afternoon, bringing home the last empty trailer and then a different driver would stay in Pontypool the next week and so on. It worked really well without a hitch!

Guildway were delighted when after much headache they received accreditation, becoming approved house builders and meeting requirements, bye laws and equivalent building regulations in Germany and France. The first such consignment was for Hamburg. The ferry route was Transport Ferry Service, Tilbury to Rotterdam.

We used a twenty-four foot platform, rigid eight-wheeled lorry. This was quite an occasion for everyone and Guildway had arranged a "reception committee", apparently complete with local television. John Hard and I set off and arrived in Rotterdam. A man emerged from his office armed with a long stick. He placed this against the loaded lorry, stood back and looked upwards stating, "you are too high for the bridges in Holland, you will have to be rerouted". It was arranged that a route would be prepared by the authorities at The Hague enabling us to avoid low bridges and this would then be despatched to Rotterdam by courier. This took all day!

Parts of the Pontypool job with trailers awaiting unloading. We had ten of these step-frame trailers built by Taskers of Andover, primarily for Guildway work, with 8.25 x 15 tyres and air-operated Girling brakes.

Trevor Duke about to unload in Luxembourg in 1985. The tractor unit is Scania 112M registration FNO 38Y. We found Scanias better suited to the job and more reliable.

We were told that we would have to arrange a police escort to get around the motorway near Utrecht and that we were not to go on the motorway toward Utrecht as all the bridges there are a maximum of 3.8 metres high and our vehicle was taller than that. We were also told not to move at night. We were now one day late and we set off. We managed, I remember not how, to obtain a police motor cyclist at Utrecht who took us around and under the motorway. As we passed under the concrete structure, there was a crunch and we jammed to a sudden halt. We reversed out, climbed on top of the load only to find our sheets ripped apart and our ropes severed. For no apparent reason, several onlookers appeared from nowhere and stood motionless, silent and staring. If they, up to now, knew no English and they listened carefully they would quickly acquire a few words not normally found in the dictionary, but with a very clear meaning.

After patching up the damage, the police rider calmly took us round the obstacle, no problem, which he could have done in the first place except that he had led us up on to the motorway toward Utrecht where we should not have been and it was getting dark. This was the point of no return. We were on a dual carriageway, heading for Utrecht. If we did not come to an exit point before we came to a bridge over the road, which would be 3.9 metres, I do not know what we would have done. We were lucky, we were able to leave the motorway and so proceeded during the night to try to make up time. We were nearing the German border at last. At about 5.00 am, when it was just beginning to get light, we came to a railway bridge dead ahead at 2½ metres, it was really only for bicycles and pedestrians but lucky for us again, an early motorist stopped, looked and said "follow me". He led us through the back streets of wherever we were to a large cornfield. He took us through the field to an open railway crossing, I was driving and John had climbed up to the top of the cab to make sure that we cleared the overhead electric cable. "Go, go, go", he shouted. There was a bright headlight in the distance, an approaching train!

We were in Germany. Too high for the bridges and no route to avoid them, our only chance was to lower the load. For most of the day, John and I lowered six of the roof trusses, one by one and hung them three each side. We then re-sheeted with the torn sheets and knotted ropes, but this made us wider. We now set off again and the last problem to encounter was that we met a fast moving German lorry and there was a bang, we had met side to side. Each stopped, some distance away from each other got out of our vehicles and stood in the road, glaring at each other in the distance. Neither wished to do battle and so we moved on.

We were eventually met somewhere outside Hamburg and conducted to the delivery site. By then, there was no reception committee and no television camera. This story sounds like a fair bit of fiction but it is not. It certainly was a pioneering exercise for both our customer and ourselves and it was a few years earlier than it should have been as later on, we did become more proficient at continental haulage.

The float we decorated for Guildford Crime Prevention Panel. Among the people who travelled on the float was Cheryl Burchett (pictured in the blue dress on the lower view), our long-term and very loyal office worker, our daughter Jessica and cousin Rosemary.

9. We acquire Warren Hill

I return to the British Rail pit at Weydon, Farnham. As the pit was emptying of ashes, British Rail commenced bringing in train loads of 'spent ballast'. The railway track is laid on a bed of clean limestone aggregate known as track ballast. On top of this, go the sleepers and then the rails. With the constant pounding of the trains and the dripping of oil and grease etc, the stone compacts down and breaks up and the track becomes non-resilient and too hard. Therefore, the material has to be dug out and replaced with new limestone. The Railway have special machines to do this, one excavates the 'spent ballast' out and loads it into railway wagons. Another machine lays the new ballast evenly and at the required depth progressively.

This operation is ongoing track maintenance and is usually carried out during nights and weekends. Trainloads would arrive at Weydon and would be unloaded by British Rail staff and machines. We then would market the material and deliver to site with our own equipment. The material was excellent for roads and tracks as it would grade out and bind down into a hard surface. This was much cheaper for the customer than the alternative material that was available from stone quarries known as scalpings.

There was plenty of demand for this material. We were buying this 'spent ballast' directly from British Rail on a monthly basis. We had no control over the quantity or the quality of the material coming through. Sometimes it would be heavily contaminated with clay or similar, if they were digging more deeply or digging new tracks. We would try to separate the clay from the stone, or move it away from the unloading area to another part of the pit. We had a bulldozer and later installed a screening plant, as well as loading shovels and tipping lorries to perform these functions. There was quite an amount of other goods that needed separating such as sleepers, old iron, level crossing gates and the like. This material was considerably heavier than clinker or ashes and so consequently, we had to progressively move toward heavier vehicles with greater carrying capacity, working at higher gross weights and costing more money.

This meant a requirement for more power from the engines. In common with others, we had already moved from petrol to diesel fuel and this solely because it gave more miles per gallon and at the time, it was less money per gallon than petrol. The government was moving steadily toward heavier gross weight for commercial vehicles and legislation was introduced requiring a power output of six brake horse power per ton minimum. In other words, a vehicle of say ten tons gross weight that is loaded weight, would require an engine producing sixty brake horse power, or 24 tons gross, 144 brake horse power. Some engines could not meet this requirement, however several manufacturers got round this.

All diesel engines have a maximum revolutions governor. This is primarily to prevent the engine from over-revving and flying to pieces. The manufacturers simply adjusted the governor to increase the maximum revolutions per minute, which increased the brake horse power, however it did not work. It gave no more effective power but it did give more smoke and more noise, together with a much higher failure rate of the mechanical 'bits' in the engine. It worsened the problem of a loaded lorry crawling up a hill ever more slowly and giving out more dense smoke than before.

What was required was more torque, at lower revs or simply more power from the drive wheels at the road surface. Many of these engines were too small, therefore underpowered for the task set for them. More time to redesign was required. Meantime, the operator spent more time broken down or washing greasy soot from the rear of his vehicle. What the industry required was not top speed from vehicles, but much improved grade-ability on hills. Loaded vehicles which could travel up hill at the same speed as on the flat or nearly, which were quieter and gave out no smoke, all coupled with improved reliability. Today, all of this has been achieved except that I feel that top speeds are now too high.

To May's Motors (Transport) Ltd all of this meant buying lorries with the requirements listed above. In addition, heavier gross weights, more powerful engines and so on, all reacted on the remainder of the machine. Most important of these were brakes, tyres and suspension systems and improved working environments for the drivers to include the fitting of powered steering. At the time of the 'engine troubles', there was one outstanding product. It was the Gardner diesel engine, which started life as a marine engine and developed into an automotive engine as well. By comparison to others, it was a high torque, slow revving engine and Gardner's achievement was to provide superb reliability, low fuel consumption, lightweight and a guarantee that it had been tested to give the performance claimed for it by Messrs Gardner. One person individually built the engines and the code number gave the identity of that individual. Naturally, demand exceeded supply so we had to wait for the vehicle if we were not prepared to accept an alternative engine. In addition, we had to pay a premium of £1000 per engine which was already more expensive than its competitors. When it started up one could not see for thick blue smoke but this would disappear as the engine warmed up and after that, it would "run forever". Unfortunately, the company ceased trading some time after the death of Mr Hugh Gardner.

One of the Guy Invincible 8-wheel tippers, 928 XPK.

We had started on this process of replacing the fleet with heavier better quality trucks and the final three Guy eight-wheeled tippers were fitted with Gardner engines. At the same time, we were using more 'artics' and expanding the trailer fleet. The Guy factory at Wolverhampton closed down and we started to buy Atkinson vehicles that were fitted with Gardner engines.

Our son Andrew was born on 1st January 1958, which made a very nice New Year's present. The sixties and seventies saw much development and diversification of traffic during that period. We started to deliver mushrooms from four local growers to the old Covent Garden market. In addition, chrysanthemum sprays from a local grower and, during the appropriate season, lettuce and other fresh crops from local growers five nights per week. We were also delivering some twenty to twenty five tons of paper-bagged potatoes to Covent Garden and sometimes Brentford Market and Spitalfields Market as well. This was nightly during the main crop season from KFF packing shed in Farnham. Some years, would find us loading twenty-ton lots of new potatoes from the Jersey boats at Portsmouth. Usually these were deliveries to Birmingham or Manchester markets scheduled for midnight delivery same day. Relief drivers would load these consignments, ready for night drivers to take over from our yard. From the mid-seventies we started running night trunks for Boots the Chemist, from the Aldershot warehouse. This involved two tractor units and nine box-trailers, six nights per week, each tractor doing Aldershot to Dartford and Aldershot to Southampton, using between them six trailers per night. The other trailers were for overspills and other additional casual deliveries.

A new Guy Warrior Light Eight, with May's bodywork and painting, supplied to E.J. Benyon on test before delivery. It was fitted with an AEC AV470 engine, AEC five-speed synchromesh gearbox and Eaton two-speed rear axle.

Another night activity was a one-ton Bedford van running Massey-Ferguson Tractor spares from Ben Turner Ltd.'s main depot at Ripley in Surrey, on a circuit of their other depots at Bishops Waltham, Chichester, Maidstone and Ripley. Thus urgent spares were delivered to all depots before they opened. During harvest periods, these deliveries were stepped up to seven nights per week. The new workshop of May's Motors (Elstead) Ltd had attracted the service and repair work of Buxted Chicken Company's fleet of twelve BMC seven-ton lorries from its Aldershot factory. These vehicles all worked at night collecting thousands of chicken, in crates, from various farms over a wide area that contracted to Buxted Chicken to produce the poor things. An interesting fact emerged from this activity about the chicken. Man's "carnivorous" requirements make the rearing and slaughtering of chicken daily a material fact.

A new Guy Warrior Light Eight tipper, supplied to T.W. Lee. It had the optional Gardner 6LW engine, 6-speed ZF gearbox, Eaton two-speed rear axle and Edbro tipping gear and body.

Without going in to the ethics of the subject or indeed, the whole question of vegetarians versus meat eaters, I must say that companies such as Buxted Chicken make every effort to make the operation as humane as possible. The chickens arrived at Aldershot in crates and in the process of unloading the odd few would get loose and wander about the concrete yard to be picked up by the staff. The good bit is that one or two did get away. Buxted lorries were brought to us in the mornings for servicing and maintenance, a journey of some nine miles. We would drive it into the workshop over a thirty-foot inspection pit to look underneath and tilt the cab to look from above. Sometimes we would find a chicken, somewhat black and oily, firmly clasping the front axle of the lorry, blinking at us but not moving. It would have bumped its way all the way from Aldershot. Another hiding place was on the top of the engine which had very little to hang on to, was very noisy and very hot. Probably the engine-cooling fan kept the frightened bird cool. But the chicken felt that its situation was preferable to its other option had it stayed in Aldershot. This happening does sound quite untrue. The aforementioned Cecil Beaven kept an open-topped tea chest, complete with a handful of corn and a bowl of water in the workshop, into which went the chicken. He would take them home and introduce them to previous escapees who gave them a bit of a rough time, which is normal among chickens. Eventually they all settled down into what can only be called 'normal chicken behaviour'. What is interesting is that it happened sufficiently often to make a provisional tea chest worthwhile.

Loading sugar beet for Kidderminster into Guy Invincible eight-wheel tipper 469 PPF. Driver Reg. Mitchell with my brother-in-law Alex Doughty standing beside the cab door.

All of the foregoing demonstrates that more and more of the non-tipping side of the business was becoming a twenty-four hour operation. Obviously, the idea was that the use of vehicles day and night where possible, cut overhead and standing costs. The problem was to cover night breakdowns. Through the years, this had been one of my activities. It was normal to never retire at night without a car or van, a well-equipped (and heavy) toolbox, petrol in the tank, a torch, small change for possible telephone calls and, in those days, cigarettes and matches (now a non-smoker for many years), another obvious requirement was a telephone by the bed. The servicing of Buxted vehicles also required that we deal with their breakdowns. Should that happen, it was usually in a muddy farmyard, on a wet cold night but it added to the problem of night-time repairs.

Another Guy Invincible 8-wheeler, 824 XPJ, this time fitted with a tanker body. It proved unsuitable for our work and I drove it to Slamannan, near Stirling and flew back the next day from Edinburgh with a cheque for £4,000.

Although we set up a sort of rota in later years, it never really worked because it was the same people at night as by day. It was never a serious problem, as fortunately it was pretty infrequent, so between us we would always do something. We had other companies locally whom we could call for some problems such as tyres and others for different problems such as electrical, so we took each incident as it came. An interesting comment, some twenty to twenty-five years later, is that our son Andrew was doing what I had done, running about at night with a toolbox, although the Buxted Chicken job had long since gone.

We had a good building, steel-framed, asbestos-clad, about fifty feet long by twenty feet in the lower part of the yard. This we leased out to Atlas Express, a parcels carrier based in London. We fixed up a lorry floor-height decking throughout the building. Atlas brought in a loaded 'artic' trailer nightly from their Birmingham depot and changed it for yesterday's trailer now emptied and reloaded. The contents were all manageable parcels destined for the Godalming, Guildford and Farnham areas and handled by Atlas staff. They were unloaded on to the decking, sorted into destinations and we had three three-ton vans onto which the sorted parcels were loaded. We delivered these to the areas as above and collected at the same time and brought back parcels for the Birmingham area, which were loaded onto the Atlas trailer. The couplings were the quick-release type, made by Scammell, as previously described, as used by the railways. Therefore our old Bedford unit (that went to and from Grantham), was able to move the Atlas trailer as required and leave it ready to be collected for Birmingham during the night.

New commercial workshop being built for May's Motors (Elstead) Ltd.

We had by now, given up the household removals side of the business as it became a much more professional operation and often required storage facilities as well. Another problem was that if a job required a crew of three or four men, it could mean standing idle the lorries that those men would normally drive. We did however, use a pantechnican type of vehicle for the Covent Garden business as it was all manhandled and required a 'walk-in' facility.

At this time, I noticed that my mother was repeating herself frequently. It was the start of Alzheimer's, which developed over six years after which she died at the age of 74 in 1967. Many readers I am sure have witnessed the distress and tragedy that this disease brings with it. The lack of understanding of the illness and the helplessness experienced by patient, family and carers who witness this thing are still unexplained and quite beyond comprehension.

An unusual purchase in 1958 was this Dennis Hefty flat truck 176 HPH. Fleet numbers were used in this period but were later abandoned. The truck is loaded with concrete products for deep sewer construction, manufactured in Aldershot.

The business activity of May's Motors (Transport) Ltd was increasing quite strongly. It required an increasing number of heavy tractor units and trailers and a lesser number of rigid vehicles, which was an ongoing situation during the seventies and eighties. In 1966, something quite unrelated took place. June and I had been looking for a property ideally on the outskirts of the village of Elstead. When dog-walking, we found a south-facing, eleven acres of dense woodland, with outline planning consent for one dwelling with a usage condition of horticulture. It was covered with chestnut and birch trees, would require a lot of clearing and it was situated on the side of a hill near Shackleford. The asking price, from memory was £10,000. We offered £9,000 in view of the cost of clearing only to receive a curt and rude response, which in effect said "don't be so stupid. It's worth more than the asking price". So that was that.

Meantime, we looked more closely at another site almost adjoining the first one, which we had envied for a long time as it had wonderful panoramic views for 360 degrees. It was in fact, a hill of some thirty acres, again covered in chestnut and birch and had been used by local farmers for shooting pheasants and rabbits. There was no doubt why it was named 'Warren Hill' even on the Ordnance Survey. We looked at this land several times and liked it more and more. It turned out that several owners through the years had applied for planning permission but apparently it was never seriously considered by the Authorities because it was an area of outstanding natural beauty and it was "no", "no", "no".

At this time, one of our customers came in for petrol and I happened to serve him. I said to him, "who owns that hill above your farm?" He said "I do, why, do you want to buy it?" I have always believed that life is a mixture of faith and fate. Man must have faith in something and fate has always played a part. However, totally against all of the advice, we negotiated £10,000 less £1,000 toward clearing some of the land, to purchase for £9,000. Out of the blue came another curt note, "your offer of £9,000 has been accepted, please advise the name of your solicitor." Now we had the choice, £9,000 for eleven acres of land with planning permission or £9,000 for thirty acres of land without planning permission. What should we do? June felt that we should play safe and take the eleven acres, whereas I favoured taking a gamble and buying the thirty acres. I felt strongly that if we were patient, we would get permission for a house eventually. Everyone without exception said that we would never get it.

We agreed to buy Warren Hill and even at that stage, we were absolutely over the moon, it was beautiful. The company May's Motors (Elstead) Ltd owed me over £10,000 in the form of a loan account. This money was tax paid being un-drawn profit to my credit, therefore a term loan was arranged between the Bank and the Company and the deeds of Warren Hill were put in as security.

After the Bedfords and the Guys, we bought Atkinsons with Gardner engines.

We had the land, now to obtain building permission! Despite the ongoing saga of all this activity and the pressure of running a developing business, the long hours, with resultant exhaustion, the constant strain of insufficient money mainly due to being under capitalised or, in other words, over-trading, which obviously brought pressure on us from the banks, it never crossed our minds to stop doing it. In fact the opposite as on the other side of the coin, we had achieved a tremendous amount.

We had brought up and educated four children, Jessica was born fourteen years after Andrew in 1972. We had lived comfortably but not extravagantly. We had built up a good and I like to think honest business. We had kept my parents in their later years as they had put their all into the business for many years before and had that not happened, there would have been no foundation on which to build.

I was throughout this time, also spending quite a lot of time on Road Haulage Association matters. This was a conscious decision as I considered that I got more out of the Association than I put in. By meeting as many people from the road haulage and allied industries of which we were a part, I consider that it was as good as a full time course on aspects of trade and more. It was certainly an insight into how others did it from a mental, financial and practical point of view, from which much could be learned. But as with all things, it needed to be kept in perspective. It would have been too easy to allow road haulage affairs to take priority over our own business. I have seen that happen. I had discussed the Road Haulage Association involvement with Alex Doughty and we could see no problems arising. John Meade was now attending meetings of the Motor Agents Association instead of myself, he was for a period, Chairman of the Farnham Section. More about the Road Haulage Association later.

With the day-to-day running of the business, such minor things as Reg Powell's car road tax came to light. He was a likeable rogue who worked in the body-cum-spray shop for May's Motors (Elstead) Ltd. He usually had a customer's vehicle in the shop for a few days at a time knocking out dents or painting out the damage. Reg considered that it was wasteful to have a paid tax disc doing nothing in his spray shop, so he would place it in his own car's windscreen until it was required on the original vehicle, at which time he would then change it for another! I must say that I had some sympathy with him.

This Rolls-Royce Phantom III, registration TP 1, belonging to Tyrone Power, had just left our paintshop.

Another 'usual' was acute financial problems associated with some of the drivers. This often resulted in a head-to-head meeting in my office with the driver to discuss the problem. The usual outcome was that our wages department paid his rent, his local weekly groceries and so on. We arranged with the shops concerned to do this and arranged the rent payment with the local council. We then deducted these payments from the employee's wages and gave him the remainder. Sometimes, we were asked to advise on divorce. It sounds extremely dramatic but it was usually sorted out. I do not wish to make it appear that these men were stupid, or irresponsible, on the contrary; they just could not manage personal monies. Their capability with large vehicles and other machinery however, was outstanding.

Arrival of one half of the new office and below, lowering it into position with Andrew up aloft and "Digger" (Fred Padwick) and Mick Reeves helping to guide one half of the new office into place, at Elstead.

I have written about how hard we worked and how money was never plentiful, but in the course of trying to research this book and finding some old appointment diaries, I am amazed at how many holidays we managed and how many different places and countries that we visited. My notes read like a holiday brochure. Apart from the United Kingdom, including Ireland, and many trips to mainland Europe, the main really distant ones were to Hong Kong and on to Tokyo to visit Jan our eldest daughter and her husband who was working in Tokyo. They arranged and paid for this trip. We also went to Australia and another time, across Canada by train, also a trip to Disneyland, Orlando being one of the Road Haulage Association conference venues (paid by the Company). In fact, Road Haulage Association conferences which were held in the autumn and started in the United Kingdom in the early years and later usually taking place somewhere in Europe, were nice autumn breaks and always to places that we would not have normally visited. The fact that Inland Revenue allowed it as a business expense made these events all the more enjoyable.

June, Jess and I were on holiday in North Wales when a phone call from Jan informed me that 'Dobber' Lawrence had died. He was one of our drivers around forty-five years of age and had been driving a thirty-eight ton gross 'artic' at Milford on the A3. He had stopped the vehicle and was later found to be dead. He had shown no previous symptoms, or given any indication of problems. We would sometimes congregate at lunchtime on Saturdays in the British Legion club, which was next door to the yard.

Our first bulldozer, a Bristol at Warren Hill, in 1966.

It was previously the farm belonging to Mr and Mrs Ellis and had been bought, converted and given to the Legion by Mr Jack Billmeir, something initiated by my father. Dobber Lawrence could order one pint of beer and then a round of drinks for his mates. Whilst this round was being prepared, he would pour his first pint down his throat like a gallon of petrol going through a funnel and then dump his glass on the counter for his second pint. He was one of the 'old school', a cheerful and always helpful person.

We went to Malta in 1967 to a house owned by a customer with Jan, Judith and Andrew and again in 1984, with the Road Haulage Association conference. I was sitting outside the house in 1967 watching the world go by when a Bedford TK came and tipped a load of sand, just opposite where I was sitting. It was our custom, on selling old vehicles, to paint out our name and sign writing. This was usually a quick cover of undercoat paint over the writing. I thought that I was imagining things, because this Bedford appeared to have our sign writing showing through where the paint had rubbed off. I could not be sure, but to my surprise it returned with another load of sand and I could confirm that it was indeed one of our ex-tippers. I could not recognise it initially because it had a different body fitted, which came about because all commercial vehicles imported into Malta were without their original bodies; this was by law and it was done to create work for the islanders who then had to build new bodywork. To complete this amazing story, we saw another of our ex-tippers the next day. Both of these lorries had left our yard, hooked up to a breakdown truck, as "non-runners!"

As time went by, progress being made by Messrs Guildway Ltd resulted in some considerable interest in their products, coming from abroad, France in particular. Therefore we had no alternative but to direct our attention to delivering these houses to these new destinations. There were plenty of our competitors looking enviously at our Guildway traffic, just waiting to pounce given the opportunity, including handling of the continental traffic. I earlier outlined the trip to Hamburg but now we had to make sure that we retained this new business and learned how to do it. There were many other operators exploring and entering this newly developing activity of direct deliveries by road to mainland Europe and beyond.

10. Continental Haulage

Developing with it were increasing options of several different sea routes, different rules and regulations in different countries, a massive increase in bureaucracy and paper work. This was a wonderful opportunity for unnecessary officialdom from border to border. There were many hours of wasted time, therefore wasted money, awaiting customs clearance at many different countries borders. We had to first obtain a road permit for the country to which we were delivering such as France, Germany and Italy. These were the early days of the European Economic Community and their rules and regulations. Switzerland and Austria for instance had their own regulations if we wished to transit their country and whereas some would allow Sunday movement, equally some would not. Livestock was special, as were perishables. Some would allow movement on Sunday if returning home, some if the vehicle was empty. I have become very hazy about all of this as it was long ago so I am probably writing some untruths. There was so much of it. It was necessary to have an Agent, usually to be found in a collection of offices at the ports and at the frontiers.

We had to submit applications to the Ministry of Transport in the UK. These permits had to be stamped at every frontier both going out and coming home and were then returned to the Ministry on completion of the journey. They had to be used by a certain date and so to not use any permits that one had was unwise, as it would probably jeopardise a future issue. The EEC had also set up customs documents known as 'T' forms of varying types and purpose. These would be raised by 'our agent' and supported by copies of the original invoice or invoices for the goods that we were carrying which had to show the value of the load.

The original permits that we had to acquire, were known as bilateral permits, and were subject to individual negotiation with each partner country. French permits were more plentiful than Italian, and the most difficult to obtain were German. After accession of the UK to the EEC in 1973, the permits became EEC permits, were multinational, and were followed by E.C.M.T. (European Conference of Ministers of Transport) permits, which were more liberal, and allowed much more freedom of movement. These were known as "books". These books were pretty scarce, but we were lucky enough to be awarded two of them. With the coming of EEC permits as above, many, perhaps most, of the individual countries' requirements or restrictions disappeared. The whole thing became more rational, and therefore easier to operate.

The above-mentioned "T" forms had to accompany the goods right through to the final Customs clearance at destination. The goods could not be unloaded, until clearance had been obtained. Much of this procedure was part related to the collection of VAT (known in France as TVA), which all member states have to effect, on the behalf of the EEC, now the European Union. What the system did, was to allow the goods to leave, for example the United Kingdom, pass through transit countries without payment and into the final country to be unloaded pending final settlement by the customer. If we had or were able to arrange a back-load, the reverse procedure would take place, the documents would be raised at the source of the goods. We would come all the way to the United Kingdom and come ashore into a parking compound at Dover or Portsmouth, the procedure was always the same. The documents would be submitted to Customs. If we had no agent, we could usually arrange for one at the home port then wait and hope. Sometimes it was quick and sometimes not, but you could not be on your way until the 'T' form was Customs-cleared.

After the Atkinsons, we switched allegiance to Scanias.

Our usual means of communication internationally was by the wonderful ticker tape machine, the Telex. Sometimes the information that we had collected for the return load could be forwarded to the agent by Telex, which could possibly speed up the clearance because then, all that was required was a sight of the original documents to confirm the facts. Some firms were specialising in 'groupage'. As the name implies, collecting up many smaller different consignments into one load and delivering to many different destinations and back-loading into the United Kingdom in similar fashion. To arrive at a frontier or the home port behind a driver clutching a fist full of 'T' forms would mean a long wait, as each individual consignment had its own documentation.

One of the "pre-accession" requirements that was removed was that France required registration of trailers, which were taxed similar to a car. In the UK, they are not taxed separately. A temporary exemption to this, by the use of a "Carnet de Passage" could be obtained from the AA in exchange for the necessary payment. In effect on entering France, this 'Carnet', which contained all details of the trailer, would be stamped, with that half being torn out and retained by the French customs. On leaving France at any border, the other half would be stamped, torn out and retained. The French would reunite each half somehow, which established that the trailer had left their country and they were no longer interested. I am sure that many people will remember this, as it used to apply to private caravans, which are trailers.

Another French requirement was, that commercial vehicles could only carry a very small quantity of fuel into France, something like fifty or one hundred litres. This meant that we had to buy fuel as soon as we entered France, whereby the French government received the duty on that fuel. A similar requirement in effect, operated in Germany. This was another source of delay at frontiers whilst being checked and measured. Interestingly, there was and is no such restriction on foreign lorries entering the UK. I am giving another history lesson with all of this but we were confronted with it at the time. I have only now woken up to the fact that I have no need to go further into the details and intricacies of Continental haulage paperwork, as other operators, such as ourselves, who also carried out some of this type of work, will have their own knowledge and experience of these matters. It will hold little interest for the remainder of my readers, who can happily skip it, if they so wish. I am sure that as operators, we were not alone at that time, in that we had to conform to this bureaucracy, as it arose, so that we could get on with the job. It was a necessary evil that had to be carried out. We did not attempt to understand the workings of the EEC. We never did know the answers to most of it, in fact, nothing much in that respect has changed. Consequently I had to seek some help in completing this chapter. My thanks go to Garry Turvey (Director-General) and David Green (Head of international transport and customs) of the Freight Transport Association

(FTA) during the years of negotiation with various governments concerning road permits for helping with this chapter.

The Road Haulage Association, under its then Director-General George Newman, was also working with the FTA during these negotiations. It is very revealing to learn that all of those years ago, these two trade associations were working so actively on behalf of their members (and what a good job that they were!). I am sure that had it have been left to Government officials, our problems would have been much greater. Garry is now Chairman of the Roads and Road Transport History Association, the publishers of this book.

As I explained, we were really forced into developing this continental haulage because we feared that if we did not, we could lose all of the Guildway work and we could not afford the risk. It was pioneering and it was exciting, we thought that it was a developing trade and that it would "thin the field". It would make us more 'specialist' and it was very much a part of the future. A fundamental difference between the UK and continental haulage was the ferry costs each way. Very few customers could afford to pay the round trip costs. Therefore we had to obtain a return load to pay at least for return ferry and fuel, disregarding the other costs of getting home.

There could be many dead miles involved in going to collect return loads that originated from further away than the delivery point of the outward load. This all meant that we were having to use "clearing houses" to provide us with a return load at their price, take it or leave it. The above situation unfolded as we went along. It was very difficult therefore to accurately cost a particular journey, for quoting purposes, particularly as most of the Guildway Bungalow traffic was a 'one off'. These were mainly France, Germany, Italy and Switzerland. Local authority housing was much easier to handle as sites would usually be thirty, forty or even fifty houses, each a repeat of the previous delivery.

We worked, for instance, for Frigoscandia dealing in refrigerated traffic from their United Kingdom cold stores. This company would arrange everything. We would collect a pre-loaded refrigerated trailer from Stratford, London, all of the paperwork would be prepared, the ferries would be booked and paid for by Frigoscandia, the return load instructions given and the rate advised. For a few years, we had two tractors, painted in their livery. We had to use our permits and supply reliable drivers who would constantly monitor the temperature settings as this could vary from load to load and the commodity being carried.

We also had this arrangement with a company in Southampton, but with their covered trailers not refrigerated in and out of Southampton. We would drop one trailer and pick up another and so on. In 1971, we also linked up with Hampshire Hauliers, a business of three haulier owners from the Andover area. They set up a traffic office at Whitchurch, Hampshire that catered for continental traffic originating from that area and similar traffic to the United Kingdom. We purchased two large "step-frame supercube" trailers with canvas-covered tilts and supplied tractors and permits for the work. The office was run by Peter Goetz who was an ex German prisoner of war who had stayed here after the war and married an English girl. Peter Goetz and I went together to France and on another occasion to Germany, making contacts with fellow hauliers that was interesting but which, from memory, did not "bear much fruit".

We had also established a very good relationship with a privately-owned clearing house in Rouen, northern France that was run by a Frenchman and his English wife. This was very useful as we could telex him in advance of a Guildway load and thus usually enable us to pre-arrange our return load.

We had a substantial operation going, into which much effort and time was expended. We had a considerable spread of customers and commodities and by its nature, it extended the need for weekend working, which fell largely on me. As vehicles returned from abroad, usually at weekends, next week's vehicles were starting to move in order to be across the Channel, with driver's rest period completed, waiting to roll as soon as possible on the Monday morning. I therefore had to prepare and check all of the paperwork involved for each lorry going out. Any last minute attention to the trucks had to be organised as well as driver's travelling money and fuel credit card etc. Unfortunately, Ray Mitchell the traffic manager, left to operate his own catering business. This created quite a void as Ray was one of our ex-drivers. He was very "hands-on", calm and a very successful traffic manager. John Milligan who had been involved with lorries from the age of seventeen and who was driving for us at the time, took on the job. He had been to Paris with the equipment for an episode of "This is Your Life" that the BBC were doing over there. He was to wait there and after the event, bring the equipment back. It was an 'eye opener' to us to learn from John that he would be delayed for a day or two because there were two pictures in the equipment that needed to be hung on the wall of the set being established but that the union would not allow anyone there to hang the pictures, as it was not their job. Therefore they had to wait for someone to be flown out from England to hang the pictures! How stupid can it get?

Over some ten years we had been replacing the fleet gradually with Gardner-engined Atkinsons. For the technically minded, these had David Brown Six-Speed Overdrive Gear Boxes and Eaton Two-Speed Axles at thirty-two tons gross. The last of these was bought around 1973/74 and was fitted with a Sleeper Cab. Compared to the Scanias that followed, it was rather primitive but it did several years work and never let us down. The first Scania 110 was purchased in 1975, followed by many more for the next twenty odd years.

It must have been at the time of the rapid development of the United Arab Emirates, Dubai and Abu Dhabi in the Persian Gulf, that an urgent demand for vehicles to take merchandise to Teheran arose. This was I presume, because the Gulf was saturated with loaded shipping waiting to unload their cargoes. At that time, Saudi Arabia simply had not the shore-based equipment to unload the vessels. Therefore, there was a severe bottleneck.

En route to Teheran. The trailer was a Taskers 12-metre step-frame supercube with tilt, hauled by Scania 110 Super JPD 716N. These vehicles operated as *Mays of England* as they spent the majority of their time abroad.

We actually completed five trips from the UK to Teheran carrying such equipment as mobile air compressors in full loads from Holmans of Camborne, Cornwall as an example. It was "go to Ankara in Turkey and turn left for Teheran!" There was a special train with ultra-small wheels on special freight wagons which could accommodate fully-loaded articulated lorries with twelve metre trailers, four metres in height and which drove on to the train from one end to the other. By boarding the train at, I think it was Cologne, which terminated in Ljubljana in Yugoslavia, road permits to cross Germany were automatically granted. The drivers were accommodated in a passenger carriage.

An overnight stop in Turkey would mean a cluster of vehicles forming a sort of compound back to back and close together and the employment of a local person, complete with his dog, for the night.

Otherwise such items as diesel fuel, spare wheels, and part of the load or anything else that could be 'lifted' would be. Another hazard was that a 'sheep minder' would see an approaching European lorry and, at the critical moment, drive his flock of sheep straight across the road, obviously killing a few sheep. The situation required to be settled at once and as soon as an eventual settlement was reached and the money paid, of course always for a higher number of sheep than it should have been, the lorries could move on. The best thing to do was to agree, to pay up and get going.

The return journey was by the same method back to Germany from where we would hope to load home. We were very lucky that we had no real problem throughout the five journeys. We could never have attempted these trips on our own as pioneers, however other companies were already carrying out this work and we simply followed their lead provided that the paper work was in order. On one occasion I discovered that one piece of paper had been left in our office. I had no alternative other than to fly out to Germany and then catch a train to the railhead and deliver the vital document to our driver.

I did not go on any of the trips to Teheran myself but I did do several journeys into France, Germany and Switzerland when no one else was available. This was usually when we were over-busy which would mean that the sleeper cab lorries with their regular drivers were away, so that I finished up with one of the older, non-sleeper Atkinson lorries that would normally work nearer home. In the course of these journeys, on the ferry crossings, there would be lots of "lorry talk". There was a company named 'Astran' who were very experienced at Middle East traffic and listening to their drivers was very enlightening. I learned that Turkey in the winter could not be attempted without double drive tractors. That means tractor units with two rear axles, both driving, called double-drive. The other frightener was listening to their tales of parking overnight on wet ground and waking up to find that they were literally frozen to the ground.

This would mean jacking up each wheel one by one, until a loud crack released a large lump of frozen soil, which was stuck to the tyre and had to be chipped off. This process could take hours. Another problem was punctures. There was no roadside tyre repair service whatsoever. Astran's own drivers had to remove the wheel and do their best themselves. Then they could not reinflate unless their vehicle had been fitted with a small air compressor on to the gearbox and it required ninety to one hundred pounds per square inch pressure to inflate a tyre. Again we had been lucky. As the autumn was approaching I decided that we should not go again, as whilst we were running to Teheran, we were not using our German, French or Italian Permits and that was not wise. I also realised that the stories that I had been listening to were authentic, had been presented in authentic truck drivers' language and description and could be believed.

On one occasion I was a few miles out of Le Havre on my way to a Guildway Site at Claye Souilly, France when I was stopped in a roadside check by French Police, I was using a 12-metre flat-bed trailer, loaded with a timber framed house. We had previously bought a batch of five trailers at one time; therefore their chassis numbers were consecutive. Each had their own Carnet de Passage however, the carnet that I had with me, was one number wrong. I had Andrew with me who was somewhat wide-eyed at the sight of a Gendarme climbing into the cab with us and directing us back to Le Havre, where we were held pending the payment of a fine. We managed to arrange the money through our "Agent" in Le Havre. Andrew was quite thrilled at being carted round Le Havre in a police car, down to the docks to the agent, back to the Gendarmerie and then back to the lorry. They were quite happy to take us about like a taxi! On another occasion, during the Suez Crisis, we had been informed that the limit on fuel carried into France, had been suspended. I therefore deliberately arrived at Le Havre with a full tank and was checked there by the police who used the handle from a broom that I had tied to my vehicle to dip into and check my tank, another fine and more money raised from our agent to pay it.

One consignment that I delivered was a twenty-three ton Hymac Excavator to an address somewhere near Zurich in Switzerland. My friend, Harold Andrews travelled with me. This was an over-width load due to the wide tracks with which it was fitted. Therefore our written instructions from the Swiss were "do not move in darkness". Because we were delayed in loading at Southampton by several hours, we were climbing a very steep hill somewhere in Zurich in darkness when we were stopped by a policeman who was waving a torch at us. Whilst he studied our paperwork by torchlight, I leaned out of the cab and pushed my delivery notes under his torch light and asked him where is this address? This diverted him from our other paperwork and he then told us which way to go whereby, I promptly pulled away and, this time, avoided further trouble.

Somewhere in Europe. This was one of the first Scanias that we purchased, after the Atkinsons. It was a 110 Super, registration TPK 697M, pulling a TIP hired 12-metre box trailer.

On these trips, there was never time to have a nice relaxing drive through the different countries and enjoy the always-changing scenery. We were ever trying to beat the clock to meet the delivery deadline and use the driving hours to best advantage to work out how to get to the reload pick-up point before they closed, thus saving another night away from home. Once we were reloaded, we then had to work out how far or how long to make the ferry for home by perhaps avoiding some country's ban on weekend movement or some other reason that would have caused delay. These efforts often resulted in a curtailment of feeding and sleeping times but we never starved!

One memorable trip that I undertook accompanied by June was to deliver a Guildway bungalow to a site high up near Chaisso overlooking Lake Como on the Swiss and Italian border. To get there we had to climb up and on the other side to descend the Saint Bernadine Pass. Lorries were restricted to certain defined hours in using the pass and we arrived a little too early, so had to wait. We were gazing up at a latticework of road bridges that crisscrossed all the way to the top. It was awe inspiring to me, a wonderful feat of engineering and to climb it and then descend without the modern aid of an exhaust brake, was quite an achievement for my old lorry as well. The assistance of power steering for all of those hairpin bends would have been more than useful. In view of the advancements in design, sophistication and engineering of the current vehicles compared to my faithful old Gardner-engined Atkinson of yesteryear, would be like putting Stevenson's rocket locomotive on to the London to Edinburgh express train. But then, what we never had we did not miss! In its day, it was a good machine and it did a good job.

Driver Ray Thorne, somewhere in Europe, with another 110 Super.

The site for the bungalow was most impressive, set out on the side of the mountains with a wonderful view and the lake in the distance. Our vehicle was much too big to get near the site and so it had been arranged for us to park in the village square below and for a small lorry to transfer our load bit by bit up to the site. The builder took us up to the site in his car which was fine, coming down however, was a different story as it was the most terrifying journey that we have ever had and the builder was quite oblivious to it all, we were obviously not due to depart this life yet. Whilst we were unloading, June took the opportunity of nipping into the nearby hotel, straight up the stairs to the bathroom to use the shower. She came down stairs very pleased with herself, boasting that she only had one handkerchief with which to dry herself.

As the years passed, the vehicles got better and better with very good mechanical reliability and properly designed and built sleeper-cabs, much quieter and more comfortable, fitted with independent night heaters, small twenty four volt refrigerators and a small twenty four volt television set. We had built up a substantial volume of continental business running four vehicles weekly for most of the time, but it was not easy. The financial return was disproportionate to the effort. My prediction that not many operators would go into this type of traffic proved to be wrong. The market was saturated with hauliers and it became extremely cut-throat. Therefore, we had the constant worry and pressure of shortage of money. We had an accountant named Ian in our office at the time who really was far too high-powered and clever for a business such as ours. He was convinced that the whole lot was doomed to failure and that we should liquidate forthwith. He arranged a meeting with an Insolvency Practitioner from Manchester and his accomplice and we met them in London. I did not know what an Insolvency Practitioner really was or how it worked. His accomplice appeared to be nothing more than an avaricious shark and for a couple of hours or so the three of them pounded me to instruct them to liquidate our business forthwith, meaning from tomorrow! "Just say the word and that is all that you need do". The more emphatic that they became and the more that I listened, the more concerned I became. I realised that they knew that they were onto a good thing. I asked them how much they would want out of this and after a pause one said "£25,000". This was around 1977. To carry it out, I had to instruct them, by the latest, the following morning.

I refused to commit to anything and Ian and I returned to Waterloo Station heading for Guildford. I think that was the worst journey that I ever experienced. Sitting in the train, feeling very low the mental fog began to clear. It was necessary to carry out some fundamental thinking. I am quite sure that in the eyes of a competent accountant, such as Ian was, that he was quite correct that a non-profitable business was doomed to failure. May's Motors (Transport) Ltd may have been heading for trouble but May's Motors (Elstead) Ltd was not.

I had slowly built up the property from "bits" into one unit. This included my sister's house and her shares in May's Motors (Elstead) Ltd. That company was guaranteeing the transport company's borrowing, but its value was far in excess of the borrowing. Obviously the "Manchester sharks" were focussing on to the property. My conclusion was that if we were prepared to hand over £25,000 and no doubt a lot more to total strangers, I would be better to gamble that £25,000 on survival. I did not bother to contact them again. It is interesting to note that we were still going some twenty years later. In addition, we had enjoyed a moderate but comfortable life style for another twenty years.

However, as a result of all of this, we did decide to form a separate company, to be known as May's Motors (Continental) Ltd. The EEC permit situation had improved, in that one could apply for an "EEC Book" of Permits for use throughout the community instead of independent permits as I stated earlier. We were lucky to be awarded two of these books in addition to our French, German and Italian permits. As these were worth money, they became assets of the new company. John Milligan, the Traffic Manager had the opportunity to go into business on his own account, which he did, and developed a good business with four eight-wheeled tippers and a couple of earthmoving machines. He was quite right to do this, as it was very successful, and all very amicable. His tippers and ours often worked side by side and he worked well with my fellow Director and brother-in-law, Alex Doughty.

Bob McKerlie, who was a thoroughbred Scot, had spent the war with large army recovery vehicles, retrieving vehicles that his colleagues had damaged, wrecked or abandoned. He was fiercely proud of his ancient Scottish Regiment, the Cameron Highlanders. Bob's post-war history was very much involved with lorries and he became our Traffic Manager and later, Traffic Director until his retirement. He was very keen on continental operations and became very good at it. He had a very clear memory, which could store a great amount of detail. He also took evening classes for the German language and became very proficient.

With the passage of time, came the inevitable changing world. Our customer, Guildway, had set up several subsidiaries or associations with marketing people or with builders in France, Germany, Italy and Switzerland as well as others. As a result, more and more of the non-UK deliveries were arranged from the other side of the channel. As has been said, "One person's back-load is someone else's outward load", therefore either price for the job is depressed. By now the volume and diversity of our continental operation, was much more than the Guildway traffic, nevertheless the progressive loss of this was significant.

Bob had discovered a German transport company who were building up their English traffic by establishing a fleet of vehicles based in and operated from England, in addition to their fleet in Germany running all over Europe. They could do this by using hauliers such as ourselves, who were licensed in the UK and who had the necessary road permits.

They traded as "Westermann" and they specialised in large volume, lightweight cargoes. They pioneered the design of the vehicles to achieve this. I have to now go a little technical by stating that to obtain the maximum capacity, by volume, they used a lorry and separate drawbar trailer, not articulated. This gave an overall legal length of eighteen metres, instead of fifteen and a half metres. By reducing the gap at the rear of the lorry and the front of the trailer, they could increase still further the total carrying volume of the whole outfit. But this meant that the thing could not move out of a straight line when trying to turn corners or to reverse.

So, they had designed a complicated steering mechanism for the front axle of the trailer, highly geometric and with many moving parts, all of which would quickly wear out and the front left-hand or right-hand corner of the trailer would collide with the rear of the lorry. This mechanism enabled the front end of the trailer to move sideways left or right, to clear the rear of the lorry in front. The result of that was that either the left hand or the right hand driver's mirror on the lorry would be partly obscured because it was looking at the front of the trailer, which had moved into view. It goes without saying that this contraption was a most difficult machine to reverse. Bob could do it, so could Andrew, but I could not. Surprisingly, no disaster befell it.

Westermann and the trailer manufacturers in Germany had evolved it and at the time, all of the Westermann vehicles were identical, both here and in Germany. Ours were built exactly the same, painted in their livery and to their specification. It was clever because wherever any of the outfits were throughout Europe and there were over one hundred of them, Westermann Traffic Department could load them in exactly the same way. They did not carry heavy commodities. Two examples of goods carried were as follows - thousands of new empty aluminium beer cans without lids, they were already coloured and printed, Carlsberg lager, Guinness, John Smith's bitter, or whatever and stacked on pallets to the roof of the lorry and the trailer. They were often taken to Carlisle for storage, to be called up for filling and "lidding" by the Brewers.

Another frequent traffic was a bare, painted body shell of a new Ford car from their factory in Spain to Ford's in Ellesmere Port, Liverpool. One body would be placed in the lorry and one or two in the trailer. It was not unusual for nine or ten Westermann vehicles to be waiting at Ford's factory in Ellesmere Port for a day or two until Ford were able to offload the lorries straight onto the production line. This incurred less cost and there was less risk of damage. They were prepared to pay a pre-agreed demurrage charge for each vehicle for a limited time. Another frequent destination was Ford at Genk in Belgium. By evolution, this early design of trailer changed to a much less complicated system known as "close coupled" which handled much more as an articulated combination. Unfortunately, the engines of these first lorries and the complicated trailers as described for Westermann were troublesome, but the concept was good and we then worked for them for many years without trouble.

We were concerned about the declining Guildway continental traffic and the poor financial showing, which could undermine and destroy the whole business. As a partial safeguard for Bob McKerlie, I suggested that he should operate a small business of his own, in addition to his job with May's Motors (Transport) Ltd. This was to be properly set up and operated quite independently. In the event, a solution came up. We had been pulling trailers, that is supplying traction, for a fellow haulier based in Kent, who was using primarily Dover as his port of entry and exit to and from the Continent. He was expanding his European activities and we were reducing ours. In 1982 Bob negotiated a deal whereby our customer "bought" our two EEC "books" (road permits), which gave unlimited use within the then EEC, each for one vehicle. There were seventy-two French, fifty-nine German and ten Italian road permits and we had to assign these permits from our company to our customer's company. They could not be bought as such, however provided that the Ministry agreed, permits could be assigned. We received a very useful £26,000 from this transaction.

At the same time, May's Motors (Continental) Ltd was taken over by Bob McKerlie. This company paid rent for parking, servicing and repair to May's Motors (Elstead) Ltd and eventually took on the lorry and trailer with the "funny steering" working for Westermann. Bob's wife Olive did all of his office work and some for May's Motors (Transport) Ltd. This arrangement worked very well for several years and certainly achieved its original objective as we intended.

None of this prevented May's Motors (Transport) Ltd from performing the odd job or two, to and from the Continent from time to time should this be required. The last consignment that I personally handled was in November 1984 and this was to take one replacement Rolls Royce Spey aircraft engine to Berlin and to bring back one faulty engine for Dan Air. It will be remembered that from the end of the war, Berlin was divided into sectors and occupied by the Americans, the Russians and the British. Berlin was isolated in East Germany at the end of a one hundred and fifty mile corridor and Berlin had the added 'attraction' of the Berlin Wall. There were two airports in Berlin, one for the Easterners and one for the Westerners. Relying on memory, the Western one was Templehoff. Only one American company, Dan Air for UK traffic and Air France were allowed to fly in and out. The road corridor was allocated for American and British traffic primarily and was rigidly controlled.

I arrived at the border crossing from West Germany into East Germany wherever that was which I found initially frightening and sinister and this, despite the fact that it was many years after the war. Ahead of me was a row of controlled "gates" and I was directed into one of these. Each one had a small hut, occupied by a somewhat belligerent female and watched by a soldier, complete with rifle who was standing outside the hut. The whole structure was built rather like passing between two railway platforms, so that as one drove in, the lady in the hut would be sitting at the same level more or less as the driver of the lorry and could therefore peer into the cab. All of the personnel about the place were military, as many women as men, and all were in drab khaki-coloured uniforms. Surprisingly, the females all wore short skirts which was most unexpected. I was carrying several forty-five gallon drums of de-icing fluid, but the paperwork was in English. Therefore, I am trying to mime what this is! I climbed out of my cab and started to perform my act, which electrified my audience. To leave the cab was not allowed and I was smartly returned to my driving seat.

It was usual to buy two hundred cigarettes, duty-free, on the ferry and maybe dish out the odd packet of twenty for no other reason than a goodwill gesture. When the presiding lady in the hut approved the paperwork and I was ready to go, I offered the soldier twenty Players. It is not much of an exaggeration to say that he looked terrified. He promptly ran around to the other side of the hut and disappeared. After the admission to East Germany, immediately behind the gate and the hut was the next stage. Here was what I can only describe as a "no man's land"; it consisted of a wide, barren stretch of land, defined by an electrified barbed wire fence with spaced white porcelain insulators.

Bedford TK truck TPK 699M with Bedford 330 engine and 4-speed gearbox loaded with a Rolls-Royce Spey engine for the trip to Berlin in November 1984.

Every-so-often was an elevated wooden watchtower with an outside walk round platform. As I drove past this inviting structure, I returned the humourless stare of a sentry on the platform complete with Tommy gun, slung over shoulder - bored stiff! Welcome to East Germany, welcome to the world of communism. It was difficult to believe that what I was seeing was true, and then to realise that all of this was really to keep the poor souls in rather than to keep others out.

Whilst speaking of Communism and European transport, I am reminded of one interesting fact that I had until now forgotten. As we started, in common with others, to roam Europe, so did the Iron Curtain countries. We would frequently find ourselves parked alongside drivers and vehicles from behind the Curtain. Most, if not all, of these trucks were carrying a passenger dressed in grey trousers, collar and tie and a smart green blazer. They were government men put there to make sure that the truck driver did not drive away further West, rather than return to their native East Europe. They were discouraged to mix or talk to the drivers from the West and rumour had it that these drivers' wives and families were placed in controlled accommodation called "hotels" whilst their men folk were away, to make sure that they returned to their home base.

However, back to the Berlin trip. I was now travelling along the one hundred and fifty mile corridor toward Berlin on what I imagine had been one of Hitler's revolutionary Autobahns, by now rather the worse for wear and simply a concrete carriageway with pot holes! I encountered a road repair gang, complete with a Barber Greene-type tarmac laying machine and all of the equipment, except that there was no tarmac with which to feed the machine, therefore the whole lot was sitting idle.

The landscape was depressing in that everything was neglected and uncared for. Fields that had been ploughed were unfinished and all of the headlands were left untouched. There appeared to be very little agricultural activity or machinery. I saw a sort of café and decided to pull in for a coffee, only to be refused as this was for Americans travelling by coach only. Filling stations that had obviously been privately operated were abandoned and derelict and where there had been a petrol pump there was now only a bare pipe sticking out of the ground and bent over. There were no shops or private facilities that I could see that were operating.

I was driving an ordinary seven-ton Bedford flat truck, it was getting toward the end of the day and I needed food, fuel and sleep. I discovered that the only way that any of this could be obtained was to go into what today would be a motorway services area. I went in and asked for a Zimmer (a room) for schlafen (sleep). "Ya Ya - police, passport". Me, "nein, nein" I repeat by sign language and they repeat "police, passport". I did not wish to do this, although I noticed later that although the East European lorries had sleeper cabs, the drivers did not use them but walked to what I imagine was some sort of dormitory. I elected to sleep across the seats in my Bedford, although I now believe that this was not allowed. I went to the restaurant where there appeared to be about four choices written up on a board, to me totally unintelligible and unreadable.

Apparently, these choices went on all day from opening to closing times with no differentiation between breakfast, lunch or dinner, just any one of the four. I looked at the food on the plate next to me and pointed to that, which is what arrived, I survived! I noticed too that I had paid with currency that was different to the locals. In the morning I had found a tap and using my own bucket, was having a wash alongside my lorry when I spotted a police car at the top end of the park sitting quietly watching. I bought some fuel and discovered that there was a small general store near the fuel pumps. I also found that these were the only choices available for food and fuel etc.

The next services would be doing exactly the same thing, although the premises might well be different, as they had been taken over by the state from the previous owners. Everything was state-owned and -operated and dictated by the authorities. Staff were completely disinterested and everything reflected this.

I arrived at Dan Air at Templehof where my load was Customs cleared, the new engine and the de-icing fluid unloaded and the worn engine loaded and 'T' forms issued. We had been briefed by Dan Air in England that when we tarpaulin sheeted the engine to make sure that the sheets allowed a clear view underneath the engine, the same needed to be applied to the return journey as this was to enable the East Germans to make sure that there was no person hiding underneath, trying to escape to the West. To help check the underneath of the engine, a large mirror on the end of a long pole was used to scrutinise the complete underside of the lorry.

There were tipping lorries carrying sand, coming from behind the Berlin Wall and delivering into the Western sector and then returning empty. There were special arrangements for checking these and they were Alsatian dogs on long leads on a raised platform with their handlers, which enabled the dogs to leap on to the top of the sand and dig into it, making sure that it was only sand.

I was now on my way home and should be back into West Germany by nightfall. Travelling along, I was receiving some interested stares from the occupants of some of the mainly Russian-built cars that overtook me from time to time. I had not noticed this on the way in but then I wake up to the realisation that I was on the wrong road. It turned out that I was in effect, behind the Berlin Wall and heading deeper into East Germany!

I saw a police car on the other side of the dual carriageway. We waved to each other and he signalled to me to stay where I was and he came across to me. By both looking at the map, he said five kilometres, Brucken (bridge), over this and down the other side, this by sign language. I found the bridge and crossed to the other side. On the bridge was a stationary police car but all of this was no problem and in due course, I arrived back at the East - West border crossing. Having passed through the inspection department, I was instructed to pull out of the way and wait and they had my passport. I had not expected this and felt a little apprehensive. Eventually a more senior official came over to me and he handed me my passport and said in English, "Mr May, you may go!" That was a great relief!

I later learned that vehicles entering the corridor were timed in and out at the other end. If they were in the corridor overnight, the police and passport performance would record that overnight stay. I had not conformed to this ritual by sleeping in the Bedford. Therefore, I have concluded that they considered that I was several hours adrift, so where had I been? I compounded this by going the wrong way when leaving Berlin. Nevertheless, I have the feeling that I was being watched.

Obviously all of this had a profound effect on me at the time resulting in so many clear recollections all these years later. It was frightening to see indeed to experience, albeit to a limited degree, the lengths that man will go to control his fellow man, but the reason for so doing is not clear. The words immoral, power and corruption come to mind. I do know that it was very calming to drive back to the tranquillity of my Surrey village. We are very lucky!

11. The Road Haulage Association

I have dedicated a complete chapter to my activities with the Road Haulage Association (RHA), as they were intertwined with both my working and our social life over a spread of forty-seven years. They also continue with my theme of an ever-changing world, thus contributing to the "full turn of the wheel".

It all started as mentioned earlier with the Farnham section of the Motor Traders Association which we (May's Motors (Elstead) Ltd) joined in connection with our Austin Car Agency. These were local meetings held in the evenings. After a year or two, I was asked if I would accept nomination for the Chairmanship of the Farnham Section. In this I was encouraged by Donald Jones, the Managing Director of Swain & Jones, our distributor, and I was duly elected to serve from 1959-1960. The appointment required the Chairman to attend the monthly divisional meeting in Great Portland Street, London and to report back to the local committee.

Obviously this divisional committee was a much more powerful committee and had representation from many of the larger motor dealers from all over the South East of the country. Again, the committee discipline was strong, as were many of the individuals in attendance, so the best thing to do was to keep quiet and listen and learn. In the meantime, from 1946, I had been attending the sub-area meetings of the Road Haulage Association in Guildford. Here the same thing applied. Good committee working, interesting people to meet and talk to and many interesting views held on which to ponder.

In 1949, I was made Honorary Secretary to the sub-area. This required writing up the Minutes of the sub-area meetings, dealing with any correspondence arising and attending area meetings in London. This went on without a break until the area office took over these functions in March 1982. From 1949 when I started attending the London meetings, many more and varied committees surfaced and required attention and these duties were spread as evenly as possible among the members of the area committee.

As my involvement with RHA increased, our manager at May's Motors (Elstead) Ltd, John Meade, took on the attendance at the Farnham Section

ROAD HAULAGE ASSOCIATION LIMITED
(Member of National Road Transport Federation)

Chief Executive Officer and Secretary: R. Morton Mitchell, B.L., D.P.A.

Area Secretary
S. H. JARDINE, O.B.E.
Assistant Area Secretary
P. S. WOODHOUSE

Tel.: LANGHAM 4911-3
T'grams: HAULFRE PHONE LONDON

Metropolitan & South Eastern Area

50a EVELYN HOUSE,

62 OXFORD STREET,

LONDON, W.1

BCF/DEH

20th December, 1955.

P. May Esq.,
Messrs. May's Motors (Transport) Ltd.,
Elstead, Surrey.

Dear Mr. May,

I should like to take this opportunity of expressing my sincere appreciation of your continued support during the past year.

During my term of office as Area Chairman, now drawing to a close, I have realised only too well the importance to the Area as a whole of the selfless duties carried out by the Sub-Area Honorary Officers, and my warmest thanks are due to you.

I should also like to convey my best wishes for a very Happy Christmas and every success in the New Year.

Yours sincerely,

B. C. Floyd
CHAIRMAN

Motor Agents Association as it was then called and started to take an active part. He also became Chairman of the section for one year and remained a useful member until his retirement.

There was so much happening within the circle of the RHA nationally, internationally, politically and technically over these many years, that it is quite impossible to record it here. It would be a manuscript in its own right! I can only make a few comments from a few sketchy notes as they come to mind, regretfully they will perhaps be somewhat disjointed.

At the time of 'the merger', when the London Cartage Association and the Associated Road Operators became the RHA, they had sub-areas in the Metropolitan areas of North, East, South, West and Central London. The South Eastern area was operated from Chatham and stretched from Luton to Dover, to Brighton and then northward via Guildford, Reigate and Redhill to join the London boundaries. The South Eastern area had many sub-areas - far too many, with each of these also requiring a chairman, secretary and committee together with associated administration from the Area Office. Each sub-area had a representative on the area committee, which subsequently was also far too big.

The membership consisted mainly of small-sized concerns with just one, two or three vehicles - often family businesses. It was not long before Chatham was closed and the areas combined to become the Metropolitan and South Eastern Area. Similarly, sub-areas began to merge and the members dispersed into neighbouring sub-areas. In 1982, Freddie Plaskett C.B., M.B.E., F.C.I.T. an ex-army Major General of high repute, was appointed Director General of the RHA. He completely reorganised the RHA structure and its finances. He reduced the number of areas from I think, sixteen to eight. Guildford sub-area and many others have long since gone. Head Office was moved out of London to Weybridge. Finances were converted into healthy balances and the voice of the Association became important.

Subsequently, the number of areas has reduced from eight to four with the South Eastern District being operated from Peterborough. I no longer have the knowledge of the sub-area structure or today's equivalent as I have been out of the industry for several years now. I still receive my monthly copy of the RHA journal "The Road Way" from which it is apparent that the Association is still very healthy, active, modern and very necessary.

Having attended the monthly area committee in London for a number of years, I was elected to the next stage up which was the National Council. To this committee came delegates from all over the country. Again for me, it was another time to sit back quietly, listen and learn. It was quite a thrill to discover that many of the delegates in that room were from some of the largest and best known road transport companies in the UK. Meetings were every two to three months.

Another activity was acting as the Road Leader on the Road/Rail negotiating committee. This only came up if and when a local member applied to vary his licence to increase his number of vehicles or to widen the conditions on his existing licence. These applications were published in each of the Traffic Areas to give operators the opportunity to object to the application should they so desire. The Railways invariably did.

The committee consisted of a Chairman, either from the Road or the Rail. The railway representative and the RHA representative called the Road Leader and the applicant would be invited to attend. This only happened if the applicant had received an objection to his application either from the railway or from a road haulier or both. In our case, meetings were held in Redhill. This committee was very useful in that it sorted out the fundamentals of the case before it required a Public Enquiry, should the Licensing Authority so decide. The main object of the meeting was to endeavour to get the objections withdrawn from wherever they came and then inform the Licensing Authority who would receive the notes of the meeting that we had held and decide whether or not he wished to hold a Public Enquiry.

Mostly, he would grant the application from his office called "in Chambers" without an Enquiry. If we could not agree to recommend withdrawal of objections, then the notes of our meeting would be torn up there and then and the application would go forward complete with the objections. Where this process succeeded in getting objections withdrawn, it saved a great deal of time and money and for some applicants, a deal of anxiety. A Public Enquiry could be quite an ordeal to some applicants as it was similar to attending a Magistrates Court. This was a voluntary activity by the Railways and the RHA and a very useful service to members.

It is evident that my involvement with RHA was increasing with time. It now required on average, perhaps two days per month in London plus the local meetings in the evening, bi-monthly plus, as described the infrequent Road/Rail in Redhill. In the early sixties, I was asked if I would accept nomination for area Chairman, which would mean one year as Vice Chairman, followed by two years in the Chair.

Time for thought! Why was I doing this? Certainly not for self-glory or for any power seeking motive, also had I both the time and the money to undertake this? Although a certain amount of expenses would be reimbursed by the RHA, it would no doubt make demands on our own business, on our time and on our personal finances. Was I up to the job? Having served under several previous area Chairmen, I would have to maintain a pretty high standard - could I do it? Now I repeat, why was I doing this? Really and truthfully, because I wanted to, however nothing, but nothing, must be allowed to act against the interests of our business or to jeopardise its future.

I was already highly involved with May's Motors (Elstead) Ltd, May's Motors (Transport) Ltd, Rushmoor Garage Ltd and from 1966, we purchased Warren Hill which soon became Warren Hill Farm of which I will speak later. On the credit side, we had established a pretty good all-round team and whilst we were not making a fortune, we were all getting a reasonable living. From a personal point of view, RHA had broadened my horizons considerably. Here I was, mixing and talking to a great cross-section of people both male and female from this very diverse and comprehensive industry, people who knew their job and their subject.

There was so much to learn and it was there for the asking. In addition, there was a social side, whereby we made many new friends and acquaintances and went to many different places and functions all of which were held together by the common link of road haulage. I am quite sure, that we received much more out of the Association than we put in and that view was strengthened as years went by. So, having discussed the subject with my Co-Director Alex Doughty and other key members of staff and realising that it would involve commitment, I accepted the nomination for Vice Chairmanship of the Metropolitan and South Eastern area of the RHA and was duly elected Vice Chairman in 1966 and Chairman in 1967. For me, it supplied a recreational activity almost like a hobby within the Industry and without detriment to our own business, in fact the opposite and plus, we enjoyed it.

I have already indicated that there were too many sub-areas in the Metropolitan South Eastern area of the RHA, there were probably about fifteen to twenty. It was customary for the Area Chairman to visit each one during each year of office, normally to attend their respective Annual General Meetings. In addition, many of them held ladies' nights, usually in the shape of Dinner Dances and the Area Chairman and his lady were normally the principal guests. So, there was a lot of travelling and a lot of speech-making. This slowed up considerably in later years.

The Metropolitan South Eastern area held its own 'Banquet and Ball' during March each year in the Great Room of the Grosvenor Hotel in Park Lane. This was the climax to the year's activity. It is a most impressive venue and June and I were the hosts for the evening. There would be approximately one thousand people in attendance and we had to wait for everyone to assemble and stand behind their chairs. At the given signal we would be played in, descending from the grand staircase and make our way to the Top Table. The first time was quite an ordeal while the second occasion the following year, was 'all down hill', as we had been there before. It was traditionally a white tie affair on which I was not keen, so I stated that I would prefer a Dinner Jacket or black tie function. This was not to be and it was made very clear to me and separately to June by the 'elders' that it would be a white tie occasion and that was that!

RHA Banquet and Ball at The Grosvenor in March 1967.

There we stood for about twenty minutes at the top of the stairs receiving our guests who then made their way down to their tables. I was dressed up like a head waiter and June as usual, was looking like royalty, both of us hoped that we looked quite relaxed and carefree but if we did, it was a complete illusion. The wonderful George Harris assisted by Miss Harrison, both excellent area staff, had as usual, thought of and arranged everything. I was very grateful when George handed me a quick double scotch just before the Reception started. During the meal, we both had to continue with the looking relaxed bit and make small talk to the principal guest and his lady and then the time to make my speech drew nigh by which time my appetite had gone, my hands were clammy and my white tie was very tight.

The time came, one thousand faces staring at me and everyone had gone silent. June sat next to me bolt upright and looking just a little tense and then it was over. As I sat down, I feared that I had missed bits out but if I had nobody really cared. After the speeches and a short break, June and I took to the floor to lead the dancing and at the end of the evening, we did the same to close the dancing. The RHA had booked us into a room at the hotel which, compared to our Surrey Village, we discovered was very noisy. At the end of the evening, we were standing outside of the hotel waving goodbye to people and watched as Freddie Bird did his usual. He helped Gladys into the rear seat of his Rolls-Bentley, then climb into the driver's seat, don his chauffer cap from under the seat and drive away! He was not a drinker but he did not wish to be stopped at that late hour and as far as I know, he never was.

When attending this function in earlier years, often accompanied by guests, it had never crossed mine or June's mind that we would one day be sat at the 'head of the table'. We had always enjoyed this event, but it was an indelible memory and an incredible experience indeed a privilege to carry out such an assignment. We must pay tribute to the area staff, with their experience and excellent organisation and with their quiet attention in the background which made our 'Banquet and Ball' such a success. Prior to the event, June and I accompanied by the area secretary, George Harris, had two meetings with the catering manager at the Grosvenor to decide upon the menu for the event. Herein June came into her own and very skilfully persuaded the catering manager to provide that little bit more within the budget.

Continuing with the theme of social activities which resulted from membership of the RHA, regular attendance of area, national council and other meetings obviously brought several of us together quite regularly and we got to know each other quite well. In addition, the winter time 'Ladies' Nights' at sub-area functions broadened this further and from this we attended the annual conferences as often as possible which were held over three or four days always in the autumn. They always had a very good social content and we always greatly enjoyed them. Initially venues were in the UK such as Blackpool, Torquay, Brighton, Bournemouth and Eastbourne. Later they moved to many different European resorts and on occasion, to Disney Land and Cape Canaveral. We had great fun and many new experiences, all of which were extremely good value for money.

Of course it was not all socialising. There was much more important work going on. At the request of the Licensing Authorities (LA), the Maintenance Advisory Committees were set up. These were usually held at the LA. Offices in the various traffic areas. It provided a useful and constructive link between the RHA and the LA's concerning vehicle maintenance. The LA could and would revoke an operator's licence where bad maintenance was evident. This link helped to establish the maintenance standards that were required and the LA's were made aware of the technical and mechanical problems involved. Information was coming from down-to-earth 'hands-on' people and the Licensing Authorities listened. The outcome was good for both parties and regular meetings were held and maybe still are.

Another small but useful activity was RHA representation on the local Crime Prevention Committee. I did this job as it was held at Guildford Police Station during an evening every two months. It was quite interesting to get inside a working Police Station without being locked up. It provided a useful local contact with the police and other organisations from the community. We used to provide a vehicle for a float to go in the Guildford Town procession, thus providing useful publicity for the Crime Prevention theme.

Holding the post of Metropolitan South Eastern Chairman for two years, carried a few 'bonus' points some of which I list herewith; a visit to the Port of London Authority Headquarters, from where we were taken to their own river craft and given a private trip into Dockland, including the group of the Royal Docks continuing down river toward Tilbury. The information that we received was most enlightening. We met British Rail on more than one occasion, in particular at York Way, where the Freightliner was being introduced. It was drumming up support from road hauliers to put their longer-distance regular traffic, primarily London – Scotland, onto its Freightliner trains and take it off at the other end. I remember their plea to Government on one particular occasion "We know how to run a railway, leave us alone to get on with it and stop interfering. We need an uninterrupted long term plan and strategy and be allowed to get on with it!"

On another occasion, we had a 'freebie' on the Dover to Zeebrugge Ferry and were then entertained by the Port of Zeebrugge Officials. Again very informative and impressive. I managed to deliver my vote of thanks in French. I never discovered if anyone understood it but it was a good trip. Barry Hempsall and I went to Iveco at Turin. Iveco was formed from Ford and Fiat Commercial Vehicles and we went in response to an invitation from them to tour their Italian manufacturing plant where we were given a comprehensive tour, conducted in English of course. We were taken to a pasta tasting session and to the extensive Bugatti Car Museum which was again a very instructive and interesting excursion. This was in April 1985.

In April 1987, I was asked to open a new Tyre Retreading Plant in Maidstone for Bandag Ltd. They had developed a very good process for reconditioning lorry tyres which I think originated from America. During the years 1985 to 1987 I undertook for the second time the Chairmanship of the Metropolitan

South Eastern Area. In this capacity, I went to Bandag at Maidstone. By 1985 it was a sign of the times that the annual 'Banquet and Ball' at the Grosvenor Hotel had to be discontinued because members could no longer afford to attend.

I understand that only two people, myself and Roy Bowles have carried out this appointment twice. Roy was National Chairman of the RHA for two years and in total, has devoted much time to the Association. I remember that he took on the Road Transport Industry Training Board at some stage and it became a long-running battle. I will only comment that the RHA were fortunate in having Roy there at the right time.

In 1987, I was elected to serve on the Executive Board of the Association. A most unexpected happening for me but I must admit, I felt rather proud that the members had expressed their confidence in me by electing me to that select body. Towards the end of my second 'reign' as Area Chairman in 1987, one remaining outstanding event for June and me took place. We were invited to Buckingham Palace to attend a garden party. We were so busy looking, watching and peering at everything around us, that when we eventually arrived at the Tea Tent the cucumber sandwiches had gone but that was the least of our problems. It was a wonderful experience and a glimpse of another world! Before and after being elected to the Board, I had been involved with labour relations on behalf of the RHA. I wish to go into this subject in some depth and have therefore left it toward the end of the chapter, enabling those readers who have no interest in the subject to move onto the next chapter.

Since 1948, wages and conditions in the industry were governed by the Road Haulage Wages Council. This statutory body consisted of Employer, an Independent and Unions. This body set national minimum wage rates. Very few paid these rates as they were very low and therefore meaningless. This developed into an opportunity for the Unions to act nationally and effectively to confront the government of the day should they so desire. Eventually the Wages Council was disbanded and Joint Industrial Councils were set up on a Regional basis instead. These councils quickly became mainly the RHA on the one hand and the trade unions on the other, which fitted very well into the various RHA areas and some sub-areas.

I recall that the Callaghan government were in difficulty in December 1974. They had decreed that there would be no wage increase and left whoever was negotiating at the time to implement their decree. There were at least two teams doing this apparently, one in London and another in Scotland and ACAS had been called in.

The situation was critical, with the threat of a national strike. The government then declared that they would go to 2.5% maximum which was not accepted. They increased their offer another 2.5% which was again unacceptable but then the surprising news came through that Scotland had settled for £1.00 per hour, (£40.00 for 40 hours) for 32 tons gross. This broke the deadlock and became the statutory minimum. It is interesting to note now that in November 1979, I was involved in negotiations for a claim of £80 for forty hours. It had doubled in five years!

To go back to the Statutory 'Road Haulage Wages Council', this body had totally lost touch with the industry and, I would suggest had 'passed its sell-by date' and so change was over due. The replacement "Regional Joint Industrial Councils" were quite different. Section 11 of the Employment Protection Act said that "agreements reached by a collection of Employers and Trade Unions on an area basis were legal and binding on all employers and employees in that area, whether or not members of the RHA or TGWU etc." Therefore these agreements were no longer national and varied considerably throughout the country, thus defeating the unions' national approach to such matters. In addition, the local contact that was established each way was invaluable.

There followed a Conservative government who rescinded Section 11 and this had the effect of changing the agreements into recommendation which are obviously without the power of law. We now have as a result, many more 'in-house' and large company deals which made the whole thing more flexible. I would emphasise that we were discussing 'wages and conditions' and it was the list of conditions that made most of the differences to the various recommendations. For example, the working week, overtime, weekend working, night work, subsistence, sickness and accident, holidays and so on varied considerably. Another advantage was that where for instance fuel tanker drivers had negotiated a higher rate of pay with their employers who were usually large specialised companies, these rates were not applicable to the 'poor relations', the general haulier.

When the Road Haulage Wages Council was disbanded, the RHA were now precipitated into a new situation. They were on the forefront of wage bargaining for the industry and this came down directly to the membership sitting on the Area Committees, me included. Most of us had absolutely no knowledge or experience of pay bargaining or labour relations but we were lucky that we had some large national companies operating in our area and on the committee who had. It was obvious that we were not being very successful in our efforts. We were then told by Head Office that the RHA had arranged for those who wished to attend a weekend intensive course at Ashridge College on the subject (we had to pay our own costs).

Several of us attended and it was well worthwhile as it taught us the thinking methods and the strategy of the unions and how to combat it to the best effect but remain fair minded with it. We were then able to impart this knowledge to our own colleagues. Progressively both the RHA and the unions settled into a routine, perhaps charade, but each respected the other and the end result was very much more realistic and less abrasive. We soon managed to establish this routine on both sides and had frequent meetings with the unions. It was not easy and either side could be tough. It is worth pausing for a moment to think back over that period of ten or twelve years and appreciate that we in the area had an excellent relationship with the unions which must have been good for our industry.

I can assure the reader that this was no accident but rather because of the consistent level-headed efforts of the negotiating team and the equally responsible response from the Unions, the 'elastic' frequently became stretched to the limit but it never broke. We had the situation whereby we could have one or two members on our negotiating team from large national companies with large fleets in our area. Sitting opposite could be their own Shop Stewards representing the union, on full pay from our member but that was no problem. It suited the large companies very well to have a small company member from the country acting as spokesman or leader and that was me, thus preventing the union from 'picking them off' and spreading trouble nationally which had been known to happen in the past. This tactic enabled them to closely monitor what was going on throughout the country, without conducting a high profile. There was nothing to stop them from making their own company deal which would probably be a little better than ours and everyone was happy.

We also had our own National Labour Relations Committee, which consisted of the leaders of the various areas who met periodically in London. This was only for exchanging information one to the other and comparing notes. There was essentially no national structure or directive from this committee. In my view, there are so many different facets of the operational side of road transport whereby the skills and experience of the workforce required is so diverse that it is quite impossible to set one rate of pay for all.

Hence the failure of the Road Haulage Wages Council and its statutory minimum wage. The flexibility of local recommendations was, by and large, very successful. Throughout my years whilst serving on area and national council committees, I had noticed one thing, whenever the question of wages came up on the agenda, quite a number of members immediately 'put up their hands in horror' and said "no wage increase, we can't afford it." The plea was always the same, "new vehicle costs are up as are the costs of fuel, tyres, insurance, road tax and spares etc a wage increase at the present time would cripple the industry." It would not be mentioned that the vehicle carrying capacity had gone up, that the fuel consumption per ton carried had gone down and that vehicle and component life had increased.

So there was a magnificent gleaming new machine, the cost of which probably equated to at least half the price of a house, but they could not afford to pay the driver a decent wage. Nevertheless, he was expected to have exceptional skills, to work long hours, to be away from home for much of the time, to encounter problems en route most of which he would have to resolve himself and to be hounded by persecuting legislation. He was and had to be, a professional. I used to sit and listen to these arguments and think how hopeless it would be to put the argument forward to the unions that we could not afford to pay an increase, so we did not use it. So it went on for several years. However it was a very enlightening and I think rewarding period. I am sure that both sides became much more professional and therefore effective with both sides contributing to the smooth running of the labour relations subject.

There was one unpleasant happening in early 1979, which was a national strike. Through the years we had twice gone through the experiences of recession and inflation. I suggest that very few businesses whilst concentrating on making a living, are trained to handle either recession or inflation. The only thing is to deal with it as it unfolds and hope for survival. Assuming one succeeds, it is inevitable that one emerges from either situation somewhat 'bruised and knocked about.'

I cannot recall what sparked off the strike. It was nothing to do directly with the ongoing wage bargaining's described above; on a regional basis. It was a national strike presumably called by the union's national officers. I have seen it written that it was caused by 'raging inflation.' It was also suggested that nobody really won that strike and that many jobs were probably lost as a result.

I was personally very upset about it and enclose a copy of a letter dated 16th January 1979 to some of the strikers in which I state ..."I appreciate that you must strike, if so called upon by your Union. I do not appreciate that our drivers, many of whom I have worked with closely for many years, consider it more important to come to our yard and picket our gate, than to quietly stay away." (Copy of full letter enclosed as 'Appendix A' on page 230).

The silly thing was that there was absolutely no fight between our company and the workforce whatsoever and in the event, it was a bit of a 'damp squib'. Some drivers ignored the strike like our night drivers on the 'Boots the Chemist' work who carried on. The non-conformist Mick Reeves and his mate Steve Gordon, carried on absolutely as normal with the situation being addressed by Mick in very colourful language, at which he was very accomplished.

Mick was also well known as an animal lover and would regularly feed a family of foxes who lived at the large fenced and concreted yard at the Boots Warehouse in Aldershot from where we operated six nights per week. Before leaving Aldershot on the first run, the ritual of feeding the foxes would be observed and once they were satisfied we could continue with the night's operations.

A very unpleasant side of the strike was as a result of the drivers who worked on the continent being abroad at the time of the strike and therefore unaffected by it and still working. A dreadful incident happened to the wife of one of these drivers who lived in Aldershot and was away at the time. Jim Moody's wife was 'threatened' with a brick through her front room window because Jim still happened to be working. I continue to fail to see the logic of this appalling action, which was not sponsored or supported by our own drivers. It does however show the dangers of the idiot fanatics.

This strike was taking place during a difficult period of trading throughout the industry and we emerged from it minus three vehicles and four drivers. It made no difference to our subsequent 'wages and conditions' negotiations that continued for years unchanged. It was little known at the time that the very able George Newman Director-General of the R.H.A. was working very hard to resolve the issue. It demonstrated the growing influence of the Association.

In 1982, we were confronted with the London nighttime lorry ban. This was a political initiative, the idea being to reduce many night-time movements of lorries throughout London or better still, ban them altogether. The exercise was apparently conducted from what was the old County Hall, the Greater London Council (GLC) Building on the embankment, nearly opposite the Houses of Parliament. I do not know if it started at government level or whether initially it was a GLC idea, I rather think that it was the GLC. The RHA on behalf of the operators and the TGWU on behalf of the unions were invited to a meeting and it was the composition and conduct of that committee that caused me great concern at that time.

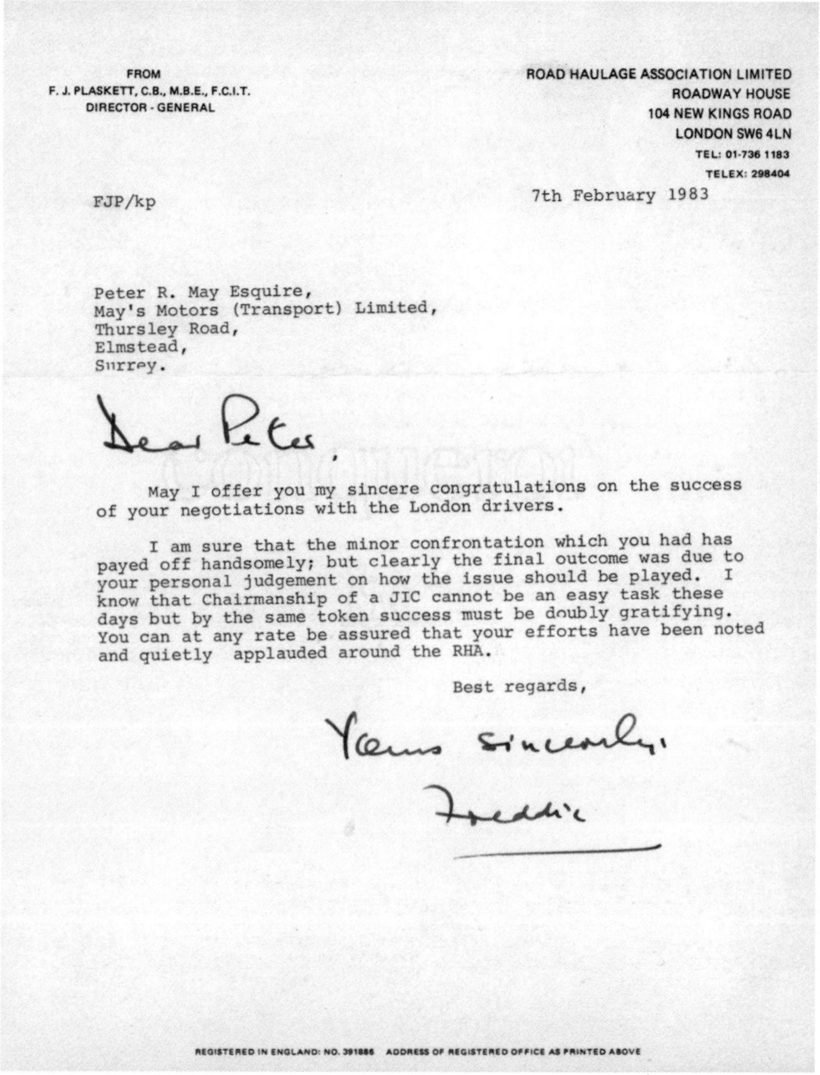

FROM
F. J. PLASKETT, C.B., M.B.E., F.C.I.T.
DIRECTOR - GENERAL

ROAD HAULAGE ASSOCIATION LIMITED
ROADWAY HOUSE
104 NEW KINGS ROAD
LONDON SW6 4LN
TEL: 01-736 1183
TELEX: 298404

FJP/kp

7th February 1983

Peter R. May Esquire,
May's Motors (Transport) Limited,
Thursley Road,
Elmstead,
Surrey.

Dear Peter,

May I offer you my sincere congratulations on the success of your negotiations with the London drivers.

I am sure that the minor confrontation which you had has payed off handsomely; but clearly the final outcome was due to your personal judgement on how the issue should be played. I know that Chairmanship of a JIC cannot be an easy task these days but by the same token success must be doubly gratifying. You can at any rate be assured that your efforts have been noted and quietly applauded around the RHA.

Best regards,

Yours sincerely,

Freddie

REGISTERED IN ENGLAND: NO. 391886   ADDRESS OF REGISTERED OFFICE AS PRINTED ABOVE

Consider for a few minutes some of the factors involved with night-time deliveries of goods by lorry in Greater London. The original Covent Garden Market, all of the tonnage brought in from the growers was taken out again each night by the buyers. The same happened for Spitalfields, Smithfield (meat) and Billingsgate (fish). There was also a large milk bottling plant at Vauxhall with road tankers bringing in fresh milk from the West Country over twenty four hours and the bottled milk being taken out for distribution on the doorstep in the morning.

The heating oil for the needs of St Thomas' Hospital at Westminster was delivered at night, as were supplies for many other London hospitals. This was often because of the traffic congestion by day. The Royal Mail was collecting bulk mail from the mainline stations all night for sorting, ready for the postman in the morning. Fleet Street had to be supplied with rolls and rolls of newsprint paper to be delivered overnight and printed as newspapers and then distributed to be delivered to the doorsteps, of course this was all happening when printing was carried out in Fleet Street. In the case of our own company, for Boots the Chemist, one of our runs was twice nightly from Aldershot to Dartford from where would be distributed the goods for sixteen retail shops the next morning.

On our second run to Dartford for instance, we would deliver the drugs for the sixteen shops as mentioned for their dispensaries to make up the prescriptions as required. Why I mention Dartford is because there was then no circular road around London as in the M25, so vehicles had to more or less cross London. In addition, all traffic moving from South to North, South to East or to North West and vice versa had no M1 motorway and so they had to cross parts of London. There was a North Circular Road which passed through many different London Boroughs, and all of it in built-up areas. Similarly, a route called the South Circular Road which was a collection of ordinary streets and which also passed through many different London Boroughs.

In the case of our own small company, we were running nightly to Covent Garden and through parts of London to Dartford and return. I recall one job when one of our articulated vehicles with a lorry-mounted crane had to deliver twenty tons of bricks over a wall in Harley Street which is a one-way street. To achieve this, the arrangement was to reverse down Harley Street the wrong way, and deliver at about 5 am and this we did. This was only a fraction of the total activity going on in London, for at least five nights per week and of course in other cities as well

The intention was for each London Borough to be included in the scheme and to be responsible for their particular area. In the event, some took it on and some did not. One could sympathise with the theory of reducing noise and traffic during the night, but theory and practice are two different things. They realised that to convince normal level-headed and clear-thinking people would call for some special techniques.

When we arrived at County Hall, we were conducted to the meeting room to discover a most unusual set of people. Of the eight of us present, five had been hand-picked from the extreme left and blindly supported any anti-lorry set up that could be found. The Chairman, we learned, had been brought in from Manchester, was paid expenses and lived on social security. There was a member from Transport 2000 or similar body and a couple of other people who held the same strong views as the others. The fifth member was a retired gentleman dressed in tweed jacket, corduroy trousers and brown brogue shoes. He held equally strong views that London should and could close down at about 5.00 pm until next morning. He was going to take down the Minutes. There was myself for the RHA and for the TGWU was the chief negotiator Ron Connolly whom I knew very well as he was usually fighting us on wage bargaining. However, on this particular occasion, we were 'colleagues' together. There was also an eighth member who had not been previously brainwashed.

There was no mystery about the views held by the RHA and the TGWU on the matter, but the 'five' were not interested. There was no debate, they had been strongly briefed beforehand and as I said earlier, hand-picked. Therefore five votes out of eight, in favour of going ahead with the proposed London night-time lorry ban, were assured. The Minutes of our meeting which were to be forwarded on to higher authority were read out to us by the 'country gentleman' for our approval. These Minutes read something like this..."After some initial disagreement, and further discussion, the meeting concluded unanimously that the ban should go ahead." This was blatantly untrue.

Ron and I were incandescent and insisted that the Minutes be re-written. With great reluctance a modified report was written which admitted that no agreement had been reached. I often wondered if that report or another was passed up to higher authority. After this event, we attended another meeting in County Hall some weeks later to consider the collective results of meetings held on the subject. This time the room was arranged like a court room. Three council staff sat at a raised table and again Ron and I were colleagues sitting below. Again there was no debate and we were ignored throughout. There was no doubt about the result, it had been cut and dried a long time previously, it would go ahead. The result of that was that permits would have to be created and issued for every HGV that came into London between certain hours.

To achieve this mammoth task, some London boroughs had to set up departments to operate the scheme. After that, the permits would have to be updated and changed as the nature of the work changed and vehicles were renewed or removed from the operator's licence. Imagine the cost to the council tax payers.

I am quite certain that the great majority of vehicles working in London at night were regular, constant and necessary. Therefore they would all require a permit. The number that need not come in and out at night and would be refused permits was minimal and insignificant. I am also quite certain, that the population of London would notice no difference in noise or traffic, at night anyway. Those that were refused could only add to the daytime congestion.

Had I not experienced the way in which this 'committee' worked and that was only from the fringe, I would never have believed it could happen. It was absolutely appalling practice. To discover that such a lot of effort had been spent to unearth these characters, they were sinister and fanatical. It was very evident that they had been briefed and well prepared, to ensure that the so-called consultation process would allow no civilised or reasoned discussion, to prevent this legislation from being passed. It was also frightening to realise how far these types of people had infiltrated local government.

In this chapter, I have condensed nearly fifty years of RHA activity. In fact it was interwoven throughout with our main activity of earning a living. There was so much more than can be put into words in the time and space available. At the end of my time in 1992, I did feel satisfied with my achievements. I had served between five and six years on the National Executive Board. Together with my colleagues, we had spent many successful years on labour relations and I hope that this did contribute a real service to our industry.

I am very proud of three unsolicited letters, one from the Area Chairman dated 1955 (see page 165), one from the Director General, Freddie Plaskett in 1983 (see page 177) and another from Director General Bryan Colley in 1992 which is reproduced opposite. In January 1993, I was elected an honorary member of the RHA, the citation reads..."In recognition of eminence to the Road Haulage Industry, and to the Road Haulage Association." I put much into the RHA and I received much from the Association in return. However, I am quite sure that the scales have been weighted in my favour! As a result of my having achieved a Higher National Certificate in Mechanical Engineering in earlier years, I was accepted into Membership of The Institute of Road Transport Engineers (IRTE). Later, I was also accepted into Membership of the Institute of Transport (IoT). As a result of being a member of the RHA, colleagues proposed and seconded me for membership of 'The Worshipful Company of Carmen.' To be accepted, one had to first be made a Freeman of the City of London, an honour which I still hold.

From: D B H COLLEY CB CBE FCIT
Director-General

ROAD HAULAGE ASSOCIATION LTD
ROADWAY HOUSE
35 MONUMENT HILL
WEYBRIDGE
SURREY KT13 8RN
TEL: 0932 841515
FAX: 0932 852516

21st April, 1992

P.R. May, Esq.,
May's Motors (Transport) Ltd.,
Thursley Road,
Elstead, GODALMING,
Surrey, GU8 6EF.

DBHC/pmb/0230

Dear Peter,

Thank you very much for your most generous letter dated 16th April, which I am circulating to colleagues at Weybridge. I know I speak for all members of the staff when I say that we have enjoyed our association with you. We appreciate your friendship, charm and wide-ranging practical experience of the industry.

Looking at your 46 years' involvement with the RHA, this really does cover a lifetime, and the changes you have experienced in road haulage over this period must be numerous. Inevitably, there must have been bad times as well as good, but I hope that, looking back, you feel at the end of the day that the bottom line on the balance sheet is in the black. From my short time with the Association, I know that it has benefited greatly from your participation and wisdom.

I hope that, although you are reducing your active commitment to the RHA, we shall continue to see you at the Conference, the Annual Dinner, TipCon and other such events. In the meantime, thank you again for taking the time to write, and our very best wishes for a long and happy retirement.

Yours ever,

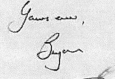

The Worshipful Company of Carmen at the Mansion House. From left to right – Trevor, Judith, Peter, Jessica, Lynne, Andrew and June.

From the IRTE, and the IoT has come a continuous stream of literature and information concerning the industry and others allied to it such as the bus, rail, and shipping industries. There are many meetings and lectures around the country but time has not allowed me to attend many of these. However, as a retired member I still receive their regular journals. From the highly technical and electronic information that continues to flow from these publications, it is very evident that these Institutes have maintained an extremely high standard of service for their members, both nationally and internationally over many years. I must admit to being very pleased in that I no longer have to study much of this in depth as I certainly no longer understand it. I now claim the privilege of old age!

The Worshipful Company of Carmen (WCC), being originally one of the many City Livery Companies is much less technical, but much more ancient. The WCC like to encourage as many 'Carmen' as possible to be members of the Company. Therefore, most of the functions contained a substantial number of RHA members. The Lord Mayor of London is the 'boss' of the City of London. His official residence is the Mansion House and the 'offices' are 'The Guildhall'. The Lord Mayor is elected from one of the City Liveries, therefore on occasions, the Carmen's Company have provided a Lord Mayor of London. It is customary for the WCC to seek permission from the Lord Mayor to hold their annual banquet in the Mansion House. This was an experience which was out of this world and we attended several times. The interior of the Mansion House is unique and wonderful. The whole place and the functions held in it are steeped in history, pomp and ceremony.

The Lord Mayor is elected by votes from the Liverymen which are cast in the Guildhall. Also, outside the Guildhall there takes place the annual 'Cart Marking Ceremony'. This was the early form of Licensing. The carts were 'marked', which authorised them to ply for 'hire and reward' to carry goods in and out of the city. A large proportion of this traffic was removal of rubbish to the outside of the city wall. At Christmas time, a carol service is usually held in The Carmen's Church, St. Michael's Paternoster Royal.

The 'Master' of the Carmen's Company is elected annually and it is customary of each Master to hold his own special event, during his year of office. Therefore, each event is different. We attended as many of these as possible as they were all so interesting. They were usually held in the evening during the summertime and, wherever possible, were exclusive to members of the Carmen's Company. Some examples were, "The Ceremony of the Keys" at 6 pm in the Tower of London.. The "Overlord Tapestry" which at that time was displayed in the Tun Room at Whitbread's Brewery in Chiswell Street. Also at this site, lived the beautiful grey dray horses to whom we were 'introduced' and which were used in the Lord Mayor's annual Show. Another occasion was a visit to Stowe House in Buckinghamshire. Another, the Port of London Authority's Headquarters.

Another was dinner aboard the Chrysanthemum which is permanently moored on the Thames embankment, I must confess that I have forgotten its history. Another, a trip on the then new Thames Water Buses between Westminster and the Thames Barrier. Another, an evening conducted tour of Tower Bridge which is a fine piece of engineering and is operated by flooding the finely balanced bascules with river water down below to raise the two halves of the bridge roadway. The bascules are then pumped out to close the Bridge. Originally, these pumps were powered by steam engines. After this, we enjoyed a buffet supper in the enclosed walkway linking the two towers at the very top of the bridge with wonderful views of London. Another was a visit to Canary Wharf before it was fully occupied. Up we went in the express lift to a floor near the top of the building. This floor was completely free of internal walls and it offered us a 360° panoramic view of Windsor Castle on one side, towards Tilbury on the other and a glorious view of the river while enjoying another excellent buffet supper. And so it will be seen that life was not all hard work and worry but that we did have our share of entertainment and fun.

12. Pig Farming!

And so we come to the subject of Warren Hill. It will be recalled, that we bought the land in 1966 without planning consent and with little hope of obtaining the same. It was an area of outstanding natural beauty, a thirty acre hill very overgrown with bracken, laurel, birch, chestnut and some beech trees with very light sandy soil and over-run with rabbits. The name on the Ordnance Survey map was Warren Hill therefore, the rabbits must have been there forever.

When one could see it, the 360° view was wonderful. It looked down into distant Sussex and was on a height level with Hindhead some nine miles away. From the other side ran the ten mile stretch of the A31 between Guildford and Farnham known as 'The Hogs Back.' We were faced with the question of what to do with it? The first thing was to selectively expose some of the view and after obtaining permission, we felled fifteen acres while still preserving all of the beautiful mature beech trees which we were happy to do, as we had no desire to root out everything in sight and by cutting the chestnut instead of uprooting it, it would shoot again. The birch cleared easily and there were plenty of self-sown saplings which were happily growing and would flourish with more light and space.

Geoff Wigley and I went to a tractor dealer in Sussex and bought an old Fordson Major Diesel tractor, complete with front loader for £150 - a marvellous machine. We obtained a tow chain for pulling out roots and an old, very heavy chain saw and a good axe. With this 'equipment', we cleared an area some 100 feet square, cut our own chestnut posts some ten feet long and built a complete cage. By covering it with wire netting, and making and fitting a gate, we had a vegetable garden, pest-proof against rabbits, foxes and birds. All of this was weekend and evening activity although Saturdays required my presence for most of the day down at the transport yard. The aforementioned member of our work-staff, Cecil Beaven, became the volunteer gardener. He was a very early riser and we often found a bag of fresh field mushrooms on our doorstep, picked fresh that morning. For several years, we each had a supply of lovely vegetables. All that we had to do was supply the seed and Cecil would do the rest. Years later, his son Alfred Beaven who was our fleet engineer, took his father's place and history repeated itself.

Bracken was a major problem on Warren Hill, particularly on the steeper slopes and it was very tall and extremely prolific. Our ambition was to build a house on the site but how to obtain permission to build? We learned that there were at least two possibilities, horticultural or agricultural use. In fact, we planted 1500 conifers, Douglas Fir I think, as we had been talking to a forestry company and we thought it a good investment for future timber anyway, but no help toward a house.

As far as I know, here in 2007, those trees are still there. They must be quite mature by now. We concluded that horticulture would not serve our purpose but that agriculture could be a possibility provided that it involved animals. The theory was, that animals required looking after by humans and as our site was isolated, someone would need to live there.

We decided that pig-keeping was worth a try as the land would be well suited to the purpose for what we called 'free range pigs', that is, outside in paddocks except for farrowing, when the mother sow would require a warm hut. In the meantime, I had acquired two small but old bulldozers. They were both similar machines, both 'Bristols'. I have never seen one since. The one machine was workable and the other was for spares, particularly to provide a spare set of tracks. We were therefore able to clear various areas for paddocks. Several of the drivers could handle such machinery and were very happy to put in a few hours casual work in the open air at weekends. We made enough mistakes to learn the hard way. For instance, we would bulldoze too big an area at a time and finish up with a large heap of bracken, soil, roots and branches that was very difficult to untangle and remove. We soon stopped that.

We also realised that we were wasting by burning too much useful wood, particularly chestnut. So by going more slowly and cutting more sensibly, we could obtain as many five or six feet posts as we would require for fencing, many of these would split to make two posts. By now, we had bought a used McConnell saw bench which was carried and driven by the tractor and used to supply us with birch logs for the fire at home. The next thing was a site hut in which we could lock up our growing number of tools as most of the time, there was no-one on site.

When on one of our Cornish holidays, I had seen living vans as used by the drivers of steam rollers working on road maintenance for local councils. These were owned by Messrs R. Dingle & Sons Ltd. who at one time had fifty such machines contracted out. The steam rollers travelled from job to job and the drivers lived in these vans at least all week.

This work originated probably in the thirties but with the influx of diesel rollers and increasing use of the motor car for travelling to work, their business was in decline. In the late sixties, I was able to buy two of these vans from the Redruth depot of Dingles, one for us and one for Geoff Wigley. As soon as we had a low-loader lorry in Cornwall, we collected these two vans. They had a large locker at the rear for our tool storage. I fixed up a Calor gas ring and light in the van. We now had a place to 'brew up' and security for the tools and we could tow it about on site as required. Later on, it became a changing room by the swimming pool and now has returned to its native Cornwall where it still resides with us and is still in good order.

A company named Willets carried out the rebuilding of the Elstead Sewage Works. At the end of the job, they sold off all of their very well-made wooden sectional site-huts. We were able to buy several and they were ideal for storing paper-bagged animal foods and all of the other gear that needed to be stored under cover. It is interesting to note, that at the completion of the work the Council changed the name of the plant to "The Water Pollution Control Works", at least that was an improvement if nothing else. Then came a piece of luck, a certain person named Dick Purse came into my office asking if there was a drivers job available.

He had recently experienced problems with his retail greengrocery business which had been closed and was therefore looking for work. Whilst talking to him and his wife Ginny, who was the Deputy Head-teacher of a private school in Hartley Wintney, I learned that he had been a farmer in his native Norfolk and at one time, manager of a large private estate near Hartley Wintney. What was particularly interesting was that his speciality was PIGS! I immediately offered him a job not lorry-driving, but with pigs.

We subsequently visited Warren Hill and discussed our plans for a pig farm. A lesser man may well have been daunted by the prospect but Dick was very enthusiastic. Once more, my theory on life came to mind. One has to have a mixture of faith and fate, a belief in something whatever that might be except that it is something bigger then mankind, so we call it faith and accept the inevitability of fate for better or worse. This time, as it turned out fate was on our side. Dick's first priority was to build some fences to surround some of these areas that we had cleared. This he did. He then purchased some pigs, a few 'Large Whites.' The next problem was an obvious one. The need for water. Our first solution was an old water tank which had been mounted on an old axle with two wheels and which Dick had bought locally in a sale.

One of us would tow this tank by tractor down to our transport yard for filling. This was usually me, as our supply was a very poor half inch hosepipe. I would go early by car before work to collect the tank which took one hour to fill. I would carry out an hour's work while the tank was filling. The next stage was that we were able to buy the use of the nearest hydrant to our farm about half a mile along the road. It cost £25 per annum for its use. Filling the tank was now only a few minutes and so June would often do this after the 'school run'. It was quite an achievement as the tractor had no cab and was open to the elements. There were no brakes fitted to the trailer and the tractor brakes were almost non-existent. It was quite difficult to turn into the property at that time but when other car drivers saw an attractive young woman smiling at them from the wheel of an old tractor while waiting to turn into the Farm, they mostly stopped and waved her in!

Dick had purchased a boar which we called Cyril and we started the process of breeding pigs. We now had to provide 'maternity wards' for the new mums and families. Up until now, the sows had moveable pig areas in Dick's new paddocks in which to sleep. I found an advert in the *Surrey Advertiser* "For Sale - ten pig farrowing units." These were purpose-built wooden huts complete with enclosed forecourts which were transportable, being approximately 7 feet wide and 14 feet long. They were being sold by a pig breeder near Woking and were in excellent condition.

The pigs at Warren Hill Farm - ready for a run.

It so happened, that May's Motors (Elstead) Ltd had sold a new vehicle to a customer and had taken in part exchange, a 7½ ton Bedford truck with a light hand-operated crane mounted behind the cab. This was just right as I was able to use it over the next two weeks before it was resold. June and I managed one trip per evening or, with a bit of a struggle, I could load one hut on my own.

On arrival back at the farm, I would park the lorry sideways on the hill whereby when I lifted the hut with the crane, the hut would swing out sideways and I could lower it to the ground. It was then easy to tow it by tractor to where we wanted it.

After that, myself and Ron Burchett, one of our longstanding drivers, laid a concrete base for each hut one by one during the weekends and established two rows of 'five a side' with a tractor run between them and two rows of concrete gullies for drainage after washing out. These gullies were by courtesy of British Rail who had discarded them with the track ballast in the pit at Farnham. They were no longer serviceable for the railway but we were able to patch them up as we concreted them into our new hut bases. We were quite proud of our maternity unit. Ron Burchett was a first class bulldozer operator as well and could nearly make it talk! In addition, Ron's daughter Cheryl worked in our Transport Office and Ron's wife Kath operated our five line telephone switchboard. This family involvement continued over many years.

By now the Bristol bulldozers had become worn out and we bought an old well-used Drott International B100 machine. This was much heavier, more powerful and effective. We were lucky that we had low-loader lorries available to move this machinery as required. On Dick's advice our intention was to produce 'weaners.' When these weaners were, from memory, ten to twelve weeks of age, they would be sold on to buyers who were set up to carry on where we left off. For most of this time, they would be running about the place loose like rabbits. They certainly enjoyed life. Dick had enough to do, cutting, splitting and sharpening chestnut stakes for fencing. He then had to drive these stakes into the ground and then strain up four strands of barbed wire and to erect gate posts and gates. It was also necessary to create controlled 'roadways' to link paddocks to each other and to link to the farrowing units. In addition, as we bought more adult pigs the number of weaners increased at any one time and it was necessary to create holding pens as the weaners became too big to be allowed to roam free anymore.

With the feeding and welfare of the pigs and the farrowing, particularly the farrowing of gilts (that is first time mums), together with his fencing etc,

Dick had his work cut out. For some of the time he had the help of his son Jim which was more than useful. Dick only had one day off per week if that and was not well paid, neither was Jim, but they kept on going. I will return to the subject of holding pens shortly. Meantime more about Dick.

I earlier mentioned fate and on reflection which perhaps comes in later life, both June and I appreciate how well fate served us. The reader will recall that our primary purpose was to obtain planning consent to build a house on this beautiful site legitimately and we had decided that we would go for pig farming. We could not afford to pay to set this up. We were working very hard on our existing occupation including bringing up and hopefully educating four children. We knew absolutely nothing about pigs.

It never entered our heads that we would not be able to handle the project from either a physical or work point of view. For knowledge on the welfare of pigs we were willing to listen and learn and from that point of view, we could have had no-one better than Dick Purse.

A pig is an obstinate, very strong and destructive animal. Its main object in life is food. When it has a family, it becomes extremely possessive and can become dangerous. This is where Dick's expertise and patience came to the fore. He would never become upset with them frustrating though they could be. He would talk to them and although the language that he sometimes used on them was atrocious, the pigs never got upset about that! When a 'gilt' was about to give birth to a litter, Dick would say that she was apprehensive and frightened. He would stay with her, talk to her and stroke her gently until the birth commenced. One danger was that a baby pig could get itself crushed by its mother. The strange thing was that despite the squealing that the piglet made, the mother pig would often not take any notice and could crush her baby. By being on hand, we could persuade her to move and thereby save the little one. This had to be carried out with extreme caution because if she realised that a human was picking up one of her prodigy, she would likely turn and bite and a bite could be serious!

On occasions a piglet would be stillborn but often a quick 'dunk' in a pail of water or literally, the kiss of life would get the piglet going and this was very satisfying. As we learned more and more from Dick, we became more competent with pig care. June particularly quickly rose to the rank of midwife and saved many little pigs. The farrowing huts were fitted with a crush rail. If this could have a heat lamp above it and some clean dry straw on the floor, it would hopefully draw the babies away from the sow's crushing back. They would soon find their way round to the other side for mum's milk and they would soon be running about.

Warren Hill Farm from a hot air balloon. The clump in the centre of the photograph with the house and swimming pool visible.

As the operation developed, two things or rather, lack of them became more of a problem. These were water and electricity. The water hydrant up the road was now visited at least twice daily and the lack of electricity speaks for itself. When we first bought the land, we were entering by an access which ran for perhaps ten yards over a track into a field alongside our property. One Sunday morning, a gentleman arrived at Warren Hill and announced that he had been advised to close this access to us. We said "OK Mister, so be it." Geoff Wigley was there at the time so both he and I consulted the Ordnance Survey map. We found what we thought was an access point from the public road within thirty yards of the one that we had been using. We promptly brought our faithful Fordson tractor with its front-loader to this point outside on the public road. We lowered the loader to approximately driver's eye level and drove the tractor into the hedge at the spot that we had selected. The only opposition was the self-sown hedge of mainly hawthorn and we had entered our property. We then discovered a bargate stone paved roadway over which we had driven which was laid between a properly built opening in the bargate stone wall. We were spot on. Now there was no need to consult the planners on this one, the gentleman's Sunday morning visit, contrary to his wishes, had done us a good turn.

Returning to the subject of the water supply, the water main terminated at the earlier mentioned hydrant. We obtained a quote from the water company to extend the main to our newly discovered entrance. This was, for us to pay 10% of the cost of the job namely, £2,500. Therefore the total cost was to be £25,000 but not to us.

Another visit to the bank was required and this was becoming a bit of a habit. The job required a trench to be opened part way alongside the public road and then for the remainder of the distance, in the road itself. In due course, the work started and then, after about two hundred yards of digging, it stopped. On making enquiries we learned that someone had registered an objection to the job claiming that the land alongside the road had been dug up without permission and that the water company had not given the statutory notice of two weeks before closing half the width of the road before digging the trench. All that happened was that the job was suspended for two weeks!

It was noticeable that as soon as the water supply arrived at our entrance, a tapping was made into the fields adjoining our property. They were using it before we did. The next subject was, that the Electricity Board requested permission to bring a supply line to Warren Hill. We asked Stan Edgington, a neighbour and he readily agreed to allow an overhead line to run alongside his boundary fence which adjoined the gentleman's boundary. So we now had water and electricity supplies to Warren Hill Farm.

We were buying our pig food and such things as barbed wire, nails, water fittings etc mainly from Southern Counties Agricultural Trading Society (SCATS), in Godalming and as much as possible from our local hardware shop. SCATS had departments dedicated to water supplies primarily for farms. They installed our basic network throughout the farm all in high quality polythene piping. From this, we were able to install automatic drinkers in Dick's new paddocks and add more as areas were developed. Hose pipe points were more than welcome. The heat lamps for the farrowing units were invaluable. They were designed especially for the job without the risk of overheating or of fire. As the pig farming progressed, the need for holding pens became more urgent.

March 1989 - the reconstructed bungalow at Warren Hill.

Another stroke of luck at the right time. The Aldershot Military Garrison was rebuilt and modernised. The main contractor was Messrs Bovis who were permitted to set up a substantial concrete works on military land, on the condition that at the end of the work, it was closed and removed. For several years, May's Motors (Transport) Ltd carried tons and tons of concrete products from these works to many destinations in the South. This was because as the rebuilding of the Garrison passed the half-way stage, the capacity of the concrete works was not being fully used. Therefore Bovis supplied products to other large jobs in the area. Among them were structures for the Metropolitan Water Board. Some of these were large circular containers presumably for water storage. These had a 'lid' made from triangular-shaped segments cast in concrete. They were placed together to form a circular 'lid' to the structure, the pointed ends being placed at the centre. They weighed approximately 2- 3 tons each and were about 8'6" wide and about 10 feet to the point.

Another job was the building of the then new AA multi-storey Head Office at Basingstoke. This was all concrete and we carried it all. Another was the carriage of pre-stressed beams and other bits for many of the concrete bridges being built on the M4 motorway. For this work, we had two existing 12 metre trailers extended by the maker, Taskers of Andover, to carry beams 54 feet in length. They were loaded onto two carrying points only some seven feet from each end to prevent the beams from cracking in transit. There were several other jobs of similar vein, some of which were wide loads therefore requiring notification to each police authority through which they passed. We were very sorry when Messrs Bovis' Aldershot Concrete Works closed down. The reason for relating all of this is because, Warren Hill Farm did very well out of it. To explain, these concrete products were all individual pieces according to their design. They were of very high quality and to exact dimensions. They all required initially, a mould or 'former' which was made by craftsmen joiners in wood. They had to hold newly-made concrete until it set hard without distorting in any way.

As most of these pieces were usually large and therefore heavy, the timber used as mould framework was of top quality and substantial. It was usual to face the mould with top quality marine ply which was screwed and glued. Some moulds were made for a 'one off' piece and others were used repeatedly according to the job in hand. There were lots of them, of all shapes and sizes. However, when the particular job was finished, the mould was no longer required. It was difficult in fact almost impossible to dismantle them, to salvage the very good timber or plyboard, they were to be burned. We offered to take it away. Bovis jumped at the idea. We would leave an empty twelve meter trailer at the works. Bovis would load it with these timber formers at their leisure with their large overhead crane. I would arrange to bring it back to our yard. During the evening, Ron and I would take it to the farm and use the bulldozer to push it off the side of the trailer. We had plenty of room.

Chaseside Loadmaster 700 shovel showing left to right John Sillence, the author driving and Dave Nash.

At the British Rail track ballast pit in Farnham, from the first Chaseside cable-operated loader, we had progressed to Chaseside 700 loadmasters. These more modern machines had a cab, power-steering, hydraulic lifting-arms and a full-width, hydraulically-controlled one cubic yard bucket. After these, we were buying the purpose-built Volvo BM shovels, which had advanced still further.

The last Chaseside was still in fair condition and was kept serviceable as a spare machine for emergencies at Farnham. Naturally I kept it at Warren Hill Farm. It was invaluable. Not only could it move and load soil, logs and rubbish etc it could lift, with a chain, our latest timber moulds from wherever we had dumped them to wherever we wanted them. We did manage to break up some of them for timber but not many.

We surprised ourselves with what we could do with it by adapting the holding pens that we were building to the timber available instead of the other way around. For example, the formers for the triangular roof panels for the water board were ideal for the ends of the holding pens. These were two rows of pens open at the front and facing each other with a ten foot gap between them. By placing our triangular formers with the pointed bit at the back of the shed and the eight foot six dimension upright, the ten feet side was on the ground and the other ten feet side formed the outer edge of the sloping roof from eight feet six inches to nothing. So four of these quite massive pieces formed the two ends of the two facing sheds and with no alterations.

We made up partitions by some cutting and hammering, making four pens each side. We concreted these out to meet more discarded British Rail concrete gullies for drainage. From another sale locally we bought a quantity of light wooden panels, rather like six feet fencing panels and we could cut out plenty of timbers for roof framing. On to this went the panels. The whole lot was covered with roofing felt. This was the most expensive item, apart perhaps from the aggregate. We mixed our own concrete using an old mixer, driven and carried by the tractor and Ron and I each had a good shovel. Despite this description they looked very good and were very snug and warm, complete with an automatic drinker and clean dry straw on the floor. Individual front panels (framed plyboard) slotted into each one which completed the job.

We were very fortunate that we could always borrow the Transport Workshop and its facilities, including a tipping lorry, platform lorry, low-loader lorry or small van. Whenever we had a slack day we could borrow any spare labour and it was surprising the number of different trades we had among our workforce. They were always willing to do a day or two 'up at the farm'. For June and I, it was non-stop as Dick, even when assisted by son Jim, could not do it all.

June and I would have to complete at weekends any jobs that we had started earlier such as repairs to fencing, gates, water-drinkers etc. One enormous bonus was the removal of bracken which was everywhere due to years of uninterrupted growth and it was very persistent. The bonus was to use the destructive power of the pigs. Bracken roots are very deep, black in colour and very juicy and pigs love them. They will burrow with their snouts deeper and deeper for hours on end, munching contentedly. The farm was a bit of a 'string and wire' outfit in that it was constructed as economically as possible but it was a true 'free range' establishment, producing good happy animals. Lots of people were interested in coming to see what we were doing and like us, they found it interesting. We were always more than happy to show them and so on we went.

Our activities at this time were quite intense. As we started to produce pigs, so they grew and the need to accommodate them became more urgent. In addition, we had to keep going in order to produce some money to provide cash flow. We quickly established regular buyers. Obviously, once we had achieved paddocks, fences, water, electricity, huts and farrowing pens etc. the job became more of a routine and we were building up numbers. It was about six years later that we applied for planning consent to build on the site. We applied for a three-bedroom house, similar to that at Elstead in which we were living. Warren Hill Farm had become a recognised smallholding although it was really a pig farm. To our great delight, outline planning consent was granted with an agricultural condition. We then had another wonderful stroke of luck. Directly after receiving planning consent, Messrs Guildway Ltd, the manufacturer of timber-framed houses for whom May's Motors (Transport) Ltd delivered their product announced their intention to replace their main show home at the Guildford Factory. This was a three-bedroom 'L'-shaped bungalow. It was to be replaced by a newly designed and much larger bungalow, requiring the demolition and removal of the original show house and it was to be offered, primarily to Guildway employees.

Their stipulation was that the original bungalow had to be dismantled and removed over one weekend three weeks hence. Bids were invited and we as contractors to Messrs Guildway were also offered the chance to buy. It turned out that the best bid from a Guildway employee and our own bid were exactly the same. To meet Guildway's time schedule, it would be necessary to have storage space available for the bungalow forthwith, the other bidder could not meet this condition and our good fortune was that we could. In addition, we were more than lucky in that we had labour and transport available.

Looking back on this operation, we still cannot believe how well it went. On the Friday evening of the deadline weekend, we arrived with two of our small tipper lorries. We had enlisted the assistance of two Guildway employees, John Sillence and Dave Nash, with the approval of Dennis Lockhart, a Director of Guildway. John and Dave knew exactly what they were doing with the Guildway product so we acted under their direction. At 6 pm off came the guttering, then with one tipper each side of the building, the Redland concrete tiles were slid one by one down a plank into the lorries with the help of three men on each side. Fortunately the light evenings assisted and by nightfall, the tiles were removed, loaded and transported to Warren Hill. These were neatly stacked the next morning to await eventual re-use.

The bungalow had a brick outer skin which was 'attacked' by our demolishers. As it was only single brickwork, it was not difficult. The resultant rubble was hand-loaded again into the tippers and delivered to Warren Hill for future use in the base. All of the inner plasterboard and ceiling board had to be torn down and carted away to tip. Andrew, who was about 16 years old, took great delight in standing in-between the now exposed roof trusses above the ceiling and kicking and hammering down the ceiling board.

When the mess had been cleared up, the free standing 'L' shaped structure was exposed. Light fittings, bathroom and toilet furniture (unusual because it was for show only and had never actually been connected), were removed and loaded. The process carried on throughout Saturday and most of Sunday. Under the rigid control of John and Dave throughout, the structure was dismantled and loaded on to our waiting articulated trailers. They had the foresight to remove all fixings, nails and screws as the various components were dismantled ready for re-use when the time came.

The various wall panels which contained the fitted, double glazed windows were very heavy, but we were used to carrying them whilst unloading on site. In this instance, we were loading them whereby all had to be lifted up on to the trailer. When originally loaded in the factory, the panels were carried on overhead conveyors and the trailer was in a sunken bay which made the factory floor and the trailer floor the same height. At 3 pm on the Sunday, the last of the loaded vehicles left a couple of us sweeping up the now cleared site. The complete package was by Sunday evening, stacked and covered with tarpaulin sheets until required again. Finally, once more by courtesy of the bank, I was able to write a cheque to Guildway for the package, the nice thing about that was that we dodged the VAT, as it came into force at midnight on the day that we issued the cheque.

We now had to submit another application to change the outline planning consent from house to bungalow and, in due course, it was granted. At the same time, we managed to add another bedroom to the plan. The great thing about the Guildway system was that we could change the interior layout freely as desired and in the course of rebuilding we did make many alterations to suit ourselves.

This is how we managed the extra bedroom. The day arrived, when 'the man from the council' came to view the site and to decide where exactly it would be sited. We had established a tractor track through the beech trees to the top of the hill and this is where were wanted to build, at the top or near to it. We were on this track, when 'the man' came.

He had a sketch map with him and asked "Where do you want it?" We would have been happy if necessary to agree the spot where we were standing but we thought let's try our luck and so whilst talking to 'the man' both June and I slowly walked towards the top of the hill. We were surrounded by dozens of little pigs running round and round us and looking very cheerful. And so were we when the man from the council put a pencilled cross on his map and said "somewhere around here?" We could hardly speak but one of us said "er yes, fine, thank you!"

We could not believe it to be true, we had achieved it, permission to build just where we wanted the building. We had arranged for John and Dave to rebuild the bungalow, that is the timber-framed structure, the refitting of the inside, second fixings, plaster board, ceiling board and skirtings etc. This was to be carried out during the evenings and weekends as required. We had to arrange and co-ordinate all of the remainder, that was to establish the drains and the whole of the site. This had to be extremely accurate for the prefabricated components to fit together progressively. In the event, they did. In addition, plumbing, electrics, roof tiling and outer skin had to be effected individually. We had no architect or trades co-ordinator, we did it ourselves.

The operation started approximately one year after the initial dismantling of the bungalow at Guildford. Overall, the job took nearly two years. June had always wanted a 'stone farmhouse' but being a free-standing structure, the outer skin was not load bearing. We settled on Purbeck stone edged with reclaimed yellow London stock bricks. Throughout the job, although we used several different builders and tradesmen, there was absolutely no friction, no overlap and no problem. We finished up with a lovely home, southwards facing on a lovely site exactly to our wishes and requirements.

We were delighted. We enjoyed the land for 31 years and lived there for 23 years.

We will always remember the first visit of the building inspector to inspect the footings. Neither of us could quite believe that where we had actually started digging the footings that he had come to inspect would be acceptable and correct. When the inspector consulted his site plan, presumably with the pencilled cross on it we waited with baited breath for him to say "this is not in the correct place" instead, he said "OK fine, carry on."

Dick Purse decided to move back up to Norfolk to set up his own pig farm. He had always said that he would stay with us until we obtained planning permission. By good luck that was the way that it worked out. The pig business was by now well established and for a few months, June and I had to do the job ourselves, with the other businesses going full steam as well. Life was not exactly relaxing but we managed. Andrew was very helpful and capable with limited availability because of school. Chris Fairbairn, a much younger man, than Dick joined us. He was also very knowledgeable and capable with the subject of pig-keeping.

I mentioned earlier that most of our supplies, including pig food came from SCATS (Southern Counties Agricultural Trading Society). They were quite active in the area and were substantial operators of farming supplies and farming services. They called a meeting of all of their pig-breeding customers at their Winchester headquarters. They proposed setting up a pig-marketing co-operative and Breeders would all be shareholders. SCATS would organise and operate the whole thing. It was to be called Steventon Pig Producers Association Ltd. Steventon would buy all of the members' pigs from weaners onwards. The pigs would be matured and then graded into pork, bacon, sausage meat or whatever. SCATS would obviously supply all of the food. This was to be a large organisation, spread over several counties. Much research and groundwork had gone into this by SCATS and the proposals were well founded and prepared. We, Warren Hill Farm, were contracted to supply one thousand weaners per annum, to the co-operative.

Suffice to say, it would have been for us a substantial commitment and expansion. We would have to be careful to not overstep the mark by becoming too ambitious. However, we felt that it could be done and we were certainly flattered by the SCATS belief that our 'string and wire' set up and the quality of our product was up to their standard. Then, just before the scheme was to start, the 'bottom' fell out of the pig trade. Apparently it was normal over the years for Europe to absorb the surplus grain produced by America. This was made into poultry, cattle, pig and similar cereal based animal foods. The cereal supply from America suddenly disappeared. We understand that the grain was being purchased for cash by unknown individuals who turned out to be Russians. The Russian grain harvest at this particular time, had been a major disaster so their government had to buy food from wherever they could get it. The resultant shortage of cereal in Europe caused the price to rocket. In fact to double and in our case, our pig food costs went from £45 per ton to £90 per ton in a very short time and this caused the fattening market to cease.

Here we were with an increasing number of sows, subsequent increasing number of weaners and no market. The longer it went on, the more the pigs grew and the more they ate. Our cash flow stopped and the overdraft spiralled. We could not go on and slowly sold a few pigs for what we could get as and when we could and gradually closed down the operation, leaving us with a large overdraft from which we never recovered financially. In the course of time, a local butcher Cyril Pride, rented the premises and produced pigs for his own shop. This had been another chapter in our lives which demanded hard work and from which we learned much and had no regrets.

Loading the 1914 Dennis fire engine (restored and driven by Nick Grenside) in preparation for the 1986 London to Brighton road run.

13. The loss of track ballast and Guildway

And so the wheel continued to turn and the world continued to change. This process has taken so long, so much has happened, so much has been forgotten that it is impossible accurately to portray the passing of some sixty odd years. Parallel to the current demise of the village shops, compared to the growth of strategically placed superstores, so the small country garage with new car agency and a couple of petrol pumps giving local service faded away. Ours was no exception. Messrs Hillbrow Bodies Ltd who specialised in truck bodybuilding, crash repairs and paintwork, leased our retail garage premises from May's Motors (Elstead) Ltd. They took on our car workshop, body shop and petrol forecourt. They also took on the existing staff of that department and continued our pension scheme as established.

May's Motors (Elstead) Ltd carried on in the large commercial workshop with the retail commercial work. This was in 1983. When June and I moved into our lovely rebuilt Guildway bungalow in around 1975, we had arranged for our car workshop foreman Trevor Balham to move into our old house. When Hillbrow took on the lease, they also leased this house for Trevor Balham.

Our traffic Director, Bob Mc Kerlie, was operating two vehicles as May's Motors (Continental) Ltd. in addition to his main job for May's Motors (Transport) Ltd. and was regularly bringing in full loads of cooker hoods from Italy for D.R. Cooker Hoods Ltd. This presented the opportunity for us to lease the small warehouse, previously used by Atlas Express to D. R. Cooker Hoods. At the same time, a fellow haulier, Fred Miller, who also worked on night work for Boots the Chemist, out of Aldershot among other things, was in dire need of premises. We leased Fred part of our yard and one third of the commercial workshop. Our fleet engineer, Alfred Beaven joined Bob McKerlie and took on the distribution of the hoods for D. R. Cooker Hoods. May's Transport transferred their fleet maintenance to May's Motors (Elstead) Ltd which was very well conducted by my cousin Bob May and his staff who could do anything! We therefore now enjoyed a useful rented income, which carried on for several years with no problems.

Our son Andrew had worked for Pickford Heavy Haulage for a few years at their main depot in Enfield and gained considerable experience. After that, he worked for Ben Turner Ltd running their transport department and moving Massey-Ferguson products, HyMac Excavators and heavy machinery for their four depots. What he really wanted to do however, was work for May's Motors, which eventually happened. He could drive anything and usually get them going again when they had 'conked out'.

We had this low-loader trailer built by Taskers of Andover, with "knock-out front-end". This allowed the platform to rest almost on the ground to facilitate loading. It is coupled to an Atkinson Borderer with Gardner 6LXB engine, David Brown six-speed overdrive gearbox, Eaton two-speed rear axle and air-brakes.

For many years we had a very substantial and active business situated near the centre of the village of Elstead and we were well known over a wide area of the Southern Counties. As with all businesses, customers and their requirements come and go and are replaced with others. As a result, we carried all sorts of different goods to and from all parts of the UK, with the exception of Ireland but including near mainland Europe. Much of this was 24/7 operation.

It was extremely fortunate that in the early twenties, my parents had the foresight to buy the whole of the Glebe Meadow from the Church, which at the time was far bigger than the area of land that they initially required. Years later, as I developed the business, I quite deliberately and progressively managed to buy some of the adjoining property. Soon after my parents had built their garage premises and their house, they sold a plot to my grandmother, alongside their building. The situation therefore was that originally my parents, my sister and I were living in one house and my grandmother and my mother's sister were living in the other dwelling next door. Subsequently in 1953, June and I added our house onto mother's. Many years later, after the death of my grandmother, her daughter Ethel, my mother and finally my father, who died in 1987 at 98 years of age, the situation was as follows.

Trevor Balham in our original house, Andrew and family in my parents' former house, and Judith and family in my grandmother's former house. Her husband Trevor now also worked for the firm. This house had been left to my sister, who lived there for many years with husband Alex. When he retired, we (the company) bought the house from my sister. This completed the property portfolio which had therefore been 'welded' into one entity.

As I said earlier, in all businesses, customers come and go and that is what happened. One of our large customers 'Streeters of Godalming' were nationally renowned as deep sewer contractors. The equipment and materials which had to be moved about the country was considerable. For instance, one subject alone was the continuous supply of compressed air, to be fed into the miles of deep tunnels to enable the workforce to breath. The diesel-driven compressors were large and heavy and spare units were always on standby. There was much more to the Streeter work than air compressors. To our concern, they ceased trading as their extensive property was sold and developed for a large housing estate.

Another longstanding good customer was the National Institute of Oceanographic Services, who were based near us at Wormley in Surrey. They are world leaders in underwater research and in mapping the seabed etc. They evolved and used a vessel called 'Gloria'. This used the Asdic principle of bouncing signals from Gloria to and from the seabed and plotting the results. In very simplified terms, a map of the sea bed was obtained by using the many Asdics obtained. It was like a 'tin fish' and was towed from a winch, anchored to the deck of the research vessel, usually the 'Challenger' or the 'Discovery'. The tow rope was actually a very heavy multicore electrical cable, wound on to the winch.

It took two or three days to connect all of these inner wires to Gloria. Due to their size, we carried Gloria and the winch on separate vehicles. The winch was a one-off and the vulnerable bit where all of these connections had to be made, protruded into the centre of a road by about two feet so that it was extremely vulnerable. Being unique, any damage whilst being transported would put the whole programme back perhaps for months. The ship would contain a mass of special equipment and scientific instruments most of which would have to be unloaded from the ship and replacement gear loaded on to the ship with the minimum of delay. This would happen, although subject to change due to weather conditions, at Aberdeen, Barry in South Wales or Falmouth. The ship had its own engineering workshop and had accommodation for scientists and everything required for a two or three month voyage, often in remote waters. We were not happy when they moved their Headquarters to somewhere on the south coast.

Following on from this, in 1986/7, British Rail announced that they were to discontinue sending track ballast into Weydon Pit at Farnham. We had been concerned about the reduction in volume arriving at the pit over recent months. This indicated that BR was reducing the amount of track maintenance in the region, therefore there was nothing that we could do about it.

As a result, we purchased a new mobile screening-plant as there was plenty of material in the pit that could be used if treated and we had just started to do this when BR made their announcement. Starting with the clinker and ashes out of Weydon as described, probably in the early fifties and then carrying on with the track ballast, we had worked continuously out of that pit for at least forty years. BR had decided to amalgamate Weydon, Yeovil and Bristol into one location for track ballast and we had one month to hand over to some firm from Yeovil. In the event, BR asked us to carry on for one more month. We managed to sell a Volvo loading-shovel to the firm from Yeovil and after a few months, the virtually new screening-plant was sold to a local company for several thousand pounds less than we had paid for it. Finding replacement work for eight tipping vehicles quickly was neither easy nor very successful. The firm from Yeovil started to bring in large quantities of new West Country stone rather than carrying materials out of the Weydon Pit. This resulted in articulated tippers queuing up outside while waiting to tip their load and return to Yeovil empty. This activity soon produced complaints from local residents and the local council with whom we had always had excellent relations for many years.

Within one year, we understood that the Yeovil firm had gone bust. We were upset that after all of those years working with BR, no consultation on the matter was ever offered or available. This setback to our economy was soon followed by another. Messrs Guildway Ltd was sold and the site redeveloped for prestigious offices. The owner and Managing Director, Major James More Molyneaux, was a real gentleman and we enjoyed working for his company for many years. The loss of the Guildway work was a serious blow and this is when we made a big mistake.

I was heading for 65 years of age and hoping to slow down and take a back seat. Therefore Andrew had been progressively taking over. Our mistake was in carrying on as always and trying to replace the work that we had lost. We did not wish to put people out of work or to reduce the fleet. As the principal shareholder, I should have said "I am going to retire and sell the business." It is easy to be wise after the event and unfortunately I did not do this: I did the opposite.

The outcome of this policy was that we had to increase our borrowing to cover the cost whilst we tried to obtain alternative work. We had been working for Redland Bricks with two articulated vehicles mounted with hydraulic cranes. Redland had a very good central workshop near Horsham in Sussex, maintaining their own fleet of some fifty vehicles which were operating in and around the area out of their own brickfields. They were mainly eight-wheelers and fitted with electric cranes. We increased the number of hydraulic cranes in our trailers from two to seven as there was plenty of work available, especially from Bexhill. Redland asked us to experiment with a remote-control arrangement, to operate hydraulic cranes electrically from a control panel hung around the operator's neck.

This would enable the operators to walk along either side of the vehicle and manhandle the lifting forks into and out of the packs of bricks that were being lifted to place on the ground. The thing was a one-off, electrically complicated, somewhat fragile and frequently went wrong. This meant that the crane was out of action until an engineer from the crane manufacturer became available to come and fix it as they were the only people who understood it. This went on over a period of several months. Eventually the idea was abandoned and the crane was converted back to 'top seat' operation. Unfortunately, the contraption cost our company some ten thousand pounds, apart from the resultant loss of use of the vehicle when it went wrong.

The availability of plenty of work from Redland Bricks came at an opportune time for us whereby we were able to keep the vehicles and the staff busy. It took time to build up the equipment required to carry out this work and the experience and 'know how' that goes with any job. We therefore concentrated on getting on with it. A peculiarity of the road haulage industry, particularly among the smaller private companies, is to be willing to work for some of the larger national companies for a rate that is given to them by that national company, rather than quote their own required rate.

It is not difficult to see some of the reasons for this. For example, take the position of, let us say, Redland Bricks PLC. Firstly it may not be appreciated that there are many different types, colours and weights of bricks, often due to different colours and characteristics of the clay used and the area from which it is dug. A company such as Redland would have many very large building and civil engineering company customers, using very large quantities of various types of brick. These customers would probably only be interested in a 'delivered to site' price.

Therefore Redland in quoting a price would have to provide that price including delivery, complicated by the very wide variation of destinations to be served. Redland would be very knowledgeable with regard to lorry-operating costs from operating their own fleet of vehicles. They would regularly have to produce a schedule of delivery charges which had to appear simple and comprehensive. We were delivering to an area approximately from the Wash to Devon and Cornwall. Therefore what appeared simple was actually extremely complicated. But this was the rates, schedule from which we were paid. Sometimes, there was a bonus from backloading from another Redland brickyard which pointed us in the direction of home and sometimes we backloaded from other brick companies, but mostly it was one-way traffic.

It follows that often we did not know what we were earning until some considerable time after the event. Redland's own figures, from which this rates schedule was compiled, were obviously very different to our own, particularly how they constructed their overhead figures and how different their buying figure must have been compared to our own. From a cash flow point of view, we were collecting what was for us, a very substantial monthly cheque. What we did not appreciate until much later on was that Redland were slowly disposing of their own fleet and using more and more hired vehicles such as our own. They eventually closed their own vehicle repair workshop.

Whilst like others in a position similar to our own, we believed that we could run on an overhead cost lower than Redland's and that we could operate on lower running costs than Redland's own vehicles, we could not. Redland's work was very heavy in terms of tons carried. Their own fleet, as previously stated, consisted mainly of eight-wheelers with a legal payload limit of fifteen/sixteen tons approximately. They then had very few articulated vehicles, whereas most of ours were. Our legal carrying capacity was about twenty tons. Therefore, in theory, for the same price rate per thousand bricks carried per load, we could carry more, therefore earn more money per load.

This was true, but we already knew that this work was very expensive particularly on fuel, tyres, brakes and maintenance of hydraulic equipment. The haulage rate that we were receiving was not enough. We were losing money. The more that we carried, the more money we lost. It was not surprising that our money problems were becoming more and more acute.

We were not alone in this, as we learned from some of our fellow hauliers. Then along came another problem.

Our longstanding customer, Messrs Boots the Chemist realised that although they were spending literally millions of pounds annually on hired transport, they were getting no publicity or advertising benefit from the vehicles that they were hiring. They therefore issued a directive to all of the transport contractors, that all vehicles working for them should be painted and sign-written in their livery.

In the case of articulated trailers like our own, Messrs Boots decreed that they be ..."no more than five years old, 40 feet or 12 metres long, smooth sided (for easy cleaning), painted and written in Boots livery and have a wide boarded rear shutter instead of either rear doors or a small slatted roller type shutter." The wide board type of shutter slid underneath the trailer roof on lifting becoming effectively a flat area that was higher at the inner edge than the outer edge thus causing water to run off and outside of the trailer. The small slatted type of shutter rolled itself on to a roller at the top, inside the trailer whereby the water from the outer side of the shutter was tipped on to the merchandise inside the trailer and so on to the floor when opened.

The fleet in transition, with both Scanias and Atkinsons visible in this mid-eighties view.

We said to Boots "OK, fine but who is going to pay for these vehicles?" and the reply was "you are!" It was fair comment, as for many years we should in theory have been putting depreciation allowance money aside for replacement equipment, but who does? It was going to cost some £130,000 for eleven trailers. Our existing Boots trailers were old and worthless and all were 33 feet long. Each new trailer's journey could and would carry additional payload equating to seven feet of extra floor space. As 'Boots' goods were not normally heavy, overloading would not be a problem.

Therefore a further increase in borrowing was negotiated. In the process of changing a major part of our traffic from Guildway to Redland Bricks, we had to contend with a major difference between the two. Guildway's timber-framed housing was bulky but not excessively heavy, whereas bricks were heavy rather than bulky. At this point, I will try to outline the law on 'weight carrying' as simply as possible. For those who have worked in our trade, they will know what I am outlining, but for those who have not it is too complicated to attempt to understand here.

I will therefore try to make it as simple and non-technical as possible. The law allowed for articulated vehicles to operate at 32 tonnes gross vehicle weight running on four axles. That is the combined weight of the vehicle and its load. Therefore if the complete vehicle weighed say 15 tonnes empty, then it would carry 17 tonnes payload which adds up to 32 tonnes gross weight. Subsequently, the law was changed for articulated vehicles only, not rigids, to operate at 38 tonnes gross vehicle weight, but they required five axles instead of four. The overall length remained as before and so the vehicle would be no longer, but could carry more again, the payload would be worked out by deducting the total weight of the vehicle when empty from 38 tonnes.

The outcome of this changeover to Redland work was predictable. The purchase of several additional hydraulic cranes, the cost of fitting an additional axle to some of the tractor units and the replacement of two of the two-axled tractors by three-axled tractors (Scania twin steers) and then the replacement of the Boots trailers was unsustainable. We had borrowed too much additional money too quickly so the interest and capital repayments were too high against the revenue. We were in effect working for the moneylenders and, as I have said earlier, we had made a mistake and that was that.

We worked and tried so hard to get back to where we were, whereas we were digging a bigger 'hole' for ourselves financially. The bank had plenty of equity initially, but banks being banks, they had got hold of the deeds of Warren Hill Farm as well, although there was no loan on the property except for the residual overdraft from the pig farm which we were slowly dealing with ourselves. By now, the bank was getting agitated and so were we. Our branch in Godalming was under the control of Guildford, which in turn was governed by Reading in Berkshire. Andrew and I were commanded to attend meetings in the bank boardroom above the branch in Guildford. We would be led into this 'sanctuary' with its large polished table and be joined by the senior clerk with whom we normally dealt. He was very human and was our telephone contact and always very helpful as far as his cut-off point allowed. There was also a junior clerk in attendance and having all assembled in the board room we waited for the arrival of the 'headmaster'. During these meetings, we would go through the normal routine of figures, forecasts and arguments which enabled us to stagger on for a bit longer. Then came the occasion when at one of these meetings, in addition to the usual party, was another gentleman, who was introduced to us as belonging to a large company of accountants and auditors. After the introduction, he remained silent and no explanation for his presence was given. To Andrew and me, accountants and auditors meant nothing. As with most small private companies, we had to create capital out of revenue. The usual method was to use bank borrowing and hire purchase. As explained, we tried to do too much too quickly and despite ploughing back every penny that we could, we were getting into deeper trouble.

This was a very stressful period of our history. In my case, it followed a pattern of suddenly waking up at exactly 4 am each morning when the mind would start going over and over the situation again and again. Every week, we would have to make sure that we could draw wages and pay for the next delivery of diesel etc. The money had to be found from somewhere and we were always eagerly looking for the monthly cheque from Redland Brick and Boots the Chemist, both of which were substantial. We had a visit on behalf of the bank from the gentleman from the auditors and accountants, accompanied by a colleague. They just wanted to 'have a look round' and asked a few questions about the operation of the business, just routine.

We had no fight with the bank for wishing to safeguard their money, but we did take exception to their methods when we realised what they were up to. As I have said, they had more security on the property than was required to repay our borrowings. I explained that the bank control passed from Guildford to Reading and in our view, this is where the blockage occurred. Reading were completely nameless and untouchable. Guildford could only go so far and then 'hit a brick wall'. Over at Reading, none of them would explain the workings of the mind of the bank's directors or their methods.

Andrew and I were completely green on such matters until we realised why the auditors and accountants had appeared on the scene. They were there to act as Receivers or Administrators of our business although we were never told. Everyone realised that things could not go on as they were going and the only solution was to sell up and clear the liabilities. A bitter pill maybe, but this is where we feel that we could have benefited from some practical advice as to how to go about it.

If only someone had come from Reading and explained to us the full and true implications of the matter, how such things work from a bank's point of view, their methods etc, it would have been sufficient to have allowed the 'Headmaster' from Guildford to give us this information himself but no, this was not allowed. The 'Headmaster' however, did have the authority to casually announce that the auditors and accountant required some money on account for advice so far given and further, casually announced that we were to pay for it! We were truly totally speechless. Eventually we asked "how much?" he replied "well for the time being, £20,000" and added "don't worry about it, I will see to it." In other words, whatever happened that particular payment would not 'bounce'. In total they took some £35,000. There was never an invoice raised, there was no information supplied with regard to hours involved or the rate per hour, nothing. We had to give Barclays Bank instruction to pay this money or authority to take it from our account. We were in no position to argue or to contest the payment. This was, at the time, before we knew the purpose of the presence of the auditor and accountant.

In the meantime, we had sought the advice of our own accountants from whom we learned a few things about receivership and the like. On the assumption that Barclays had ideas about administration of our business, using auditors and accountants as administrators, it could mean that they would try to sell the business as a going concern. In that event, I would question the ability of the two gentlemen who had so far been involved in the matter.

However, Andrew and I had a far more urgent and serious matter to consider. I said earlier, that the bank had made sure that they held the deeds of Warren Hill Farm which were really not required. As a result of work that we had done at Warren Hill and the fact that we had obtained planning consent, coupled with rapidly increasing prices of land, it had become extremely valuable in relative terms and it was suggested to us 'on the grapevine', that Barclays were anticipating prices to rise further still, therefore they could afford to wait longer by keeping us going for as long as they wished. We made our minds up and started the process of placing a part of the property on the market and then informed Barclays of what we had done.

14. The Wheel is now Turning Faster

By taking the initiative ourselves, to place part of the premises on the market, we prevented the bank from forcing the issue and this took a large amount of stress away from Andrew and myself for reasons already given. The reason for offering only part of the site for sale was because the remainder was still occupied by our tenants. Messrs Hillbrow Bodies Ltd. It is worth reporting at this point that the eventual sale repaid the bank in full. Messrs Hillbrow's tenancy was unaffected and we retrieved the deeds of Warren Hill Farm.

Once more, we were now entering what was to us, a new and unknown world, the world of the property developers. We had working for us at the time, an accountant who recommended a commercial estate agent to us whom we eventually appointed. Prior to doing this, we had verbally explored as many avenues and different ideas as possible.

It was such a traumatic period for us that the memory is now somewhat hazy as to the actual happenings or the sequence of events. I think that we had conditioned our minds into assuming that we would simply move our operation to another nearby location by paying off the bank and finding something to rent. Visiting the local Planning Office and discussing the subject with them produced a list of some premises that could be available from the surrounding area, including Guildford in Surrey and in the opposite direction, Aldershot in Hampshire.

The problem was that we needed lots of space, good access for large vehicles and a location near to a trunk road with at least one large building available for a workshop. Our fleet comprised 18/20 vehicles and 35 trailers. Fred Miller was, at that time about 12 vehicles and some 20 trailers and growing. Never would many of these trailers be in the yard at any one time as most were stationed at various customers' premises over a wide area and being continually changed over. However we still needed lots of space.

Having explained our requirement to our local Planning Dept, the list of sites that they offered was absolutely unbelievable. It was obvious that they had not understood anything that we had explained, or what we required. In the whole list there was nothing large enough for more than about two vehicles and none with access for 'artics'. I am not knocking or complaining about our local planners, I had come across this problem at RHA meetings many times together with fellow hauliers.

All of our work and that of Fred Miller's originated from roughly twenty miles of our base at Elstead. We were an essential service industry serving local business and needs. Therefore the need for our presence was indisputable. There were many other operators with the same problem. From the early days many of the hauliers were, as we were, local family concerns that had started with one vehicle.

This often became father and son becoming two vehicles and probably stabilised at three or four lorries for many years. As these early trucks were small, space was much less important. As the years went by, some packed up, some merged with others and obviously some were or became large companies who got bigger. However, in general terms, the situation served its own local community very well and developed slowly in its own right. Planning restraints were either minimal or non-existent. The point that I think emerged, is that there was no apparent problem or difficulty that arose from lorry movements or their parking around the villages or towns. Therefore, no action was as yet necessary on the part of the local authority. Neither had they any plans or ideas in mind.

One quite significant factor regarding the question of land usage was the coal merchant. He started with a horse and cart and would no doubt draw his supplies of coal from the nearest railway station. He would need to unload the railway wagon with a shovel on to his horse and cart and transport it to his 'yard'. A railway truck would contain several loads for the horse and cart therefore, he would locate as near as possible to the station. He would probably rent a piece of land from the railway or buy a field or part of a field nearby and eventually build a house as well. Most coal merchants became local hauliers to diversify, as the coal trade was not busy during the summer. The world moved on away from the horse and cart and the two-ton lorry. In cases such as our own, we had the space and our development took place where we were in the centre of Elstead.

We were at that site for seventy years. It is not surprising that much change had taken place in that time. Planning matters had become very much a part of local government whereby control of most activities for better or worse had been affected. In cases such as ours, we had escaped the net, as we were there more or less before planning really got going. Technically we were operating without planning consent. To rectify this, we could if we wished and if we knew about it, apply for an 'Established Use Certificate' which did what it says. We obtained one of these. I suppose therefore, that we could stay there for another seventy years so long as we did not change the use.

This brings me back to the point of no provision whatsoever for operating centres for transport providers as the need arose. This is not a criticism, it is understandable. No-one had really told the authorities why it was even necessary. Our operation had become a twenty four hour, seven day activity and vehicles had become very much larger. Yet throughout all the years, we had not received one complaint about our being there. We had provided a considerable amount of employment and gave work to local people as far as possible, but now we were going to have to move. I started the process of trying to find other premises and this is when I received the useless list of possible locations from the local council.

I then commenced a search of substantial areas of Surrey, Sussex and Hampshire, looking for anything which even remotely could be a possibility to replace our existing yard. I looked at very many different sites and properties, but however hard I stretched my imagination, I had to face reality in that absolutely nothing came even remotely close to our requirements. Indeed, had we found something then planning consent would have probably been insurmountable. The obvious places to search in this modern day and age are the various industrial trading estates. This I did. Wherever I went I found the same problem, no open space but always a building in the centre of the site with the usual perimeter track, one vehicle-wide either on one side or both. Then I found a possible on Farnham Trading Estate, a large site with good access alongside the A31 with a derelict building. I again came up against the usual trouble, that of price. The owners would only consider selling with a new building. Of course, because it was industrial building land and not open space land.

This site would also require a change of use and so we talked to the Planning Office who stated that should we submit a planning application, it would be unlikely to succeed. In any case, it was way beyond haulage contractor's money. There was another possible site also on the edge of Farnham, a disused gravel pit. Planning consent was a possibility, but information was extremely vague. The access was directly on to the A31 carriageway. There was a gap opposite the entrance to reach the other carriageway. This would mean that an articulated vehicle some fifty feet long overall would, on turning, be blocking both fast lanes of the dual carriageway. This of course was totally unacceptable. The response from our local council was that it was a matter for the Highways Department of Surrey County Council and nothing to do with the council. It took no skill for us to realise that it would be a very expensive job and that there was no sign of any money coming from Surrey County Council. Here was yet another case of a lack of 'joined up thinking' from the various authorities. It does show how unrealistic they really are.

The next one was very near to Warren Hill Farm. There had been a substantial business dealing in fruit and vegetables. It was a family business and for many years, they had operated some twenty or more lorries. They worked the London markets, Covent Garden etc and collected potatoes from the Lincoln area and other produce from the eastern counties and cauliflower from Cornwall. They had about a dozen rounds supplying and delivering wholesale products to vegetable shops in the surrounding districts. Their property was on both sides of the A3 away from housing. On one side of the A3 was their parking area for trucks and staff cars together with a repair workshop, which also contained a large, sunken inspection pit. It had controlled access to the A3 from slip roads and an underpass serving either direction. Eventually the property was broken up and the lorry yard and the workshop came up for sale.

The 'Established Use Certificate' regarding the use of lorries, contained the words, "in connection with fruit and vegetable produce" and so we could not operate a haulage yard from there unless our lorries carried 'fruit and vegetables'. Our tenant, Fred Miller, was able to rent part of the warehouses on the opposite side of the A3 for only part of his fleet. His 'O' licence was in jeopardy as the Licensing Authority took the view that he was an illegal operator because the planning consent was not in order. Fred as far as I know did manage to reach some compromise, but it cost him much worry and money and took several years to quieten down. And so we drew another blank with the planners and the site was sold for a nine-hole golf course.

The final site was also very near to Elstead at Milford alongside the A3 London to Portsmouth Road. Alterations to the A3 effectively bypassed Milford. It was some two years work and the main contractor was the well-known civil engineer, W.S. Atkins. Our local council, probably on behalf of Surrey County Council, arranged for W.S. Atkins to have a compound adjoining and linked to a new roundabout which they built spanning the new bit of the A3. This was created on land belonging to a local farmer whom we knew very well. This compound was laid down with a surfaced hard-standing, water and electricity connected and fenced. It contained the site offices and all the stores, equipment and heavy machinery that went with such an operation. It was away from housing and had a safe access to the A3. It was hardly noticeable and appeared to cause no problem to anybody. As the job was nearing completion, I visited Atkins site and asked about the future of the compound.

I was told that the original field had to be reinstated including ripping up the hard-standing at the end of the job. They said why not approach the council? This site would have been ideal, as indeed would have been the previous one that became a golf course. Before going to the council, I went to the farmer who owned the land. He was very keen to sell the compound to us and Atkins were happy to pass it on. The council however stated that it had to revert to agricultural use. Whilst they could not prevent an application being submitted by whomever, they made it absolutely clear, though not in writing, that it would not even be given consideration. I have always failed to see the logic of this negative, dogmatic attitude, particularly as eighty acres of land nearby, indeed adjoining Warren Hill Farm, had been 'set aside' for five years. This meant that taxpayers' money was paid to farmers not to use their land as it was not wanted for agricultural use.

As I mentioned earlier this situation, or similar, repeatedly came up at RHA meetings all over the country and time and again it was raised by the RHA to various Ministers as they came and went. Never could we establish the required link between government and local authority whereby they listened and learned about our problems or even showed some interest. The sad fact I am sure is that they simply did not understand. They do not appear to have anything in their guidelines or their manuals or whatever bible they use to help improve the situation, therefore it goes on unchanged.

Whilst this search for a replacement yard had been going on, Andrew had been busy with Chris Burt. Chris was drawing plans for developing our site, as it was obvious that the council would hardly be upset at such a proposition. We had known Chris for years as he had become the son-in-law of George and Sylvia Harris the Metropolitan and South Eastern Area Secretary of the RHA. George and I worked very closely together during my two terms as Chairman of the Metropolitan and South Eastern Area and we became very good friends. Our children were similar ages and Chris and Andrew have kept contact. Armed with some beautiful plans for approximately 20 houses, Andrew and Chris carried out several sorties into the council Planning Office and eventually emerged with a plan which hopefully when submitted would be approved, at least in principle.

We considered that if we could offer a site to developers, with planning consent already approved, it would smooth the way and speed up the entire process. As said there were three dwellings on site. However hard we tried, we could not avoid knocking down these three houses in order to affect the new plan. So this went forward and was passed. We had thoughts about developing the site ourselves, but we were just not sufficiently knowledgeable. In fact, very much the opposite! Time was running out anyway and so was the money. So the selling process was put into gear, complete with its newly-granted Planning Consent and the new experience of dealing with property developers and agents. This was the time soon after the European Union had introduced a law requiring certain building land to have an inspection and report carried out with regard to contamination of that land, or words to that effect. Quite naturally, developers and agents quickly came to understand this legislation. By now, there were several prospective buyers interested in our site. Someone, we know not who, arranged for a machine to come in and take several random soil samples.

One particular developer employed a consultant to do the initial investigation of any site that came up for sale, ours included. The consultant visited our yard several times and we got on very well. Then came the day when the developer himself was to give us a visit. He arrived with his consultant, parked their car and walked off down to the lower yard. I thought that I would be introduced on their return. I was waiting outside my office but to my surprise, on their return, they ignored me and drove away. I was not very impressed by that however the great man then met Andrew on neutral ground somewhere locally and agreed a deal. It was now time to get contracts produced etc. but to our concern nothing happened. Time went by and still no action. Eventually, one Wednesday afternoon, I remember Andrew phoned his office and was told the Mr X had gone to Majorca for a few days. On the following Friday, two days later, Andrew again telephoned the developer's office and Mr X answered the phone himself. He must have had a quick flight home! He said that the deal could go ahead immediately and be completed within one week but the price would be £100,000 less. However hard pressed we were and however strong the pressure from the bank, we told him where to go!

We were eventually recommended by our agent to accept one particular offer. The earlier-mentioned soil report on contamination had been circulated, presumably by our agent, to interested parties. Our agent informed us that the report concluded that it was necessary to strip one metre depth of soil from the entire site and replace with one metre depth of new top soil costing approximately £300,000, therefore this offer reflected this fact. We knew that contamination was not extensive and that the report was inaccurate but our agent reiterated that this was the best offer obtainable and we should accept. Under the circumstances, unhappy though we were, what else could we do? And so we accepted.

It was only recently in fact that I learned more about a meeting that the developer had requested and arranged with Andrew. It happened shortly before we accepted his offer and had contracts prepared. He met Andrew and confronted him with £20,000 in notes. His idea was to get the price down by £30,000 and the £20,000 in front of Andrew was his! Full marks go to Andrew for refusing to have anything to do with it!

Contracts were prepared and exchanged and the deposit paid. After that we hit some problems. We could not obtain a completion date from the purchaser and it became obvious that we were dealing with a person who was very competent at his trade. His competence was in his ability to delay and delay but somehow, according to solicitors, we could do nothing to force him to announce a completion date. It became a desperate time for Andrew and Judith. They were completely unable to do anything regarding re-housing or to arrange for new schools for their children, or generally think about their future. They both repeatedly telephoned the purchaser personally and pleaded for a date to enable them to plan but he would not commit. He was a hard man and it was very distressing. There would be produced a small-sized site plan, not very clear, with the boundary marked in with a thick line. This made the exact definition difficult, so time was taken to clarify the exact position of the boundary. Another area of time-wasting activity was that of discovering a few ancient covenants on our ex church land and these had to be investigated. Another source of fun was the subject of access points to the deconsecrated land that was to have been the extension of the cemetery.

These points were on the Glebe Meadow that we had owned since about 1920 and terminated on the land that we had leased for twenty-one years from the Church and subsequently purchased from Church Commissioners. Needless to say, none of these enquiries produced anything except delay. This delay, believe it or not, was seven months. Perhaps the delay was to enable the purchaser to raise the money to complete the purchase of our land. Rumour has it, that on the day of or very soon after completion, he sold the property on for an additional £250,000. We accept that this is business and open to all and it explained the reason for the delay in completion of the contract and how clever it was.

History relates that clearance of contaminated land from our ex-site was minimal. I guess some two days' work for two eight wheeled tippers. This was quite a long way from £300,000. Needless to say, no new top soil was brought in but then, one cannot win them all. Property development appeared to be a better business than haulage contracting. Subsequently, Messrs Hillbrow Bodies Ltd, our tenants since February 1983, decided to retire after 17 years. We naturally agreed to release them from the lease, leaving the remainder of the original Glebe Meadow property vacant. This was in the year 2000.

We decided to sell this remaining portion for housing. This time, we did not use an agent: we approached a developer that we personally knew and our experience was totally the reverse of our previous encounters with developers. We initially met on site one afternoon by arrangement and within one hour, had agreed a deal including the subject of land contamination. Eventually, six houses were built. We agreed to pay a maximum of £25,000 toward decontamination and in the event, the actual figure was under £8,000. It really does take all sorts to make a world.

This was the end of May's presence in Elstead, 1920 - 2000, overall approximately some 80 years. The garage business had now ceased and the remnant of the transport business was split with Andrew taking a few vehicles and Trevor taking a few vehicles all of which, with the exception of one job has also ceased.

It now remains for me to add a final chapter to this narrative, which will consist of a few random after-thoughts, a few 'just remembers' and perhaps a few sentiments, but it will make no difference to the story. Contributing to the making of this story has been a long, interesting, sometimes difficult, but enjoyable period of time. It had taken some eighty years to complete the 'full turn of the wheel' after which, it had reached the end of the road.

Here we are using two Brockhouse extendible, tri-axle trailers for an "abnormal load" bulk storage tanks. We had to notify every police force in the country whose area we needed to traverse and the route to be taken, in order to receive authorisation. This permission would give the date and time for the movement, and any alteration to the route (if any). It would also state whether a police escort would be provided.

217

15. The Completion of "The Full Turn of the Wheel"

We had not anticipated that the completion of the 'full turn of the wheel' would end as it did. I think we had assumed that it would go on indefinitely, but we had a growing realisation in the back of our minds that it could not. Our vehicles had become much longer and more intrusive. We had many more of them and then added Fred Miller's onto the total number of vehicles using the site. The village had grown considerably and was now occupied by a newer and younger population who no doubt thought differently about lorries from us.

The approach to Elstead from the west was by a beautiful but very old river bridge. During the war, another bridge had been built alongside the old one to enable army tanks and heavy equipment to cross the river. In very recent years and in response to an EU directive, the old bridge was rebuilt to carry 44 tons gross traffic. It retained its original looks and dimensions but was not really very suitable for modern large vehicles. The council placed a 17½-tonne gross vehicle weight limit on its use. If they had put the weight restrictions on first, they could have saved an awful amount of money!

This resulted in all articulated vehicles being able to enter Elstead via the newer wartime bridge but unable to leave the village for Western destinations by the old bridge. The solution was a twelve mile detour to regain the route. Back to the yard, once we had learned the completion date, progress could be made to move out. Andrew and Judith were now able to find replacement houses and schools and we were able to pay deposits for those houses. We ceased working for Redland. I managed to find space for a portakabin and a few vehicles in a fellow contractor's yard near Borden in Hampshire and Trevor operated three lorries and took on a few of the smaller May's customers. Andrew took similarly the Boots and Weyburn Camshaft work. The camshaft job required a daily delivery of camshafts from Elstead to Perkins Engines in Peterborough and Land Rover in Birmingham.

So came the day when the premises were no longer ours. Until now, we had been struggling to hang on, we had been worrying about everything and dealing with so many things that cropped up all of the time. We were now involved deeply in a subject and happening about which we knew nothing. That of closing down. We had not had much time to think clearly or to think ahead of late. It was certainly a great relief to be clear of the bank, to have retained the portion of the property leased by Hillbrow and to have recovered the deeds of Warren Hill, but it was not a happy relief it was a very hollow and sad relief.

I drove into the yard a day or two after completion to find strange people there all over the place. I was not recognised, I was ignored and that was when it hit the hardest. I do not remember very much about anything around that period. I never did go over to where the houses had stood. I did go to the site one day and saw the flattened workshops and wreckage all around. I know that it mattered deeply to Andrew as well, but nothing was ever said, we took it inwardly.

When my parents were alive, the old man would often question "why buy that land? You don't need it", or a vehicle or a piece of equipment, or "what a waste of money". He would moan about all sorts of things and then forget all about it. But he would delight in bringing people into the workshop, or into the office or down the yard to see the fleet all lined up. He was really so proud of the whole set-up. I was very pleased that they were not there to witness the present destruction. What I did notice however was that there was no sign or evidence of any top soil being stripped off and being replaced by fresh soil.

Having got Trevor fixed up as best we could, we could not find anything to re-establish Andrew. We therefore set up a temporary, somewhat primitive base at Warren Hill Farm for about four vehicles. We knew very well that it would not be long before the council came rushing up there saying "you can't do that" and they did. We reckoned that it would take them a year to get us out. We put up a fight which was always a delaying tactic, but that is another story. As an aftermath to all that had happened, June and I were confronted with a situation to which I had given no thought. Although I was now 72 years of age, we had virtually no income other than us each receiving an old age pension.

When the law was changed to allow us into the company pension scheme (see Chapter Eight), because we were always ploughing money into the expanding business we could never afford the 'catch up' money to enable us to join. Therefore the next upheaval in my and June's life was to realise that we could not afford to stay at our beautiful Warren Hill Farm for much longer and we came to the heartrending conclusion that we had to sell the property to release some of our capital and supplement our pensions. In the past, we had often visited the Porthleven area of West Cornwall and talked of retirement there, but that thought was always far away, now it was coming much nearer and fast. We had to tackle this with a totally different mental attitude to the one of past years. We did not want to leave Warren Hill, we had both put so much into it. We were so delighted and privileged to be able to buy it in the first place. Rather like the business, Warren Hill was in our minds forever. Hence the need for a complete change of mental attitude. So we had to be realistic, face the facts and accept that we could not stay there. We had owned the hill for 31 years. We had lived there for 23 years. How lucky we had been and how much we had enjoyed being there; we could look back over all of those years with pleasure, not regret.

We managed to sell the hill rather well. Neither of us will ever forget our driving slowly down the front drive for the very last time, on our way to Carsluick Barn in Godolphin Cross in Cornwall. June was flooding with tears. I was very misty and had a job to see to drive. We were both left with our own random, mixed thoughts.

16. A few more reminiscences

During the war food production the 'Dig for Victory' campaign was all-important with great accent on farming. This concentration went on immediately post-war. Hay was an important animal food product and it was essential to pick it up from the field immediately it was 'ready' and thoroughly dry. Wet weather at haymaking time could ruin the hay, thus losing valuable winter feed. As with many things, the methods used today are quite different. It can be cut green, baled, wrapped in plastic and stored in the field awaiting use in one operation to make silage. If real hay is required, yes, it must be turned by machine and be dry then it can be baled, wrapped and stored as above. Before the machinery for making silage and for baling and wrapping appeared, it was traditional to collect the turned and dried hay from the field, probably by horse and cart, take it to the 'rick yard' at the farm and to make a hay rick.

This was started off on a bed of birch faggots as used in the bread ovens. These allowed air to circulate under the rick (and the field mice) and to keep the bottom of the rick dry. As the loose hay was brought in from the fields, it was hand-pitched on to the developing rick. Manpower on the rick built it into a circular shape and as they were working on the rick, they were therefore walking on it which compressed it. This was important to make it stable and it also affected the ultimate interior temperature of the rick to some critical figure, which prevented it from heating up and so the hay could mature. This building of the rick would go on until one could no longer pitch any higher. It was finished off by shaping the top into a cone.

After this it would be straw-thatched to keep it dry. When required for feed it would be cut from the rick by an enormous flat knife blade with a handle made at right angles to the top of the blade whereby a man could apply his full weight on to the thing to cut out a slice of hay, very hard work. Here endeth the lesson on haymaking. The reason for this story is because one local farmer hired us to collect from the field and transport to the enlarging rick.

Due to the critical timing of the hay being ready and the weather dry, he would give as much warning as possible and when ready, the operation usually started at about 4 pm. We would then carry on until it was dark or the dew came down or we had cleared the fields. We still had the wartime attitude, quite rightly, to do everything possible to gather it in. June loved haymaking, she loved being in the fields and fresh air. If she was off duty, (she was at the time a diet cook at Farnham Hospital) she would come over and join the haymakers. I taught her how to move my old Bedford lorry slowly across the field in first gear as this would enable me to help load the lorry, making an extra hand. Happy days! I am pretty sure that a hayrick is a thing of the past and the skills to create one are possibly also lost.

We had a five-line telephone switchboard which was very busy. We had a full-time operator who, from time to time, would probably be one of the driver's wives. Being married to a lorry driver had probably broadened the vocabulary which enabled them to handle most situations. We had to collect a new four-wheeled trailer from near Chichester and bring it to our yard. I must explain, that an independent four-wheeled trailer is quite different to an articulated trailer. It is hooked on to a rigid lorry and it follows the path of the lorry. The big difference is in reversing it. We sent one of our older drivers who unfortunately stuttered a little to collect the trailer. The phone rang and the conversation went "I am in Petworth car park and I can't get the f....thing out". Flitting back through the mind, several things were remembered. The staff set up our own social club, kids parties, kids outings, that sort of thing.

We had one or two very successful 'Treasure Hunts'. There was no treasure but there was pleasure. The organisers would search the local surrounding villages and area looking for landmarks or items to become clues along the road, which became a circular route from our yard back to the yard. The great thing about this was that the entire family including grandma could take part, subject to how many people could get into their car. Having assembled in the yard, usually on a Saturday afternoon, each car driver was given a typed list of clues all of which relied on observation as they went along. It was quite remarkable how clever and entertaining the use of words became to camouflage the article being sought. The cars would leave at three minute intervals and the quest would take roughly two and a half hours. Afterwards, we would all assemble next door in the village hall where tea etc would be served and the organisers would adjudicate on the returned clue sheets. The firm would subscribe a couple of prizes and the event would be much enjoyed particularly by the children and, where appropriate, Grandma.

Another thing quite unconnected with the above, but which has emerged from the memory was the supply of work clothes to the drivers. We supplied two pairs of poly-cotton trousers and one jacket per year in spruce green with a breast-pocket badge which proudly said May's Motors. It was left to the user to keep them laundered. It did add something to the image of the company. We were also proud of the presentation of our fleet of lorries. We tried to keep them tidy and clean in their livery of dual green and clearly sign-written.

We had learned with the passing of time, confirmation of the much-used comment "You get what you pay for" and "you cannot get a quart out of a pint pot". This applied to our tools of trade, our lorries. Progressively we had built up a fleet of some fifteen Gardner Engined Atkinsons, which in their day, were nearer to the top end of the scale and five or six Bedfords or similar, for the lighter type of our work. Subsequently, the Atkinsons were outdated and superseded by Scania 110,111,112 and 113s (this bit for the technical). There is no doubt that this strategy whilst initially more expensive, was more efficient in that the mechanical failure rate provided that it was not caused by neglect, was very much lower. The same could be said for the Atkinsons and Scanias. There is also no doubt, that the strategy attracted a superior type of driver who took pride in their work and their vehicle.

Another thought comes to mind that for many years, I personally always took a prospective driver for a driving test and always with a loaded lorry. This exercise held no fear for the professionals as most of them were. There is no possibility of my being able to do that any more, I would not know where to start! We had at some time achieved BS.5780, being a British Standard which recognised quality and competence of our ability within our industry. Some companies required this qualification, before they would employ us. I earlier mentioned a contemporary of my parents, Harry Rackliffe, who together with his wife had built up a good transport business in Guildford. He was nationalised and subsequently managed to buy back his premises and some vehicles after de-nationalisation. They had one son, who took over after the deaths of his parents. Eventually events overtook and the property was sold for housing, as Rackliffe junior's health deteriorated. We purchased the business only from the developer for the work that it brought, which filled a gap at the time. Another of the early operators gone, Harry Rackliffe was a member of the Guildford Sub-area RHA or maybe associated Road Operators before I was.

Thinking about past years, right up to the present, I still hold the view that both road haulage and the railways have been badly let down, primarily by the politicians. In my memory, no party leader has ever awarded the road and rail industries the attention and importance that they deserve. It is not in their interests, as politicians, to think long-term. They appear to all favour short-term power and glory. In the early part of this book, I made reference to the word 'transport' as being all embracing, to include freight, passenger, air, shipping and pedestrians. Its importance goes unrecognised.

My very simple theory would be to make the subject an all-party non-political authority, who would be led by a well-paid individual with a proven track record, surrounded by a team of 'hands on people' drawn from the road, rail, air, and shipping industries and who would be accountable. "OK silly theory, not possible, wouldn't work, you are talking rubbish". Maybe, but please tell me the sense in having a succession of Ministers for Transport who almost never come from a background with any knowledge of these industries. They come, they make pronouncements, they make promises, then usually move on very quickly. Experience and knowledge of this subject is never a requirement of office.

In answer to my comments, I would make three observations. Look at the state of the railways. Look at the persecution of road transport by regulation and the dangerously low level of profitability and get someone to research how many 'Ministers of Transport' and I mean the top men in charge, have there been over let us say the past thirty years. It would be a frightening number and I would not be alone when I say that I cannot remember any of them. It is absolutely without sense and can never work. There is no continuity of thought or purpose.

I can well understand people whom I will call 'some members of the public', who are strongly and actively anti-lorry. They are entitled to their view and sometimes they have reason to complain. However, I feel that this is on occasions, a little hypocritical and impractical. What about when we require a top-up of oil for central heating? How does the weekly collection of our household waste happen? When we wish to build an extension to our house, how do the bricks get there or the ready-mixed concrete, the sand, the tiles etc? When we move house how does the furniture arrive? Several questions - one answer, by lorry. I am nearing the end of this narrative.

I am nearly eighty-three years of age, therefore I claim the privilege of age and say that I enjoyed writing the previous few paragraphs. I have been wanting to do that for a long time!

I now return to the subject of May's Motors (Transport) Ltd. and May's Motors (Elstead) Ltd. and write a few words regarding our staff. It is pretty obvious that we would not get very far without drivers, supported by the mechanics. As I have told, we were a small private concern who concentrated on the practical, rather than the financial. As a result, we had close contact with each other and everyone, as they say, 'knew the score'.

I pay tribute to the many people who worked for us over this span of many years. It was never a highly paid industry and always required long hours. It was really the overtime that brought the driver's money up. This was of course, the nature of the job. General haulage is probably the most demanding type of work of an extremely diverse industry. Whilst a considerable amount of our work was repetitive, much of it was not. These one-offs were usually the most challenging and whilst we naturally had our problems from time to time, I recall very few failures. These men were required to leave the yard often at the most unearthly hours to meet a delivery deadline. Some were arriving home as others were leaving. Their vehicles were large. Often, their loads were also large and required special skills, but it almost always happened more or less to plan. We must not forget the sometimes adverse weather. I think perhaps the worst condition to handle was fog, after that ice and snow.

Our night drivers on the Boots work, for years Mick Reeves and Steve Gordon, had although on repetitive work, all of this to contend with night after night. I cannot remember the occasion when the drugs that we carried to be dispensed in the shop the next morning, did not arrive. I mentioned earlier that they were professionals, there is no other way to describe them and in my view they were never overpaid.

As the business grew so we had to delegate and appoint managers. Manager for May's Motors (Elstead) Ltd. was John Meade who joined us as a car mechanic and retired as manager. Robbie Morgan joined us as a mechanic, together with his wife Edna, who was our book keeper. They both took on Rushmoor Garage Ltd. when we bought it and very successfully managed it until retirement when it was sold. Edna with a bottle of ink and a pen was as good as any computer.

Joyce Clarke, wife of driver Alan Clarke, worked for May's Motors (Elstead) Ltd. with Edna Morgan for years, sadly she died far too young. My brother-in-law and a co-Director, Alex Doughty, ran the tipper department through to retirement. A most upright and honourable man he was assisted by ex-driver Bill Ellis who became assistant traffic manager until retirement. Ray Mitchell was an ex-driver and worked as a traffic manager very successfully for many years. John Milligan, another ex-driver, became another successful traffic manager and finished up with his own business, operating four eight-wheeled tippers.

Robert McKerlie, a proud Scot and a man with the highest of principles, as well as an expert in UK transport, became an expert in continental transport. He had a memory like a computer. His wife Olive assisted with the office work and with Bob's company, May's Motors (Continental) Ltd. When I wanted a really well presented letter typed, I would go to

Olive. Since retirement, Bob and Olive have been very active with a charity helping Romanian school children. They have taken several lorry loads of 'scrounged' materials to Romanian schools or orphanages and then remained to fix up often non-existent plumbing or electrics. They now have their own bus to take the volunteers to and from Romania. Bob has kept up his heavy vehicle driving skills.

John Robinson and Eric Pattison, both joined us more recently and made significant contributions to the well being of the company. Unfortunately, neither were allowed much time for retirement.

Bob May who operated the commercial workshop is still an amazing person. He can do almost anything with particular accent on electrical installation. He was trained by Southern Electricity Company and has his own lathe to make things from metal. He can build brick chimneys and walls and is an excellent carpenter and an excellent welder. He is also an excellent car and commercial mechanic and used to delight in heavy vehicle recovery. A first class gardener, he also usually takes several prizes at the local garden club functions. In retirement he has now finished a total and complete rebuild of an early Austin Seven in which he now travels all over the place as a member of the Austin Seven Club. It doesn't sound true but it is.

In earlier years, our fleet engineer was George Taylor. He used to completely rebuild our 5-ton 'O' model Bedfords. He could make a vehicle engine 'talk', unfortunately he is another sad case of an early death from cancer. He was assisted by Cecil Beaven, the man you may remember during the war who could straighten buckled bicycle wheels. He was also a marvellous gardener and started the garden at Warren Hill. He was with us until retirement. His son, Alfred Beaven, who started as a driver became fleet engineer after George's death and he was assisted by his father Cecil. Alfred was another who could do almost anything. He eventually joined D.R. Cooker Hoods as a Director when we leased part of our workshop to Fred Miller and Bob May took on both our own and the retail commercial maintenance work. One of our drivers of many years, Ian Davis, came off the road and went into the workshop. He was a trained mechanic anyway and was a quiet and thorough man. Throughout the time we had many trainee mechanics several of whom stayed on for years as skilled men and they were very good.

There are many more names, too numerous to mention, particularly drivers. The reason for mentioning this matter at all is because with very few exceptions, all of these people had one very strong common thread running through, which I sum up as follows, reliability, integrity and expertise. Therefore, management was made much easier. I like to think that, for most of the time at least, we were a happy firm.

Andrew had arranged for his 'Boots' vehicles to be based at their premises in Aldershot, the trailers were there anyway and one rigid Scania to be based at Weyburn Engineering, as it did the daily run to Perkins and Land Rover. This was and is still driven by Fred Padwick. He worked for us for many years on the tippers and then carried on with Andrew, who is now working in the building trade but had kept a few vehicles running, that is Boots and Weyburn. Meantime, Boots have closed the Aldershot Warehouse and turned the site into a large housing estate so that job is finished. Fred keeps going, he is a big man and big-hearted. He is now well over 70 years old and always willing to help anybody and still does. He holds millions and millions of miles with a marvellous record. To me, he has always been the same. I do not remember him ever losing his temper.

Before we move to Cornwall, one final short story. One Saturday morning we were preparing a vehicle for a local carnival. We did several of these each year around the villages, obviously for free, but we though it good PR for us. "Dobber" Lawrence ran a nasty splinter into his finger and a fellow driver produced a large 'boy scout' type of clasp knife and proceeded to act as 'surgeon'. He set about excavating the splinter with this great instrument when a yell from Dobber said "Don't cut my bloody finger off" the reply from the 'surgeon' was "I can't do that cos you won't stand still long enough!"

The move to Cornwall was another completely different, perhaps final, stage of our lives. West Cornwall is a beautiful part of the country and is to be enjoyed and this we are able to do, no problem. Throughout this book, I have used the two themes of 'a changing world' probably influenced by Charles Darwin and the double influence of faith and fate and I would say a word about my comprehension of the word 'faith'. Quite simply, I suggest that man has to believe in something greater than he, were that not true, then man could control everything. A little sensible thought to that would confirm that he cannot.

King Canute thought he could turn back the tide of the sea, he could not and he got his feet wet. Take the time to closely examine a fully-grown bloom on a rose bush. Tell me who designed it? Having designed, who made it? I am quite sure that it was not man! There are many thousands of other examples of this. In the absence of answers to the above questions, it becomes my definition of the word 'faith' because it is individual to all of us and none of us really understand it, but we don't have to. The meaning of the word fate is unalterable anyway.

The view from the conservatory, Carsluick Barn, Cornwall.

During our nine years so far in Cornwall, we are still busy doing nothing. I became a Watch Keeper for the National Coastwatch Institution (NCI), a totally voluntary organisation allied to HM Coastguard. The object is to help safeguard life on the lovely coastline footpaths and on the sea. I completed six years together with others providing a daylight watch for every day of the year which we all find greatly rewarding. Here we met and became good friends with the Station Manager, Treve Harris and his wife Maureen. Treve was able to offer me a one-fifth share in a 20ft cabin cruiser. We have been able to repeatedly enjoy the world-famous Falmouth Bay and River Fal waters, including the Helford River. So another lifelong ambition fulfilled.

I was 'pensioned off' from the NCI at 81 years of age when I was made an honorary member of Bass Point (Lizard) NCI. This is an honour, together with my Honorary membership of RHA that I will cherish for the remainder of my days.

June has been enjoying her spinning and weaving and her garden but never has enough time for any of it. However, because she is such an excellent cook and this is so time-consuming, we do 'eat' very well. We both enjoy the ever-changing sea to which we are very near and the dog reinforces our view! I repeat an old saying, "sometimes I sits and thinks, sometimes I just sits!"

I close with a few of my "thinks".

After watching the ever changing sea, the sky, the clouds and the sunsets, having looked at the flowers, the birds and the landscapes and at the wonderful magnificence and mystery of a clear and starlit night and having considered the design and the perfection of all that has gone and still goes into this wonderful universe, one has discovered the meaning of the word 'God' which is only a word and is essentially your own interpretation, as indeed it is meant to be. This to me is the true meaning of religion and is the same in any language, it always has been and it is not 'man-made' All other religions are!

Austin Ten service van photographed with the 1938 Bedford 27 h.p. GPH 996, the latter owned originally by A. Wilkins of Guildford. The service van was known as "the mobile dictionary" on account of its excessive signwriting.

Appendices

A. Letter to strikers in January 1979. See Chapter 11

Members R.H.A.

MAYS MOTORS (TRANSPORT) LTD.

Directors : D. May, P. R. C. May, A G. M. Doughty

Reg. No. 423511 England
Telex No. 858366

Reg. Office
ELSTEAD, GODALMING, SURREY
GU8 6EF
Telephone : ELSTEAD (STD 025122) 3255 (5 lines)

16th January, 1979

Dear Sir,

It is with more than extreme reluctance that I, as Managing Director of May's Motors (Transport) Ltd., issue the following statement –

It is well known that this Industry is going through a difficult economic period, whereby costs generally are exceeding revenue.

This leads to a situation, whereby there is very little, or no reserve, with regard to cash availability, to survive a period of low activity.

Every year, during the months of December and January, due to what in effect is nearly two weeks of very little work, and sometimes even more affected by bad weather, Companies are often at a very low ebb. If under these circumstances, further problems are encountered, it is the responsibility of Management to forecast the financial position of the enterprise, and assess the position.

Accordingly this has been done, and the outcome is a forecast deficit by the end of March 1978, of some £20,000. This means in plain language an increase in overdraft of £20,000. This forecast includes the wage increase currently being paid of £60 for 40 hours on 32 ton vehicles.

One can also assume that this overdraft increase will be refused by our Bankers.

Normally, one would fight back against these odds, with a will to win, and eventually overcome the problem. This is particularly applicable to a Private Company, such as ours, even more so, as my whole working life has been devoted to building up, and maintaining this business, and this I have tried to effect fairly and honestly, and to honour my obligations and loyalties to all of my staff.

Cont......

Members R.H.A.

MAYS MOTORS (TRANSPORT) LTD.

Directors : D. May, P. R. C. May, A. G. M. Doughty

Reg. No. 423511 England
Telex No. 858366

Reg. Office
ELSTEAD, GODALMING, SURREY
GU8 6EF
Telephone : ELSTEAD (STD 025122) 3255 (5 lines)

- 2 -   15th January, 1979

Cont....

Today, the 15th January, 1979, has made me realise that modern Trade
Union loyalties are stronger than I. They are stronger than loyalties to the
employing Company.

Obviously, I must accept this as a fact of life from now on. Today I
have been appalled and completely disillusioned, in the defeat that I
personally have suffered.

I appreciate all of the pressures and so called principles of modern
Trade Unions, and that this is part of our modern way of life. I appreciate
that you must strike if so called upon by your Union. I do not appreciate
that our Drivers, many of whom I have worked with closely for many years,
consider it more important to come to our yard and picket our gate, than to
quietly stay away.

Furthermore, some of the activities of a few of those involved, show
clearly that their true desire is to crush the Company, in favour of their
Union principles.

It may well be that ultimately, they will win. I cannot exclude any,
that have picketed today. The choice was their own, and this choice they
have made.

As a Company, we will not go bankrupt, providing action is taken,
sufficiently early. Accordingly, I am forced to the conclusion that all
drivers to whom this letter is given, must consider themselves under formal
notice of dismissal from this Company. This is due to their refusing to accept
such work that is available, by withdrawing their service, and particularly due
to their obvious preference to further the interests of the United Road Transport
Union, than that of their employers.

It is still a fact that we cannot continue on our present course, if
for no other reason than that of finance. What this document does achieve,
I trust, is to demonstrate exactly where we all stand.

Whatever the outcome, I must state that however old fashioned and out
of date that I may be considered to be, whatever modern legislation is loaded
against my Company, and others, that I no longer have any obligation to
any of those who have today demonstrated their preference for loyalties
to those other than their own Company.

Any driver who wishes to have this notice withdrawn, please contact
me individually, when the matter will be discussed.

Yours faithfully,
for MAY'S MOTORS (TRANSPORT) LTD.

P. R. C. May
Managing Director

B. List of buses and coaches operated by the company

1920s

registration	chassis	body and seating capacity	date new	notes
??	Ford TT	9 seats		seats fitted to lorry body
??	Maxwell	charabanc		
PC 9906	Maxwell	bus	1923	
PD 2136	Guy	bus	1923	
PD 7199	Fiat	B14F	1923	
CB 2803	Fiat	Ch14	1921	ex J.S. Leaver, Eanam, Blackburn, Lancs. 1925
TP 837	Ford T	bus	1925	second-hand
PF 8777	Guy B	B24F	1927	
PH 4623	Dennis 30cwt.	Spicer B18	1927	

Sold with the business to Aldershot & District Traction Co. Ltd. 2nd January 1928 were CB 2803, PF 8777 and PH 4623 plus a Ford (probably TP 837). Aldershot & District operated PF 8777 and PH 4623 (until 1929 and 1932 respectively).
Note that the registration of Dennis PH 4623 is quoted by Surrey Constabulary (in error) in its letter of 17th October 1927 as PH 4263 (see Chapter 1, page 20)

Post-war

registration	chassis	body and seating capacity	date new	notes
HKJ 531	Bedford OWB	Duple B28F	1945	ex Ashline, Tonbridge, Kent
HKJ 533	Bedford OWB	Duple B28F	1945	ex Ashline, Tonbridge, Kent
TMK 215	Crossley SD42/7	Santus C33F	1949	ex Fountain Coaches, Twickenham
TMK 216	Crossley SD42/7	Santus C33F	1949	ex Fountain Coaches, Twickenham
SML 10	AEC Regal III	Duple C33F	1947	ex T. Gibson (Lily Coaches), London, N.9

The Bedford OWBs were replaced by the Crossleys and were sold to a local Bedford dealer. They received new Duple dual-purpose seats (DP28F), roof luggage compartments and rear shock absorbers shortly after purchase.
The Crossleys were withdrawn late 1953; and the AEC Regal was withdrawn around March 1954.

C. May Family Tree

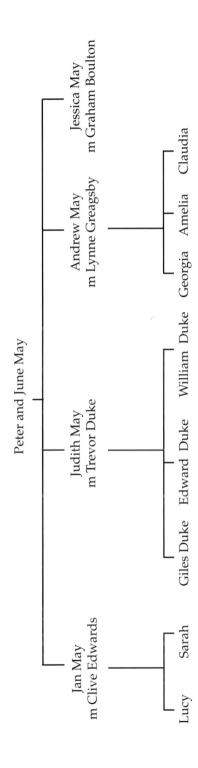

Family photograph taken by son-in-law Graham. The back row (left to right) shows June, Peter, Trevor and Judith Duke, Amelia, Lynne, Claudia and Andrew May, Clive Edwards and Jessica Boulton. The middle row shows Edward and Giles Duke, Lucy and Jan Edwards while the front row shows William Duke, Georgia May and Sarah Edwards.

Son-in-law Graham.